CRITICAL INSIGHTS

Gender, Sex & Sexuality

CRITICAL INSIGHTS

Gender, Sex & Sexuality

Editor
Margaret Sönser Breen
University of Connecticut

SALEM PRESS
A Division of EBSCO Information Services, Inc.
Ipswich, Massachusetts

GREY HOUSE PUBLISHING

Copyright © 2014 by Grey House Publishing, Inc.

All rights reserved. No part of this work may be used or reproduced in any manner whatsoever or transmitted in any form or by any means, electronic or mechanical, including photocopy, recording, or any information storage and retrieval system, without written permission from the copyright owner. For information, contact Grey House Publishing/Salem Press, 4919 Route 22, PO Box 56, Amenia, NY 12501.

∞ The paper used in these volumes conforms to the American National Standard for Permanence of Paper for Printed Library Materials, Z39.48-1992 (R1997).

Library of Congress Cataloging-in-Publication Data

Gender, sex & sexuality / editor, Margaret Sönser Breen, University of Connecticut. -- [First edition].

pages ; cm. -- (Critical insights)

Edition statement supplied by publisher.
Includes bibliographical references and index.
ISBN: 978-1-61925-403-9

1. Sex in literature. 2. Sex (Psychology) in literature. 3. Gender identity in literature. 4. Love in literature. I. Breen, Margaret Sönser. II. Series: Critical insights.

PN56.S5 G56 2014
809/.933538

LCCN: 2014945579

PRINTED IN THE UNITED STATES OF AMERICA

Contents

About This Volume, Margaret Sönser Breen	vii
On Gender, Sex, and Sexuality: Reading Gender, Sex, and Sexuality Through Memoirs of Trauma, Margaret Sönser Breen	xv

Critical Contexts

Writing Gender: Authorship and Authority, Frederick S. Roden, with Joseph J. Portanova	3
Who's Counting? Sexes, Genders, and Sexualities from Ancient Myths to Fin-de-Siècle and Twentieth-Century Literature and Theory, Katerina Kitsi-Mitakou	20
A Queer Time for Sex in Matthew Lewis' *The Monk*, Lisa Blansett	36
"What to Become?" Religion, Masculinity, and Self-Determination in *A Visitation of Spirits*, *Parable of the Sower*, and *Parable of the Talents*, Marlon Rachquel Moore	54

Critical Readings

Whistling Past the Grave of the Phallus: Aristophanes' *Lysistrata*, Roger Travis	73
Shining Genji and the Women of the Heian Court in the *Genji Monogatari*, Sara R. Johnson	87
Sexual Disgust and the Limits of Tolerance: Learning about Regulatory Regimes from Sanskrit Drama, Patrick Colm Hogan	106
Unsexing Gender in Shakespeare's *Macbeth*, Greg Colón Semenza	123
"their sex not equal seemed": Gender, Sex, and Sexuality in Milton's *Paradise Lost*, David Gay	138
Sexuality and Gender in Victorian Sensation and Other Fiction, Thomas Recchio	153
Making Herself "for a Person": Gender and Jewishness in Anzia Yesierska's *Bread Givers*, Lisa Marcus	167
Claustrophobia: Containment and Queer Spaces in *Tea and Sympathy* and *Cat on a Hot Tin Roof*, Brenda Murphy	181

Killing the Queen: Yeats, McDonagh, and Punk, Mary M. Burke   195

A Road More Travelled: Gay and Lesbian Lives in Irish Fiction Since 1989, Rachael Sealy Lynch   211

Trans/Forming Girlhood: Transgenderism, the Tomboy Formula, and Gender Identity Disorder in Sharon Dennis Wyeth's *Tomboy Trouble*, Michelle Ann Abate   226

Border-Crossing and Evolution: From Violence to Love in Cristina García's *Monkey Hunting* and *The Lady Matador's Hotel*, Barbara Frey Waxman   244

Resources

Additional Works on Gender, Sex, and Sexuality	263
Bibliography	267
About the Editor	271
Contributors	273
Index	279

About This Volume

Margaret Sönser Breen

It is hardly surprising that issues regarding gender, sex, and sexuality are so often at the heart of literary works. Our understanding of our bodies, ourselves, desire, love, family, kinship, community, religion, law, society, health, education, language, and even our relation to time and space can depend on these three key aspects of human existence—aspects whose definitions, at times, are particular and unyielding and, at other times, are abstract and malleable.

What does it mean to be a man? What does it mean to be a woman? What does it mean to fit comfortably in neither category? What does it mean if our gender expression is seen as transgressive or our sexual desires or sex acts are deemed immoral or illegal or, again, given our age or dis/ability, inappropriate? And what if one is not considered fully human: how does this abject status affect our understanding of our gender and sexuality and shape the ways in which we write about them? These are just some of the kinds of questions that this volume—in its examination of the imbricated theme of gender, sex, and sexuality in literature—provokes.

How we interpret and experience gender, sex, and sexuality, as well as their interrelationships, depends on our historical, geographical, and cultural locations. Interpretation and experience depend, too, on situational context. At times and in various places and, indeed, until relatively recently in the West, people have held that one's sex predicts one's gender and that this ostensibly natural relationship between sex and gender in turn produces "normal" [hetero]sexuality as well as "normal" sex acts. Particularly over the last century, scholars, scientists, activists, and writers have demonstrated the problems that attend definitions of gender, sex, and sexuality that assume organic or intrinsic linkages among the three. For example, one's biological sex may be ambiguous; one's external gender may be at odds with one's internal gender identity; or again, one might not be heterosexual. These are just a few of the possibilities that point to the limitations of a narrative that neatly aligns sex, gender, and sexuality. In their lived experiences, in their fantasies and desires, in their biological facticity, many, many individuals and, indeed, whole categories of people rupture that narrative. As an examination of literature across times and cultures can attest, the interrelationships among these three important aspects of our humanness are diverse and complex. What follow are a few examples of how literature's engagement with gender, sex, and sexuality can vary dramatically according to location and context.

So, for instance, we might consider the history of the sonnet. As we know, the sonnet is a poetic form specifically dedicated to the expression of love. But what kind of love? And love of whom and what? The form is, of course, identified with the fourteenth-century Italian writer Petrarch, whose sonnets to Laura inspired Renaissance writers across Europe. In these poems, Laura, whose name encodes wordplay on the noun *l'aura* (aura or wind), proves inaccessible, unobtainable; the object of Petrarch's unrequited love is more godlike than human; she is unreachable because she is an etherealized, spiritual presence. Some two centuries later, in England, Wyatt and Surrey translated Petrarch's sonnets and, in so doing, offered their versions. In some of those, instead of Laura, it is Anne Boleyn, the second wife of Henry VIII, who is the object of love, where love is not simply unrequited, but forbidden. Shakespeare offered his own innovations to and parodies of the form; he also wrote same-sex sonnets, as did Michelangelo—far better known for his sculpture and painting—even before Shakespeare. For his part, Romantic poet John Keats conceived of the sonnet in a very different way. His 1816 "On First Looking into Chapman's Homer" describes a young man's love of Chapman's translation of Homer: this is a love poem whose object is not a person, but rather literature itself and, more specifically, literature in translation. The sonnet calls attention to the class limitations of Keats' own education. George Meredith's 1862 sonnet collection *Modern Love* in turn implodes the definition of the sonnet as a love poem: the collection records the failure of his marriage. Finally, writing just over a century later, Adrienne Rich breaks the conventional sonnet form in "Twenty-One Love

Poems," which celebrate lesbian love. These poets' understanding of gender, sex, and sexuality shape both the content and the form of their sonnets.

Let's now reverse the relationship and consider how literature produces understandings of gender, sex, and sexuality—in this case, through its depiction of food. Yes, food. While there are many famous examples from which to choose (one thinks, for example of *The Alice B. Toklas Cook Book*), the comparison of William Carlos Williams' treatment of the plum in his 1934 poem "This is Just to Say" and Virginia Woolf's contemplation of the prune (a dried plum) in her 1929 essay *A Room of One's Own* illustrates the point nicely. In Williams' twelve-line love poem, the speaker admits he has eaten his wife's plums. The poem is intimate and sensuous. It is even sensual, quietly racy; after all, he has eaten her fruit. By contrast, in Woolf's essay, which describes the restrictions that delimit women's (even well-to-do women's) access to education, the prune, devoid of the plum's flavor and juiciness, functions as a metaphor for women's educational and, more broadly, cultural deprivation. The woman who wishes to study and to write faces severe gender restrictions; moreover, as the prune metaphor implies, she can herself hardly be the object of sexual delight; she is simply too dried up. It is worth noting here that, as the organization for women in literary arts, VIDA, underscores, women writers in the twenty-first century still face daunting obstacles regarding recognition and respect.

Concerning literature's engagement with the multifaceted theme of gender, sex, and sexuality, my hope is that not only the above examples, but also the seventeen essays that follow offer the reader much food for thought. *Critical Insights: Gender, Sex, & Sexuality* is divided into four parts: an introduction that includes this preface, as well as an opening frame essay; a section titled "Critical Contexts," comprised of four essays that lay out different methodological perspectives on themes of gender, sex, and sexuality; a section titled "Critical Readings," consisting of twelve essays that analyze works such as Aristophanes' *Lysistrata*, Murasaki Shikibu's *Tale of Genji*, Shakespeare's *Macbeth*, and Cristina García's *Monkey Hunting* and

The Lady Matador's Hotel; and, finally, a bibliographic section that provides suggestions for further reading.

This collection begins with my own introductory piece. "On Gender, Sex, and Sexuality: Reading Gender, Sex, and Sexuality through Memoirs of Trauma" considers two literary works, Charlotte Delbo's *Auschwitz and After* and Mark Doty's *Heaven's Coast*. For Delbo, who survives the Auschwitz concentration camp, and Doty, who loses his partner to AIDS, memoir-making proves a form of advocacy. The writers record a suffering that is specific in its gendered and sexual effects. Their memoirs of trauma rupture conventional notions of linear time and, in so doing, grant visibility and validity to their experiences, as well as those of others like them (particularly women for Delbo and gay men for Doty), whose voices would otherwise not be heard.

Following this introductory essay is the "Critical Contexts" section, the first essay of which offers an historical approach to literature. In "Writing Gender: Authorship and Authority," Frederick S. Roden, with Joseph J. Portanova, explores the ways in which western women writers (beginning with the Greek poet Sappho) asserted their agency, even as they inhabited cultural and political spaces that insisted on their silence. Following this piece is Katerina Kitsi-Mitakou's overview of theory, "Who's Counting? Sexes, Genders, and Sexualities from Ancient Myths to Fin-de-Siècle and Twentieth-Century Literature and Theory." Kitsi-Mitakou begins by recounting the myth of the three sexes, as told by Aristophanes in Plato's *Symposium*. Paying special attention to late nineteenth- and early twentieth-century formulations of gender, sex, and sexuality and, relatedly, works by the writers Oscar Wilde and Virginia Woolf, Kitsi-Mitakou demonstrates the ways in which writers and theorists some one hundred years ago both made use of earlier models and formulations of gender and sex and laid the groundwork for writers and theorists of the late twentieth century. Lisa Blansett's essay, "A Queer Time for Sex in Matthew Lewis' *The Monk*," in turn models an application of theory for readers. In this case, Blansett draws on queer theory in order to explore not only Lewis' novel, but also the subgenre of gothic literature, to which the novel belongs. For Blansett, "Lewis' addition to the Gothic canon takes the reader into an imagined world where gender and sex slip into shifting configurations. In this world, narratives do not account for the practices of desire, chronology does produce or represent a genealogical imperative, and all bodies are queer." Rounding out this section is the compare-and-contrast essay, "'What to Become?' Religion, Masculinity, and Self-Determination in *A Visitation of Spirits, Parable of the Sower*, and *Parable of the Talents*," in which Marlon Rachquel Moore examines works by Randall Kenan and Octavia Butler. Situating them within an African-American literary tradition of "anti-Christian discourse" and paying special attention to issues of gender and sexuality, Moore considers the similarities and differences between the two writers' "depictions of the tension between religious tradition and the quest for individual self-determination."

The third section of this volume, "Critical Readings," consists of twelve essays arranged in chronological order, the first three of which turn our attention from Ancient Greece to tenth-century Japan to tenth-century Kashmir. The first essay is Roger Travis' "Whistling Past the Grave of the Phallus: Aristophanes' *Lysistrata*." Written in the fourth century BCE, this ancient Greek comedy turns on a sex strike that Athenian women organize in order to put an end to the Peloponnesian War. According to Travis, *Lysistrata* should be read as a feminist play, not least because it exposes Athenians' gender anxiety, specifically regarding the erosion of male dominance. Sarah R. Johnson, in turn, focuses on the first world novel written by a named woman author, the tenth-century Japanese classic, *Genji Monogatari*, known in the West as the *Tale of Genji*. In "Shining Genji and the Women of the Heian Court in the *Genji Monogatari*," Johnson adopts a comparative approach that allows her to make connections between novels written in Greek under the Roman Empire during the first through fourth centuries and Murasaki Shikibu's masterpiece and, in the process, highlight the uniqueness of the Japanese novel. Overall, Johnson lays out for readers the highly gendered context not only of the Japanese imperial court, but also the Japanese language in which Lady Murasaki wrote. For his part, Patrick Colm Hogan introduces readers to another tenth-century text, this one from Kashmir. "Sexual Disgust and the Limits of Tolerance: Learning about Regulatory Regimes from Sanskrit Drama" examines Bhaṭṭa Jayánta's *Āgamaḍambara*, particularly its treatment of non-normative sexualities. *Āgamaḍambara*, Hogan argues, "suggests the profound importance of sexual liberation—not only for sexual minorities, but for a range of groups that might be subjected to social exclusion."

The next three essays offer analyses of English literary texts. "Unsexing Gender in Shakespeare's *Macbeth*" by Gregory Colón Semenza and "'their sex not equal seemed': Gender, Sex and, Sexuality in Milton's *Paradise Lost*" by David Gay consider two well-known seventeenth-century works. Semenza focuses on "*Macbeth*'s thematic preoccupation with socially constructed gender roles, . . . especially on their psychological impact on both male and female characters." Gay, in turn, explores gender, sex, and sexuality within Milton's epic poem by teasing out its biblical subtext. Following these two essays is Thomas Recchio's "Sexuality and Gender in Victorian Sensation and Other Fiction." By offering readings of three mid-century texts by Braddon, Gaskell, and Trollope, Recchio demonstrates how "sexuality and gender played a significant role in the forms of Victorian fiction that both challenged social-sexual orthodoxies and opened out ways to imagine social formations that enable more gender equity."

With the next two essays, the focus shifts to American literature. In "Making Herself 'for a Person': Gender and Jewishness in Anzia Yesierska's *Bread Givers*," Lisa Marcus examines Anzia Yezierska's 1925 novel, in which "Yezierska's protagonist Sara Smolinski works to 'make [her]self for a person' in an America that cannot comfortably assimilate this immigrant daughter, and in a Jewish community that cannot seem to abide female ambition and defiance against patriarchal tradition." As Brenda Murphy makes evident in her comparative piece "Claustrophobia: Containment and Queer Spaces in *Tea and Sympathy* and *Cat on a Hot Tin Roof*," discomfort also characterizes Robert Anderson's and Tennessee Williams' exploration of sexuality and the metaphor of the closet in their 1950s dramas. "In both plays," Murphy argues, "the women offer the promise of normality to the men by means of affirming their 'manliness' through heterosexual sex. In doing so, they return stability to an unstable sexual dynamic by reaffirming the heteronormative values of the plays' social institutions, the school and the family."

The themes of claustrophobia, transgression, and normativity also recur in Irish and British-Irish literature. For Mary M. Burke, in "Killing the Queen: Yeats, McDonagh, and Punk," these themes characterize the plays of mid-century dramatists Frank Carney and Tom Murphy, as well as contemporary punk playwright Martin McDonagh. Their plays center on the vexed gendered relationships that Irish immigrants experience with regard to Ireland and Britain, where both countries are cast as failed mothers that have economically and culturally either abandoned or denied their native or immigrant children. Counterpointing this experience of exclusion is the movement toward inclusion that, according to Rachael Sealy Lynch, marks the development of gay and lesbian Irish fiction over the last quarter century. In "A Road More Travelled: Gay and Lesbian Lives in Irish Fiction Since 1989," Lynch explains how, in marked contrast to early twentieth-century Irish literary treatments of homosexuality, which end in characters' exile and death, for example, depictions of gay and lesbian relationships in the works of such well known contemporary writers as Mary Dorcey, Colm Tóibín, and Emma Donoghue emphasize the everydayness of same-sex desire.

Rounding out the volume are the pieces "Trans/Forming Girlhood: Transgenderism, the Tomboy Formula, and Gender Identity Disorder in Sharon Dennis Wyeth's *Tomboy Trouble*" by Michelle Ann Abate and "Border-Crossing and Evolution: From Violence to Love in Cristina García's *Monkey Hunting* and *The Lady Matador's Hotel*" by Barbara Frey Waxman. Both of these essays are concerned with various kinds of border-crossing. Abate, in her essay—a version of which appeared in the journal *The Lion and the Unicorn* in 2008—examines Wyeth's children's picture book. Abate argues that Wyeth, in conjunction with illustrator Lynne Woodcock

Cravath, resists perpetuating gender stereotypes for her young readers. Instead, *"Tomboy Trouble* advocates a gender identity that transcends the categories of maleness and femaleness, or one that could be cast, in the lexicon of contemporary LGBTQ studies, as transgender." Similar to Wyeth, Cuban-American writer Cristina García confronts and implodes gender stereotypes. For Waxman, García's preoccupation with the movement across "linguistic, cultural, religious, and gender borders" facilitates not only her characters' confrontation with bias and intolerance, but also their heightened understanding of the richness of human experience.

Gender, Sex, & Sexuality is suggestive rather than exhaustive in its treatment of literature. Comprising seventeen essays in total, the collection engages a range of literary texts from a variety of cultures, some contemporary, some long past. My hope is that the volume will deepen readers' understanding and appreciation of the power of literature not only to identify and represent individuals' and societies' investment in definitions of gender, sex, and sexuality and their interplay, but also to challenge and remake those definitions again and again. Think of the texts that this volume has not considered. Which would you add to your own literary study?

On Gender, Sex, and Sexuality: Reading Gender, Sex, and Sexuality through Memoirs of Trauma

Margaret Sönser Breen

What role or roles do gender, sex, and sexuality play in literature, and how do those roles affect the particular kind of literary writing or genre an author employs in order to explore them? This is the doubled, overarching question of this essay, which considers a particular genre, memoir, specifically memoir of trauma, and its engagement with gender, sex, and sexuality in two texts, Charlotte Delbo's *Auschwitz and After* (1965–70 in French; 1995 in English) and Mark Doty's *Heaven's Coast: A Memoir* (1996).

How are we to understand the interplay of gender, sex, and sexuality? Feminist and queer theorist Judith Butler offers us one response. She writes, "There are no direct expressive or causal lines between sex, gender, gender presentation, sexual practice, fantasy, and sexuality. None of those terms captures or determines the rest" (25). Yet, if there are no intrinsic links, we are still well aware of the ways in which cultural, medical, political, and religious discourses, to name a few, can insist on those links. Societies can determine which genders and sexualities and sex acts are normal or healthy or legitimate or moral.

Lesbian poet and theorist Adrienne Rich adds to this discussion; her foundational feminist essay "Notes toward a Politics of Location" (1985) offers a useful starting point for considering the interplay of gender, sex, and sexuality in literature. She writes, "I need to understand how a place on the map is also a place in history within which as woman, a Jew, a lesbian, a feminist I am created and trying to create" (64). In other words, we must recognize the ways in which our location within a particular culture and historical period determines—produces the range of possibilities for—the ways in which gender, sex, and sexuality interact and are narrativized. And, of course, these aspects of our humanity are affected by and linked to other aspects, like our age, for instance; our race; our ethnicity; our physical and/or mental dis/ability; the language(s) we speak—all of which may and, in some cases, do change over time and according to the place or places we live.

Born in 1928 in Baltimore, Rich is keenly aware of how geography played a crucial role in determining her life. Had she grown up in a European city overtaken by Hitler, she might well have become a different person, or she might not have survived into adulthood. Rich explains:

> The body I was born into was not only female and white, but Jewish—enough for geographic location to have played, in those years, a determining part. I was a *Mischling*, four years old when the Third Reich began. Had it been not Baltimore, but Prague or Łódź or Amsterdam, [I] might have had no address. Had I survived Prague, Amsterdam, or Łódź and the railway stations for which there were deportation points, I would be some body else. My center, perhaps, the Middle East or Latin America, my language itself another language. Or I might be in no body at all (68).

Rich's words make clear that the stories we tell about ourselves are, in so very many ways, determined by the stories we as human beings are allowed to live. Our ability to recognize and define our gender, sex, and sexuality, including their interconnections as well as disconnections, is not simply up to us. Instead, the ways in which we might exercise that ability are already determined by "a politics of location."

To varying degrees, all of the essays in this volume consider how historical and cultural contexts produce writers' exploration of gender, sex, and sexuality. In literature, that exploration is also crucially tied to form, that is, the genre that a given writer uses. One striking aspect of Rich's essay is its memoiristic pull, especially when she urges us to consider not only where she was born, but also where she was not born. Her language regarding her gendered and raced embodiment is propelled by a traumatic insight: "Had I [been born elsewhere], I would be some body else. . . . Or I might be in no body at all." Rich's self-understanding is inevitably tied to the haunting presence of the Holocaust, an event she never explicitly names, and it is that haunting that, to my mind, most powerfully conveys her consciousness of the ways in which cultural violence can shape and reshape the body, and can even eradicate it. Rich's words provoke the following questions about memoir as a form: What does it mean to write a memoir with the certain knowledge that the context for understanding one's story, in particular one's gendered story, is always, necessarily linked to the potential, if not the reality, of violence? How can experiences of trauma, particularly violent assaults on one's gendered personhood, shape narrative form and authorial claims of agency?

I have been thinking a lot about memoir of late, and so the questions continue. What does it mean to tell one's own story? Whose stories are most likely to be told, written, and published? Another version of this question is which stories are worth telling; or again, since one meaning of "to tell" is "to count," which stories count? How much of a given story is already scripted? What are the tensions between the memoirist and the memoir form? How much control does the memoirist have over what he or she recounts? What can he/she withhold, and what are the implications (ethical, moral, cultural, political, and aesthetic, for example) of such withholding? How do narrative conventions, that is, the scripts for telling stories, which vary across cultures and times, determine the kinds of events that should be mentioned; the ones that should be overlooked? What if the stories one has to tell demand that one defy those conventions? And what does it mean to tell a story (of oneself or on behalf of others) when that story exposes, indeed derives from the limits of time, the lack of a future? These are just some of the questions that I have been asking.

In part, my fascination with memoir is deeply personal. My mother, who is in her eighty-eighth year, has been reminiscing. No, that's not quite it. Much like the queers who are the subject of Lee Edelman's *No Future: Queer Theory and the Death Drive* (2004), for my mother of late—and when one has passed eight-seven years one has to speak of the lateness of life—linearity is no longer a compelling, reliable, or even easy framework for imagining life.

Nor does she find the concept of the future a particularly meaningful one, even as here in the United States we live in such a future-oriented society. Instead, events from her past, in particular from an adolescence bracketed by war, have been much more vivid for her, and it has become a matter of urgency for her to communicate stories—moments in her early history—to me. So my present, particularly my shared present with my mother, is necessarily bound up with, inextricable from her past. The power of the present is, in many ways, determined by the immediacy of her past. That past in not past, after all.

My mother's turn toward memoir has set me thinking about the interplay among gender, sex, and sexuality in memoirs of trauma. That interplay, in particular the ways we narrativize or tell stories about it—is the subject of this essay, which considers works by two writers, *Auschwitz and After* by Charlotte Delbo (1913–1985) and *Heaven's Coast* by Mark Doty (b.1953).

In *Auschwitz and After*, Charlotte Delbo recounts her experiences as well as those of others interned in the camp. Her primary focus is on the women prisoners. As the doubleness of her memoir's title suggests, Auschwitz is not simply a narratively contained memory of a camp survivor in 1940s–1960s France; instead, Auschwitz lives on as a ghostly presence in the aftermath of the war and in the lives of multiple survivors. Memoir writing, *Auschwitz and After* makes clear, should be read as an ongoing response not simply to a historically discrete experience, but to sustained psychic violation—violation that the writer offering testimony, in part because she is speaking on behalf of others, cannot herself fully apprehend.

Similar to that of *Auschwitz and After*, the narrative structure of *Heaven's Coast* reflects an ultimately unknowable grief. In *Heaven's Coast*, Mark Doty attempts to come to terms with the loss of his partner, Wally, to AIDS. In the process he, too, tells stories about others whose stories fit neither easily nor comfortably within conventional narratives of middle-class familial and social progress. Doty's memoir may be said to grapple with how to honor the lives of those whose futures have been cut short by accident and disease, and, too, by indifference; those whose gender, sexuality, and sex acts were perhaps never even recognized as fully legitimate. *Heaven's Coast* may thus be understood as at once Doty's memorial for his lover and friends and a denunciation of a homophobic culture impervious to its own implication in those deaths.

While many disciplines have demonstrated that storytelling can function as a therapeutic response to trauma, Doty's and Delbo's turn toward memoir, recalling Rich's, teach us that such healing is ineluctably experienced through an epistemology of haunting, whereby healing exists alongside of and mediated by a trauma that is never fully psychically contained (Davis 9). As they explore how resilience can exist alongside unimaginable and inarticulable loss, both Delbo and Doty craft memoirs that necessarily transgress both cultural and narrative conventions of gender, sex, and sexuality.

Delbo: Testimony, Healing, and Haunting

Charlotte Delbo was born in France in 1913. A member of the French Young Communist Women's League, she worked for actor and theatrical producer Louis Jouvet and was in with his company in Buenos Aires when the Nazis invaded France in 1940. Upon hearing the news she returned to France, where, along with her husband, Georges Dudach, she joined the Resistance. In March 1942, she and Dudach were arrested. While he was executed, she, along with other female members of the Resistance, was sent to Auschwitz.

Delbo's writings center on her experiences of the Holocaust. These writings include *Spectres, mes compagnons*, the posthumously published *La mémoire et les jours*, translated as *Days and Memory* (1990), and her best known and most substantial work, *Auschwitz et aprés* or *Auschwitz and After* (1995), which consists of three volumes: *None of Us Will Return, Useless Knowledge*, and *The Measure of Our Days*.

Speaking of the Holocaust and the purpose of her writings, Delbo famously exhorted "*Il faut donner a voir*"—"one must make them see," and her writing style manifests that intent. She blends poetry and prose to create, as Lawrence L. Langer describes it, a "lyrical rendering of atrocity that is alarmingly beautiful, an aesthetics of agitation" (xvi).

That aesthetics turns on rupture—and not solely the rupture that is a signature of modernist and postmodernist writing, the movement across genre boundaries, in Delbo's case, is the juxtaposition of poetry and prose. Delbo continually collapses the boundaries between narrator, subject, and reader. Most striking is her commitment not simply to record stories of women prisoners, whom she encounters in Auschwitz, but also to speak on the women's behalf. In this mode, rupture may be understood as a form of advocacy that, feminist in its effect, stems from her ideals of political solidarity. "Most of the time [Delbo] will speak through a collective '*nous*' ['we']," writes Rosette C. Lamont. Delbo's is ". . . a self-conscious attempt to transmit 'a Voice from the Chorus'" (248).

Delbo's writing also enacts a rupture of temporal and spatial frames. As Judith Greenberg points out, the phrase "'Auschwitz and after' calls attention to the issue of chronology" (361). Importantly, this phrase forecloses the possibility of imagining a future or, even, comfortably, a present separate from the experience of the death camps. This issue of a foreclosed future—what, in a different context, Lee Edelman has termed "no future"—is especially evident in the original French title of the first volume *None of Us Will Return*: *Aucun de nous ne reviendra*, in which "ne" (or "not") negates the future-tense verb "*reviendra*" (Greenberg 361). And as with the trilogy's title, the first volume's title announces the psychic proximity of Auschwitz for those who lived through it.

So, for example, in the first volume, the vignette titled "One Day," collapses Delbo's memory of a starved prisoner, a woman, a Jew, who is killed by an SS dog and the present (the now) of composition, of recording the memory. This piece ruptures the boundaries between the Auschwitz death camp and post-war Paris:

> I no longer look at her. I no longer wish to look. . . . I turn away to look elsewhere. Elsewhere.
>
> . . . Standing, wrapped in a blanket, a child, a little boy. . . . It's a woman. A female skeleton. She is naked. . . . A dancing female skeleton. . .

Presently I am writing this story in a café—it is turning into a story.

A break in the clouds. Is it afternoon? We have lost all notion of time . . . Hours have passed since I succeeded in not looking at the woman in the ditch. . . . Her back hunches, shoulder blades protruding through the worn fabric of her coat. It's a yellow coat, like that of our dog Flac which had grown thin after being ill, and whose whole body curved, just before he died. . . .This woman is going to die.

. . . The SS has his dog on a leash. . . . The dog leaps on the woman, sinks its fangs in her neck. . . . I feel the dog's fangs in my throat. I scream. I howl. Not a sound comes out of me. The silence of a dream.

The plain. The snow. The plain.

. . . And now I am sitting in a café, writing this text (26–29).

"One Day"'s movement between a memory of Auschwitz, a childhood memory of a pet's death, and the present moment of memoir composition attests to the dislocation and incoherence of the "I" marked by trauma. Neither Delbo, the camp prisoner, nor Delbo, the survivor, wishes to see the skeletal woman before her; yet, in each case, "not looking" fails to produce an "elsewhere," a place or time of psychic repose unyoked from this Auschwitz memory. Who is this woman? What is she thinking? What is *she* seeing? We do not know. In contrast to Delbo, the prisoner, and Delbo, the survivor, Delbo, the memoirist, insists that readers recognize the imperative of looking—and not because looking will engender answers. Instead, the memoirist's as well as readers' looking discloses how much of the trauma of Delbo's experience of Auschwitz gathers around the awareness of her text's suffusion with a gendered suffering never really apprehended, though perhaps fleetingly gestured toward, as in this case, in the description of the starved Jewish woman torn apart by a dog. Within Delbo's account, the woman is a cipher of suffering that signals a textual excess, opaque and unknowable to writer and reader like. As Jennifer L. Geddes, citing Cathy Caruth (vii), observes:

> There is a danger . . . of assuming survivors of different atrocities . . . experience the same thing just because we use the same words to describe what has occurred. . . . We need to attend to the cultural, historical, and political particularities of situations of extreme suffering and to attend to the particularities of individuals that may make their responses to the same atrocity quite different . . . ("Toward" 2–3).

Through her layered account of looking and not looking, Delbo, the memoirist, calls upon her readers' ethical engagement with the specificity and limitations of her Holocaust testimony and trauma.

Auschwitz and After captures not only Delbo's recollections, but also those of fellow female camp survivors. That the latter speak through her in the memoir both reflects Delbo's aesthetic enactment of her politics and records the violent fracturing and destruction of self that Auschwitz has engendered: an ethical commitment to offer narrative solidarity and a collective voice to those who would otherwise not be heard (Lamont 248) or who have experienced the violation of a coherent subjectivity, what Colin Davis terms "an impairment of the self-understanding of the witness" (9).

Decades later, survivors in France find themselves still in Auschwitz. In volume three, *The Measure of Our Days*, Delbo records the thoughts of her fellow survivor Mado:

> since I came back, everything I was before, all my memories from that earlier time, have dissolved, come undone. It is as though my past has been used up over there. *Nothing* remains of what was before. My real sister is you. My true family is you, those who were with me there. . . . Presently, I am *no* longer alive. I can take full measure of this difference, but *neither* sentient knowledge, *nor* lucidity can be of any assistance. *Nothing* can fill the abyss between other people and myself, between myself and myself. *Nothing* can bridge this gulf, nor narrow it (258-59, emphasis added).

Mado continues, "I'm *not* alive. I'm imprisoned in memories and repetitions" (261, emphasis added). She concludes:

People believe memories grow vague, are erased by time, since nothing endures against the passage of time. That's the difference; time does *not* pass over me, over us. It *doesn't* erase anything, *doesn't* undo it. I'm *not* alive. I died in Auschwitz but *no one* knows it (267, emphasis added).

These passages are marked by erasure, emptiness, distance; by negation: "nothing," "neither," "not," "no one." Mado's is an identity fractured and disordered across space and time—so much so that the division between life and death has become a vacuous episteme. In *Days and Memory*, Delbo writes:

Auschwitz is so deeply etched on my memory that I cannot forget one moment of it.—So you are living with Auschwitz? —No, I live next to it. Auschwitz is there, unalterable, precise, but enveloped in the skin of memory, an impermeable skin that isolates it from my present self. Unlike the snake's skin, the skin of memory does not renew itself. . . . Alas, I often fear lest it grow thin, crack, and the camp get hold of me again (2).

In this passage, Delbo asserts that the self houses two sets of existence, the memory of Auschwitz and the present consciousness, which remain divided by an "impermeable skin." (Later in the text, she distinguishes between these two sets as "deep memory" and "common memory," respectively [Langer xi].) Yet, both the vignette "One Day" and the section devoted to Mado attest that this is not the case. As Langer observes, "Delbo seems to believe that the two kinds of memory can remain insulated from each other. But her own experience, as well as that of countless other survivors, violates her theory" (xi–xii). The "present self" remains vulnerable to memories of Auschwitz, which, as Davis' work on the 1977 text *Spectres, mes compagnons* suggests, are never "fully [its] own" (15). Both Delbo's and Mado's subjectivity is marked not by integration but by siege.

It would be a mistake, however, to read passages, such as those above, simply as testimonies of victimhood. They are expressions of Delbo's agency as both a writer and a survivor, as well as the agency of the women on whose behalf she speaks. These expressions of agency offer alternatives to conventional definitions of family, community, and time. Within those conventional definitions, the interplay of gender, sex, and sexuality, as well as the privileging of linear narrative, with its neat ordering of past, present, and future, could not possibly render the aesthetic or psychic complexities of Delbo's account and Mado's self-understanding either credible or compelling. "My real sister is you. My true family is you, those who were with me there" (258–59), asserts Mado.

Writing with regard to volume two, *Useless Knowledge*, Jennifer L. Geddes states:

> [Delbo's] many accounts of the ways that the women around her formed a community of support that enabled her to survive point to the possibility of hope, to the possibility that helping and healing connections can be made between women, between sufferers, and even between those who have suffered and those who have not. But these connections will not be based on the redemption of extreme suffering as something that gives us useful knowledge ("Banal" 112).

The knowledge that Delbo as a memoirist and survivor transmits *is* ultimately useless, where "uselessness" should be understood as a political category. In their records of healing and haunting, of life amidst trauma, the stories of human intimacies that she recounts exceed and so destabilize a cultural vision of gender, in which heterosexual reproduction and a politics of the future prove central.

Doty: What to Do with the "Presence and Weight of Their Stories"?

As for Charlotte Delbo, so for acclaimed contemporary American gay poet Mark Doty: memoir-writing entails various kinds of temporal and spatial dislocation. In *In a Queer Time and Place: Transgender Bodies and Subcultural Lives* (2005), Judith Halberstam identifies various conventional concepts of time: reproductive time, family time, and "time of inheritance." This last one, Halberstam explains, "connects the family to the historical past of the nation, and glances ahead to connect the family to the future of both familial and national stability" (5). In contrast to these kinds of time, there is "queer time," a concept born of the AIDS crisis (2), which she defines as "those specific models of temporality that emerge . . . once one leaves the temporal frames of bourgeois reproduction and family, longevity, risk, safety, and inheritance" (6). While one might argue that it would be anachronistic to apply the term to Delbo's writing and to her exploration of memory in particular, "queer time" nonetheless gives us a way of understanding the aesthetic and political significance of temporal disruption in *Auschwitz and After*.

There is no such question about the term's relevance for Mark Doty's *Heaven's Coast*, a text that Halberstam explicitly cites (2). A "weird interpenetration of ongoingness and endings" (Doty 60) marks Doty and Wally's last years together, as well as Doty's devastation after Wally's passing. Beginning with the title of the prologue, "Is There a Future? April 1993," Doty draws attention to his awareness of their loss of a shared future. The question haunts the entirety of the memoir. He explains, "The virus seemed to me . . . like a kind of solvent which dissolved the future, our future, a little at a time. It was like a dark stain, a floating, inky transparency hovering over Wally's body, and its intention was to erase the time ahead of us, to make that time, each day, a little smaller" (2). *Heaven's Coast* reflects Doty's "struggle . . . with the way the last four years have forced me to rethink my sense of the nature of the future" (3). Comprised of numerous essays, written across time and from different perspectives, *Heaven's Coast* is a text whose unevenness records the emotional tricks of time, the interplay of the passages of days into months and years with the temporal stoppages and replays exacted by grief. Intermixing rather than integrating accounts of Doty and his lover Wally's life together with the stories of friends and the legacy of those lives and losses, this AIDS memoir may be understood as a meditation on queer time.

Doty is aware of the immediacy of illness and death in the lives of so many of his acquaintances and friends and of gay men in general. Revisiting the Boston neighborhood where he and Wally first lived together, he realizes:

> Until today, I have never felt what I've heard other men I know say, that they don't understand why they're alive, when so many are gone. I am alive walking down this street in the early March sun and all the men I knew in that house, that stacked repository of time and memory, are dead. Wally and Bobby, David and Doug, others I never even knew. I am here today, in 1994, walking a city street indifferent with its own hurrying life, and I am filled with the presence and weight of their stories. What am I to do with them? (57)

Doty's awareness engenders in him a narrative responsibility that recalls Delbo's. What he does with the "presence and weight of their stories" is speak on the men's behalf. For Doty in *Heaven's Coast*, memoir-making entails granting social validity and power to the lives of those with no future.

This understanding of memoir counterpoints the widespread attitudes of indifference, incrimination, and even hostility directed toward people infected with HIV in the US during the 1980s and 1990s. In her landmark text *AIDS and Its Metaphors* (1989), writer and public intellectual Susan Sontag analyzes the discourse surrounding and in particular the metaphors associated with AIDS and, more generally, of disease. She writes, "With AIDS, . . . shame is linked to an imputation of guilt. . . . Indeed, to get AIDS is precisely to be revealed, in the majority of cases so far, as a member of a certain 'risk group,' a community of pariahs" (112–13). Guilt and pariah status are augmented, Sontag explains, by the strategic (rather than intrinsic) linkage of the disease to non-normative sex acts and to homosexuality: "The sexual transmission of this illness, considered by most people as a calamity one brings on oneself, is judged more harshly than other means—especially since AIDS is understood as a disease not only of sexual excess but of perversity" (114). The understanding of AIDS as a primarily sexually transmitted disease and its metaphorical equation with plague (152) helped ensure that HIV-positive people were consistently shunned and neglected and even treated with hostility and violence by families and doctors.

The abandonment of people living with HIV played out on local, state, and national government levels as well. In his memoir *Borrowed Time: An AIDS Memoir* (1988), writer Paul Monette recalls the Reagan administration's initial dismissal of the AIDS crisis during the early 80s: "We came to understand just how deaf the collective Reagan ear had been in the first four years of the calamity" (109). Government officials' attendance at the first international AIDS conference in 1985, Monette writes, was prompted by the realization that "the disease was a threat to 'the general population'" (108), and not simply to socially marginal, even undesirable, groups, such as gay men, IV drug users, hemophiliacs, and Haitian refugees.

Playwright and AIDS activist Larry Kramer's critique of government negligence in *Reports from the Holocaust: The Making of an AIDS Activist* (1989) is particularly powerful, not least because of the text's central metaphor. It is, of course, problematic to equate the AIDS crisis with the Holocaust: the two events are not the same. Nonetheless, this metaphor is useful, for it underscores the general citizenry's culpability in the crisis because of their unwillingness to help, their readiness to ignore, those infected. Moreover, the metaphor exposes that, as in the case of the Holocaust (Bergen 3), the targets of systematic mistreatment during the US AIDS crisis of the 1980s and 1990s were people marked out because of their sexual practices, sexuality, gender, dis/ability, and race. (These aspects of personhood, particularly when seen through the lens of Rich's "politics of location," continue to be relevant for any analysis of the most vulnerable populations in the ongoing global AIDS crisis.) Sontag, Monette, and Kramer help us understand the cultural context into which Doty is writing in 1996.

So Doty questions those metaphors that implicate the person with AIDS (PWA) in his/her illness. He writes:

> That arrogance which says *I alone* bear the responsibility for my body, for my fate, can suspend compassion. What are we to do . . . when people we love fail to stay healthy? What if we "fail" to be well ourselves; mustn't that then be a moral or spiritual failure? And if we *ask* for what we get, if all our suffering and illnesses are brought upon ourselves . . . then what is the role of compassion? Just last night, at a benefit, a man who's lived with AIDS for more than a decade was applauded by the crowd. He said he owed his life to the love of his partner, and the love of his friends and family. . . . But so many men

who are dead were deeply loved, too, and finally this statement erases them, denies the validity of their real passions, of what was felt by and for them (159, emphasis in original).

Memory work for Doty is about honoring the lives of people he has known, and it is also a means for critiquing the metaphoric equations that align AIDS with "moral and spiritual failure."

Doty's analysis above recalls a central point of Sontag's work: Being loved or, for that matter, lovable is not a cure for a disease. In its absence or presence, love does, however, testify to the boundary between the sordidness of rejection and the grace of intimate caring; between the refusal and the embrace of our responsibility with regard to the people in our lives. He explores this boundary in his accounts of his friends Bobby and Bill, both HIV-positive, and Phil, Bill's partner.

So Doty describes Bobby's treatment by hospital staff and family alike:

> . . . It seemed impossible, in 1991, that the nurses were reluctant to enter his room; they put on their latex gloves outside the door. (Later, when Bobby began to have dementia, I took him back to the hospital for an MRI. . . . [T]here wasn't a body fluid in sight, but I watched the technicians arm themselves with latex charms. I don't begrudge anyone their protection, but paranoia's ugly, as is making our fear obvious.)
>
> . . . [Bobby] had a prescription for something to prevent seizures. But no antivirals, no preventative medication for pneumonia. No doctor monitoring his case. No insurance. No income. No lover. No home— just his belongings, left in the house he had been booted out of, and a family that didn't seem to know if they wanted him or not. His mother told him not to cry in the house, on her couch; she didn't want those germs around (195).

Doty's passage is an example of writing back. Latex gloves and homelessness attest to how both hospital staff and family keep Bobby at a distance. The series of negations that describe Bobby's isolation and maltreatment—"no" and "not"—mark, not his contagion, but rather his ostensible caretakers' abnegation of responsibility. Insofar as metaphoric equations of moral failure are in play here, they apply to the medical personnel and to Bobby's parents.

In contrast to Bobby, Bill is treated with love. Partner Phil transforms Bill's hospital room from "some precinct of hell" into "a revelation" (87):

> The walls are covered with paintings from Bill's house, the windowsill thick with flowers and leafy plants, the whole room redolent of warmth and human habitation, an aura—in opposition to the severity of every floodlit room we passed to arrive here—of civility. This might be Bill's little studio apartment . . . ; room just for bed, tiny refrigerator; and the non-negotiable requirements of the civil life: flowers, paintings, music (88).

Through Phil's agency, Bill defines the hospital room and not vice versa. For Doty, "This is the gift that Phil's love is giving to Bill. In the absolute endangerment of illness, here is safety. In the face of reduction, identity. In the face of indignity, respect. In the face of erasure, here is intimacy, the sustaining of context which preserves the self" (91).

Yet, significantly, there are limits to the legacy of this love. Doty draws our attention to the inability of Bill's family to honor the men's partnership once Bill dies. At the funeral service, Phil describes a game of dress up that Bill played with children in his family. "'Are you a man or a woman?'" they wonder. When Phil recalls Bill's response—"'I'm a drag queen'"—the family, Doty records, is "not . . . amused." "'Why . . . did you have to tell people *that*?'" Bill's mother asks (287, emphasis added). Doty decodes her anguished question: ". . . [W]hy did you have to tell everyone my son was gay, why did you have to talk about it? Meaning, if my son wasn't gay he'd still be alive" (287–88). Shortly after the service, the family puts up the house, in which he and Bill had lived, for sale. ". . . [I]n the whirlwind of grief," Phil, writes Doty, "was also separating their possessions, packing up his things, displaced" (288). The family's investment in conventional narratives of gender, sex, sexuality, family, and inheritance work to write Phil out of their collective story once Bill has passed. *Heaven's Coast* records the erasure and, through its account of Bill and Phil, restores primacy to that relationship.

The title of Doty's memoir is open to various interpretations. "Heaven's Coast" refers to Provincetown, the town that, at the tip of Cape Cod, is known for its LGBT and artist inhabitants: the place where Doty and Wally lived together, where Wally died, and where Doty wrote the memoir. The title also brings into focus the text's larger twinned project of Doty's tribute to socially stigmatized communities of people, particularly gay men living with AIDS: *Heaven's Coast* not only memorializes Wally and others who have died from the disease, but also pays tribute to those who, like Doty, remain haunted by those dead. From this perspective, both the dead and those grieving them reside on "heaven's coast," an affirming meditative space that, set apart from the pull of linear time, intermixes queer experiences of death, loss, and marginalization. This is the space from which Doty writes.

Conclusion

While they examine historically distinct events, in their explorations of trauma, both Charlotte Delbo in *Auschwitz and After* and Mark Doty in *Heaven's Coast* challenge conventional understandings of time, gender, sex, and sexuality. "No future" orders the psychological reality of their memoirs' subjects. Even as they recognize their inability to do so fully, both Delbo and Doty bear witness to those subjects' experiences of disease and death; psychic violation and gendered violence. These are haunting experiences, which can be neither psychically nor narratively contained. "No future" also orders the form and political message of the two memoirs. For both writers memoir-making proves a form of advocacy. Both speak on behalf of those who cannot speak for themselves, and both insist on the humanity of their subjects, who find meaning and sustenance in relationships not tied to biological family or reproduction. So Delbo underscores the ethical power of memoir-making. She responds to the Holocaust by recounting the stories of her fellow prisoners in Auschwitz: both those women she has only barely encountered and those who, like her, have survived. Doty, in turn, insists that we consider the "presence and weight" of gay men's stories (57). He reclaims the dignity of lives overlooked or erased by a homophobic culture during the US AIDS epidemic of the 1980s and early 1990s. The stories of gender, sex, and sexuality that Delbo and Doty tell attest to the ethical power of their memoir-making.

Works Cited

Bergen, Doris L. *War and Genocide: A Concise History of the Holocaust*. Lanham, MD: Rowan & Littlefield, 2003.

Butler, Judith. "Imitation and Gender Insubordination." *Inside/Out: Lesbian Theories, Gay Theories*. Ed. Diana Fuss. New York: Routledge, 1991. 13–31.

Caruth, Cathy, ed. *Trauma: Explorations in Memory*. Baltimore & London: Johns Hopkins UP, 1995.

Davis, Colin. "Charlotte Delbo's Ghosts." *French Studies* 59.1 (2005): 9–15.

Delbo, Charlotte. *Auschwitz and After*. Trans. Rosette C. Lamont. New Haven & London: Yale UP, 1995.

_____. *Days and Memory*. Trans. Rosette Lamont. Evanston, IL: The Marlboro P/Northwestern UP, 2001.

Doty, Mark. *Heaven's Coast: A Memoir*. New York: HarperCollins, 1996.

Edelman, Lee. *No Future: Queer Theory and the Death Drive*. Durham & London: Duke UP, 2004.

Geddes, Jennifer L. "Banal Evil and Useless Knowledge: Hannah Arendt and Charlotte Delbo on Evil after the Holocaust." *Hypatia* 18.1 (Winter 2003): 104–115.

_____. "Toward an Ethics of Reading Survivor Testimonies." *Studies in the Literary Imagination* 41.2 (Fall 2008): 1–15.

Greenberg, Judith. "Surviving Charlotte Delbo's *Auschwitz and After*: How to Arrive and Depart." *Teaching the Representation of the Holocaust*. Eds. Marianne Hirsch & Irene Kacandes. New York, NY: MLA, 2004. 360–371.

Halberstam, Judith. *In a Queer Time and Place: Transgender Bodies, Subcultural Lives*. New York & London: New York UP, 2005.

Kramer, Larry. *Reports from the Holocaust: The Making of an AIDS Activist*. New York: St. Martin's P, 1989.

Lamont, Rosette C. "Charlotte Delbo: A Woman/Book." *The Faith of a (Woman) Writer*. Eds. Alice Kessler-Harris and William McBrien. New York: Greenwood Press, 1988. 247–52.

Langer, Lawrence L. Introduction. *Auschwitz and After*. By Charlotte Delbo. New Haven & London: Yale UP, 1985. ix–xviii.

Monette, Paul. *Borrowed Time: An AIDS Memoir*. New York: Avon, 1988.

Rich, Adrienne. "Notes Toward a Politics of Location." *Women, Feminist Identity and Society in the 1980s: Selected Papers*. Eds. Myriam Díaz-Diocaretz & Iris Zavala. Amsterdam and Philadelphia: John Benjamins, 1985. Rpt. in *Arts of the Possible: Essays and Conversations*. By Adrienne Rich. New York & London: W.W. Norton & Co., 2001. 62–82.

Sontag, Susan. *Illness as Metaphor and AIDS and Its Metaphors*. New York: Doubleday, 1989.

CRITICAL CONTEXTS

Writing Gender: Authorship and Authority
Frederick S. Roden, with Joseph J. Portanova

The conversation about "gender, sex, and sexuality" in a historical and cultural context begins with the recognition of bodily difference. As feminist theorists have demonstrated, the dichotomy of male versus female defines, if not all, then certainly almost all societies. In the development of western culture, with which this essay will be concerned, we find a binary of difference, wherein the female body, perspective, and voice challenge a dominant patriarchal discourse. Most often, in the historical trajectory that we will consider, there is a claim to the right to speak by indirection rather than through direct discourse. Throughout the history of Western culture, women's voices have been silent and silenced. We often find their exercise of power behind rather than beside men's.

In the past half-century, the feminist reconsideration of women's agency has produced various methods to recover and discover women's deployment of power and voice in the western tradition. As this essay will show, tracking this history depends on the reliance upon experience or practice over theory, the paradoxical assertion of right through the acceptance of a position of weakness or secondary status, and the claim of the importance of prophecy. For women in the West, revelation almost always trumps philosophy, insofar as both formal learning and access to legal authority remained the domain of men. With this in mind, readers face two areas of subject exploration. These areas frequently intersect in the figures considered here. Literature, as an "art" of representation, allows us to see how language and the metaphorical—the indirect rather than the direct—serve women's voices in creating alternate realities to the avenues of power open to them in the world. Religion—a term meant here to encompass all aspects of the sacred, non-rational, and spiritual—likewise offers this invitation. The following essay seeks to chart how these two areas of discourse provided ways for women to resist—even as they complied with—the regulations and expectations imposed on them by Western culture. This reading of women's "experience" will offer insight into "gender, sex, and sexuality" by illuminating the assumptions about each of those categories that the array of moments highlighted here demanded.

Beginning with the ancients, the essay provides a brief overview of women in the Greco-Roman world. One could argue that the memory and legacy of the poet Sappho (sixth century BCE) has meant more than the actual woman herself or her literary output. One might say the same about the figure of the Virgin Mary, the subject of novelist Colm Tóibín's recent *Testament of Mary* that speaks from her perspective. Mary may have embodied the Word, in the understanding of Christ as *Logos* and the mystical idea of her womb giving voice. But apart from acquiescing, agreeing, indeed submitting, her mouth has been silent. Taking this pair, Sappho and the Virgin Mary, for cultural mythology, we have, on the one hand, the intellectually, artistically creative woman whose band of female apprentices/lovers pales in significance compared to her leap into death following a failed heterosexual love. On the other hand, we have the physically creative foremother, the sacred trope for all fecundity, whose virginity and holiness became both the bane and hope of later women.

Ancient Greece had many goddesses, creating myths of the jealous wife (Hera), dangerous power in desire (Aphrodite), virginity (Athena, Artemis), the fruits of the earth (Demeter), and the hearth (Hestia). Priestesses, and particularly Sibyls, suggest later examples for women's encounters with the holy as well as the literary arts. At the moment around the Common Era's dawn, we find the first tangible historical record of the public role of women in two Roman empresses. No Roman empress ever ruled alone, although several wielded tremendous influence as the power behind the throne. On the death of her husband, Emperor Caius Octavius "Augustus" (the venerable), Livia (58 BCE–29 CE) was given the title "Augusta." In his *Annals of Imperial Rome*, the historian Tacitus implies that she had a direct hand in the deaths of her stepchildren and possibly grandchildren, wishing to ensure her son's succession to the throne. Agrippina II (15–59 CE) married her uncle, the Emperor Claudius, and assured that her own son, Nero, would succeed, perhaps by poisoning her husband. Agrippina sought to rule the empire through her son and found herself thwarted, first by his tutors and, ultimately, by Nero himself. We are limited to male historians, such as Tacitus, for knowledge of her tale, but Agrippina may have seduced her son in a final bid for power. He resisted and, after several failed attempts, finally succeeded in assassinating her. Agrippina could win power for Nero, but could not keep any for herself. This limitation led to her downfall.

The career of the Byzantine empress Theodora (c. 500–548) shows that Greek and Roman restrictions on women continued under Christianity. We rely on the male writer Procopius for the history of her rise from humble birth by cleverness and sexual license. When Emperor Justinian fell in love with her, she came to power. Procopius portrays her as a vengeful nymphomaniac, yet he also constructs Theodora as a successful collaborator in ruling with her husband. The couple even pretended to quarrel to confuse rival constituencies. While Procopius scripts Theodora as promiscuous before marriage, he paints her as a faithful wife to Justinian, even though she encouraged other wives' infidelities for political purposes. Theodora established a convent for former prostitutes, a "magdalen home" (the Christian term alluding to the supposed profession of Saint Mary Magdalene). Procopius finds Theodora's interference with the Christian Church to be scandalous. Her enemy Photius was dragged from the altar of the Church of Hagia Sophia, while the priests "stood to one side and suffered her to do as she willed" (Procopius 19).

In contrast, early Christianity is filled with stories of virtuous women. While some of these are literally urban legend, others stand out. The third-century Saint Perpetua, a Carthaginian patrician convert, kept a diary during her imprisonment. It depicts a young wife, daughter, and mother of a nursing infant who chose to die for her Christian faith. She describes the abuses inflicted on her physical body as warfare that transformed her into a man. Her martyrdom was the "hour of her glory," like Christ's ("Passion of Perpetua" 23). Her slave Felicity, "milk dripping from her breasts," dies with her

("Passion of Perpetua" 23). Christianity became a means of rejecting traditional gender roles. The fourth-century Saint Pelagia of Antioch masqueraded as a eunuch monk in Jerusalem, in order to live out her vocation. Early Christian hagiography offered such types for devout women's aspirations. These examples demonstrate the intersection of legal and gender transgression in the subversive Christianization of the Mediterranean world. But models of the new faith always engaged in some way the *mores* of the old. The Anglo-Saxon epic *Beowulf*, often cited as a religious text *manqué* for its struggle between heroic and quasi-Christian values, displays the noblewomen Wealhtheow and Freawaru presenting gold and bearing cups to victors. Some scholars have suggested that a "return" of "repressed" female power can be found in the monstrous representation of Grendel's mother, who emerges from her primordial ooze to wreck the peace of human civilization in that story. Anxious examples abound in European mythology. The legend of Saint Patrick driving the snakes out of Ireland may refer to banishment of the wisdom serpent, symbolizing pagan Irish female deities. In a positive light, the woman who headed a college at Kildare, the fifth–sixth century Saint Brigit, may have been considered an incarnation of the ancient Irish goddess Brigit.

Inversions of gender go hand-in-hand with the inversions of a new faith. Early English literature includes many retellings of Biblical tales, literally and figuratively "translating" them for a new audience of Germanic tribes living under a warrior code. In the Anglo-Saxon poem *Judith*, the Hebrew heroine is transformed into a vengeful soldier for Christ. "God gave Judith glory at war" (*Judith* 122). As in "The Dream of the Rood," where a warrior Christ mounts the tree of victory, heroic culture could not abide humility in its saviors. Even women were towers of strength. For this reason, the age produced women of religious authority, from the seventh-century abbess Hilda of Whitby to Saint Hildegard of Bingen (1098–1179). The later German saint described herself as a feather on the breath of God, crediting her agency to God's authority. Her letters chastised bishops, abbots, and even the pope. Hildegard claimed that she had been called by God to "'cry out . . . and write'" because she lived in a womanish age (61). Hildegard sought not to assert a feminist utopia, but to suggest that the men of her time had failed to speak as they ought. Therefore, a woman would be used as God's instrument. This default empowered and justified her speech. Hildegard used the prophetic voice in her political writing and her visionary works, extensive theological *summae* that explain cosmology through word and image worthy of Jung's *Red Book*. She is known as the Sibyl of the Rhine, having written lavish songs for her community of nuns' devotional use. These works glorify the bodies of virgins. Scholars have noted homoeroticism in such woman-song, and have commented on Hildegard's Jeremiah-like laments for Richardis, a beloved companion who left to found another convent and died.

Hildegard's justification for speech would be at odds with modern feminism. She imagined gender complementarity, not "equality." Basing authority on her aristocratic birth as much as Divine inspiration, her views on class are not ours. She maintained that one would no more mix noble and common women in the convent than place horses and donkeys in the same stable. Hildegard's view of the material world's standards could subvert, as in her pedigreed permission to speak out with few repercussions. Still, Hildegard found herself subject to the authority of "Father" Church. Her convent was temporarily denied religious sacraments because of an irregular burial. No matter how powerful in mundane or spiritual terms, premodern women were subject to male control. Saint Paul's statement that in Christ there is neither male nor female (Galatians 3.28) applied to heaven, not earth.

Complementary to the inheritance of Germanic heroic culture is the art of courtly love popularized by Provençal troubadours and trouvères. It is found in the Arthurian literature of Norman England. The Madonna-like lady might receive adoration from a knight who pledges his service to her, but whose "plaint" she cannot grant with carnal consumation. This literature depicts an incestuous culture where infatuations are inevitable but adultery's risk of bastard birth would undermine a dynastic system. Women's agency is commodified in sexual power to grant or deny favors, to maintain or destroy bloodlines. Women's bodies are volatile in the biologically procreative world. As in the tales of the Roman empresses, woman's authority is defined by her individual relationships with particular men who authorize her body. The twelfth-century Anglo-Norman Marie de France is commonly regarded as the first "English" woman author, even though she composed in French. Her *lais* are moral tales of transgression and redemption plotted on a matrix of romantic love. In *Bisclavret*, a husband's body enacts a male menstruation by morphing monthly into a werewolf as a test of his wife's fidelity. Relying on his clothing to return to humanhood (clothes make the man), the wife's treachery ensures he will remain in his lower animal nature. But the true gentleman is inside of him: when he recognizes the hierarchy of rulers, his humanity is recovered—although not before he bites off his wife's nose. Her infidelity is marked on her body, and her future offspring lack noses as well. While the outcome may be a metaphor for inheritable venereal disease from infidelity, cutting off the nose was typical punishment in medieval Italy when adultery was charged. In the *lai Lanval*, male loyalty is rewarded and female treachery punished. The knight Lanval is granted the favors of a magical lady whose only rule is that their relationship remains secret. Meanwhile, the earthly queen attempts to seduce him. When he rejects her advances with a comparison to his lady, the queen accuses him of propositioning her. The queen's duplicity is revealed as his lady forgives his verbal transgression and transports both of them to the spirit realm. This woman writer's fantasy of female perfection includes both carnal consummation and personal agency.

The most canonical male author of medieval England presents a challenge to read the female body and a female character. With the rise of authorship (Geoffrey Chaucer [1343–1400] is our first "known" author mentioned here, save the ancient historians), the question of "authority" in reading emerges. In the *Canterbury Tales*, Chaucer sketches the character of the Wife of Bath, a laywoman who interprets the Bible through the lens of her experience. Critics debate whether she is a nightmare from clerical antifeminist literature or a sympathetic portrait. The body of her text and the text of her body present the challenge of secular modernity: who has the right to interpret? The prologue to her tale is longer than the tale itself.

It provides her autobiography (a fiction, since she is a character recalled by "Chaucer," a character in the *Canterbury Tales*, scripted by Chaucer, the poet . . .). Alys of Bath recounts abuse by a clerical husband who tormented her by reading stories of wicked wives. After she tears a page from his book, he beats her. A happy marriage is restored with his agreement to return authority to her body and her property. Chaucer raises the subject of perspective here and in the formal tale, an Arthurian story of a rape. There, a fallen knight, a failure at courtly love, must learn what women want. When he discerns the answer is freedom of choice, he is granted the pleasure of a beautiful and loyal wife. While it might be easy to imagine Chaucer as a proto-feminist, this text is an intellectual reckoning of authority. The female body serves as a pawn in the struggle for the right to read: to interpret for oneself, the hallmark of modernity. In the patient Griselda of the Clerk's Tale, the wife named "Constance" in the Man of Law's Tale, and *The Legend of Good Women*, Chaucer deployed gender to explore changing dynamics of power in a world where authority could no longer be centralized in Church and state. Future texts embody the conclusion from the Clerk: Griselda is dead, and so is her patience. The world in which blind faith and blind obedience submitted to others' readings of the text of one's own life had ended.

Chaucer's representations must be compared to three extraordinary female contemporaries. In 1405, Christine de Pizan wrote *The Book of the City of Ladies*, a corrective of the antifeminist literature. Three female guides read against the errors in the western tradition's negative representations of women. Deploying the dream-vision formula, Christine de Pizan makes herself as student of these enlightened teachers. A far homelier and humbler text is *The Book of Margery Kempe* (c.1430s), often called the first autobiography by an Englishwoman. There, we hear Margery's desperation to tell her story, for she is illiterate and depends on a clerical scribe willing to write it. Prone to postpartum psychoses, Margery experienced many disappointments in middle-class life and marriage. Aware of the special recognition brides of Christ had, Margery longs to be in relationship with God as His special spouse. Her husband frees her, forgiving her marital debt (sexual intercourse) in exchange for payment of his literal debt. Prone to mad fits of weeping, Margery traveled on many religious pilgrimages. (This was how the fictional Wife of Bath occupied her time, and how people of that upwardly mobile merchant class practiced their increasingly international trade.) In Margery's text, we find audacious and skillful defenses of her right to speak publicly. Her female lay authority, willingness to challenge prelates, and determination to tell her story are extraordinary.

One of the few references we have to the English theologian Julian of Norwich (c.1342–c.1416) is found in Margery's book, where she mentions a visit to the holy hermit of that town. The thirteenth-century *Ancrene Wisse*, or rule for anchoresses, describes how a woman pursuing the eremitic (solitary) way should live. In the later Middle Ages, when some spiritual seekers were disenchanted with corruptions in monastic life or some circumstance prevented them from pursuing that path, they often opted for the "Desert Fathers" (and Mothers) model of the early Church. Julian of Norwich was one such person, whose enclosure (if one can call it that) came after a sudden illness. The little we know about the woman attached to the church of St. Julian's in Norwich comes from historical references to her presence there. We have two texts she wrote based on a religious vision she experienced while comatose. The first version recounts details with keen spiritual insight. The second version, probably composed two decades later, parses out the theological meanings of her "showings," as she calls them. Julian's hermitage was located in a busy market town where people like Margery sought her out. With one window to the world and one to the church, the anchoress' cell was a liminal space between this world and the next. Julian's texts are extraordinary because of her self-consciousness as a writer, but also for the sophistication of her theology. Informed by the best education available to women at that time (presumably from wealth and male relatives' belief that she should learn), Julian's thought weaves together the two major trajectories of late medieval Christianity. The philosophical approach of Scholasticism is wedded to the affective theology of

Divine Love in the deceptively simple conclusion that love is God's meaning. Much attention has been paid to Julian's use of maternal imagery in discussing God as mother. But Julian was not the first Christian writer to do so, and many of these voices (Saint Anselm, for instance) were male. Julian's uniqueness is in her deployment of maternal metaphors to suggest both the Creation (of everything) and the Redemption (Christ's passion) as literal "labors" of love. Biological parturition serves as the central trope for both physical and spiritual existence. Julian's scholarly abstraction is coupled with remarkably cogent and accessible counsel, sound advice from a spiritual director. In as radical a manner as Chaucer, Julian levels the hierarchical playing field, unifying the cosmos in a theology of "one-ing." Julian's refusal to attribute dichotomous thinking to the world God created is reflected in her theology, ethics, and indeed politics of gender. God is not only mother, but also father, spouse, friend, and every imaginable relationship. In reading Julian's texts, we may find it difficult to remember that a medieval Christian woman, socialized to articulate categories of difference, is speaking. She allows no separateness within her vision of unity.

Although a brilliant and iconoclastic theologian, the Blessed (not Sainted) Julian of Norwich has never been named a doctor of the Church, the title bestowed on the great teachers in the Roman Catholic tradition. The first women given such recognition were Saint Catherine of Siena (1347–1380) and Saint Teresa of Ávila (1515–1582), and these two not until 1970. Only two other women have been awarded the title: Saint Thérèse of Lisieux (1873–1897) in 1997 (for her theology of love and devotion that lends itself well to submission) and Saint Hildegard in 2012 (besides her prolific productivity, her thought is perhaps the most systematic of any medieval woman writing theology). One might argue that the sheer orthodoxy of Catherine's voice advanced her candidacy more than Julian's (Catherine did not learn to write until three years before her death; like Margery Kempe, she dictated most of her works). But however much Teresa may be called a "mystic"—consider the familiar statue by Bernini of her "ecstasy," her heart pierced with the arrow of Divine Love—she was, in fact, an extraordinary administrator. In the highly policed world of sixteenth-century Spain, this granddaughter of a Jew who had suffered the Inquisition succeeded in reforming a religious order. All of the women considered here are extraordinary for their claim to the voice of experience to speak from authority. If Julian stands on the cusp between medieval and early modern, writing sophisticated theology through a human lens, Teresa moves forward in perfecting and differentiating new genres for women. Her autobiography recalls Augustine's *Confessions* (397) and is the first work since that ancient prototype to offer such a candid portrait of the self-inviting spiritual and psychological transformation. Teresa's *Interior Castle* provides a step-by-step guide to deepening one's relationship to God. Despite formulaic language of modesty befitting her time and place, there is no question that Teresa speaks authoritatively in both of these texts.

Taken together, Julian and Teresa present us with a glimpse of a changing world where even a woman might speak boldly. Of course, this period coincides with the emergence of Reformation thought and changes in structures of power with respect to religion and the individual. While many examples could be provided, the story of Anabaptist martyr Janneken Munstdorp (d. 1573) articulates these themes. Despite modest family and humble education, Janneken could read and write. She considered her personal study of the Bible to be both consolation and her way to Heaven. Pregnant when arrested as a heretic, she was spared until the birth of her child, whom she smuggled out of prison. Before being burned at the stake, she left her infant daughter a letter exhorting her to be true to her faith and proud of her parents, whom she compares to the prophets and apostles. Janneken urges her to "take up a book, and learn to seek there that which concerns your salvation" (985). She should "give diligence to learn to read and write" (Munstdorp 986). Janneken bids her daughter to be an obedient child only "so far as is not contrary to God": to discern right and wrong for herself, not submit blindly to authority (987).

The career of Sor Juana Inés de la Cruz (1651–1695), a nun in Mexico City, New Spain, illuminates some of the advantages and liabilities of learned women during the Catholic Counter-

Reformation. Although a girl of strong intellect, she was prevented from passing as a man to pursue university education. Self-taught, her poetry brought her recognition and patronage at the viceregal court. She chose the convent over marriage. There, she assembled one of the best collections of books and musical instruments in the New World. Sor Juana studied, wrote, and taught, directing musical and dramatic productions at the convent girls' school. With the help of the vicereine, Sor Juana's first book of poetry was published in Spain. She was called the "Tenth Muse of Mexico." Her poetry celebrates educated women, such as Saint Catherine of Alexandria (287–305) whose reason confounded male philosophers. Sor Juana wrote in the Villancico VI from "Santa Catarina" (1691), "gender is not of the essence / in matters of intelligence. . . . It is of service to the Church / that women argue, tutor, learn, / for He Who granted women reason / would not have them uninformed" (Juana 3–4, 61–64). Sor Juana's downfall came when a bishop published her letter disagreeing with a minor point of a Jesuit priest's sermon preached fifty years earlier. The same bishop later wrote a critique of Sor Juana's focus on secular learning, warning of vanity and pride. Her masterful *Response* cites historical precedents and argues that learning is part of her nature. Sor Juana found herself without patrons or protection. She surrendered her library and musical instruments to the archbishop, signed a confession of faith, and died of plague the following year. Despite the public gesture, one-hundred books and one-hundred-eighty-five bundles of letters were found in her rooms after her death. Even in New Spain during the Inquisition, resistance was possible.

This debate between sacred and secular also informs our reading as we consider the cultural history of religion and literature. As we continue to see, the two are not polar opposites as much as crossroads, intersecting yet faithful narratives. The most significant literary development of the succeeding eighteenth century was the so-called "rise" of the novel. The evolution of narrative from the epistolary form emphasizing private life and particular experience underscores the significance of the individual, lay, and indeed female reader and writer. To be the author of one's own text reaches its climax in the masterful novels of Jane Austen. Although admired by a male audience, they are pedagogical guides for young women that teach negotiation of a perilous society and the longings for an inner life. The question of the "inner life" returns us to the discourse of religion. When the Wesleys and other second- or third-wave Protestant Reformers placed an emphasis upon revelation, they authorized the experience of laypeople regardless of class and re-affirmed the long tradition through which women could speak their truth. In 1859, novelist Mary Ann Evans (writing as "George Eliot") would depict this phenomenon in *Adam Bede*. Set some half-century earlier, the novel's humble Dinah Morris draws audiences for evangelical revivals with her gifted rhetoric. Methodism would ban women preachers. Samuel Johnson compared a woman's preaching to a dog walking on its hind legs: neither is done well, but one is surprised to find them done at all. Yet the preaching that women could no longer practice publicly Eliot claimed elsewhere. The genre of the novel became a rhetorical space for Biblical reinterpretation. Eliot was a former Evangelical Christian, and her works exemplify the literary output of the Victorian approach to the Bible as literature. Sacred typology might offer a humanistic guide for living in a secularizing world.

The nineteenth century witnessed an abundance of female writers claiming the pen in multiple genres. Abolitionist rhetoric and early feminist prose argued from religious imperatives. While intellectual novelists like Eliot wrote secular scripture and elite poets flourished in classical forms, "lady" hymn writers and other devout women produced volumes of works. The blind Fanny Crosby wrote some eight thousand hymns. Whether relying on philosophy, the muse, or the spirit, female authors wrote experience into their texts. When Crosby pleads that God not "pass [her] by," we hear the voice of a faithful Christian woman and a person with a disability. This century of "subjectivity" would establish the place of the first-person voice for men as well as women. The period literature displays sophisticated engagement with theological questions about woman's place. Florence Nightingale's 1852 *Cassandra* focuses on how women's time is considered to be dispensable. The title refers to the mythic female seer, tragic in that her prophecies are not believed. Nightingale laments what the world has lost by the expectations placed upon women. She asserts that Christ raised women to be ministers of God in moral activity. Had Christ been a woman, she says, he would have been dismissed as a "great complainer" (Nightingale 14). The "next Christ will perhaps be a female Christ," but the world first has to be made ready (Nightingale 14). Nightingale observes that if women were to ask "Who is my mother? And who are my brethren?" (Matthew 12.48) as Christ did, making relationship ties secondary to vocation, they would be accused of destroying the family. In her extraordinary 1857 *Aurora Leigh*, a novel in verse about the development of a female artist, Elizabeth Barrett Browning argues for woman's vocation. The poet must "choose to walk at all risks" (Barrett Browning 2.120). A would-be suitor—a philanthropist cousin looking for a helpmate in a wife—denigrates women's particularity as evidence of incompetence in repairing the world. Unlike Christ, he argues, women fail to see the big picture. The title character affirms that "'every single creature, female as the male, / Stands single in responsible act and thought" (Barrett Browning 2.472–473). Woman has a vocation to fulfill. These voices recall Mary Wollstonecraft's extraordinary 1792 *Vindication of the Rights of Woman* that blames poor education for the wrongs of women, that their observed nature is the result of socialization not essence. She anticipates twentieth-century feminist Simone de Beauvoir's famous declaration that one is not born, but rather becomes, a woman.

Many other nineteenth-century women engaged theology. The poet Christina Rossetti's 1862 "Goblin Market" tells a moral tale of Christ-like sacrifice by one "sister" for another who has "fallen." Rossetti's typological tropes transform woman into a literal savior, a Eucharistic feast to consume for redemption in vicarious suffering. Rossetti, a devout Anglican, was active in the "magdalen home" movement to rehabilitate former prostitutes. This literature had a redemptive purpose of its own for both the "fallen" and the "saved," offering hope to society's pariahs and meaning to middle-class rescuers. The poet inverts gender in her Renaissance-inspired sonnet sequence, "Monna Innominata." There, a female sonneteer acknowledges that, like Dante (with Beatrice) or Petrarch (with Laura), the female poet might use a male body as a vector for transcendence to the Divine. Rossetti is keenly aware of the silence of the woman of the Renaissance sonnet tradition. She prefaces her poem with an explanatory paragraph imagining had "such a lady spoken for herself" (Rossetti 558). Despite these subversive gestures, Rossetti's poetics, and indeed her life, were often defined by the claim of the "Lowest Place," a title of one of her poems. That humility is necessary in the imitation of Christ is an argument deployed by women throughout Christian history. Inhabiting the inferior place made them holier than men could be. The quintessential girl-saint of Divine Love, the idealized and infantilized Thérèse of Lisieux, thought so. She wrote that, longing for intimacy with God, she wished she could be priest, or even pope. But as just the little girl that she was, Thérèse affirmed she was closer to God than any male clerics could be. Thus religious thought that subjugates women has also been used for resistance and affirmation. Katharine Bradley (1848–1914) and Edith Cooper (1862–1913), an aunt and niece who wrote under the pen name "Michael Field," were lesbian lovers and literary collaborators. Their partnership was transformed upon conversion to Roman Catholicism. "New Women" of the *fin de siècle* who had studied at Cambridge, they were inspired by Sappho's *poësis*. They went on to create a trinity of their own with a beloved Chow dog standing in for the male Christ. The passion and death of Whym Chow enabled Field to re-imagine their human suffering and partnership beyond the grave. Lesbian writers would invigorate twentieth-century literature about Christianity, from Radclyffe Hall's extraordinary novel *The Well of Loneliness* (1928) (which, like Eliot's works, rewrites Biblical typology) to Jeanette Winterson's 1985 *Oranges Are Not the Only Fruit* (depicting a young lesbian coming of age in an Evangelical home). Some literature emerged directly out of the modernist canon, such as Vita Sackville-West's *The Eagle and the Dove*, a study of Teresa of Ávila and Thérèse of Lisieux that suggests the former was a lesbian.

Although far from complete, the above essay endeavors to recount this history with some representative figures that elucidate a particular arc of consciousness with respect to gender in the Western context that readers of this guide will be familiar with. Besides many individual voices we have not discussed, this essay has not attempted a cross-cultural perspective, and its focus on religious/literary discourse has engaged only Christian figures. Within the Western tradition, we cannot neglect certain "internal others," namely Jews, who despite French emancipation and American affirmation at the end of the eighteenth century (and similar British and German gestures in the nineteenth) remained on the margins of Western culture. Movements toward full participation in the societies in which Jews lived transformed traditional Judaism and changed Western culture. Becoming part of modern life also freed Jews to help make modernity. From the extraordinary memoir of merchant Glückel of Hameln (1646–1724) to the literary output of nineteenth-century writers, such as Grace Aguilar or Amy Levy, from salon ladies to the extraordinary Lily Montagu (1873–1963) who preached, led a congregation, and co-founded the British movement of Liberal Judaism, Jewish women in the West have made outstanding contributions that mobilized the gender-inflected advancements in the world they inhabited. The twentieth-century lineage from Regina Jonas (1902–1944), the first woman ordained as a rabbi who ministered in the Theresienstadt concentration camp, moves to the subject that concludes this essay. Jewish women were leaders in Second-Wave feminism, feminist literary criticism, and the transformation of the culture of the last third of the twentieth century.

This shift was the realization of the social message of the voices considered here: the right of woman to voice and agency, the rejection of an essentializing view of a limited "nature" of woman, and the recovery/rediscovery of women's voices throughout history that makes the study we present here possible. The revision of the canon of what we read and value was based on the Second-Wave feminist belief that the "personal is the political," that experience has intellectual value and practical purpose. This revolution promoted exchange between the academic work of the ivory tower and grass-roots activism. As in abolitionism and nineteenth-century feminism, religious women raised their voices, from radical Christians, like Mary Daly and Rosemary Ruether, to many Jewish women who applied their hope for *tikkun olam*, repair of the world, to feminist change. This sea change, in turn, informed religious practice, status, and agendas, as most western religious denominations moved toward full participation by women in all areas of spiritual life and teaching authority. It also led to expansion beyond feminist questions to encompass questions of sexualities, from the gay and lesbian to the bi, trans, and queer. Today, policy think-tanks for reproductive rights are affiliated with religious denominations. First-rate scholars of gender and identity write on religion, as Judith Butler has recently done. We have come full-circle from a historical moment where religious discourse served as an indirect avenue to power for those who are disenfranchised. Instead, the formerly disenfranchised—women, homosexuals, and others—play leadership roles in religious institutions and secular scholarly institutes. And it has ceased to be a novelty to examine a work of literature that interrogates both religion and gender/sex/sexuality.

This essay has sought to introduce the experience of gender, sex, and sexuality in Western culture through the experience of voice, using the lens of religion to discuss historically how we have read and why we have written. In a cultural moment that affirms "spiritual, but not religious" identities, we remain devout in reading, and speaking, the self. Whether we blog, tweet, or use no social media, we cannot deny the twenty-first century desire to tell our stories. In reviewing the historical context of this deeply human longing, our own age supersedes "chick-lit" ghettoization of disclosure and confidence. Yet the past shows how thoroughly the experience of gender has inflected our ability, indeed our will, to read as well as write our selves.

Works Cited

Barrett Browning, Elizabeth. "Aurora Leigh." *The Broadview Anthology of British Literature: The Victorian Era*. 2nd ed. Eds. Joseph Black et al. Peterborough, ON: Broadview Press, 2012. 143–168.

Black, Joseph, et al., ed. *The Broadview Anthology of British Literature: Medieval Period*. 2nd ed. Peterborough, ON: Broadview Press, 2009. 93–102.

Crosby, Fanny. "Pass Me Not, O Gentle Savior." *The United Methodist Hymnal*. Nashville: The United Methodist Publishing House, 1989. 351.

Hildegard of Bingen. *Scivias*. Trans. Mother Columba Hart and Jane Bishop. New York: Paulist Press, 1990.

Juana Inés de la Cruz. *Poems, Protest, and a Dream*. Trans. Margaret Sayers Peden. New York: Penguin, 1997.

Judith. Trans. Stephen O. Glosecki. *The Broadview Anthology of British Literature: The Medieval Period*. 2nd ed. Eds. Joseph Black et al. Peterborough, ON: Broadview Press, 2009. 93–102.

Munstdorp, Janneken. "[Testament] Written to my own dearest daughter, while I was (unworthily) confined for the Lord's sake, in prison, at Antwerp, A.D. 1573." *Martyrs Mirror*. Ed. Thieleman J. van Braght. Trans. Joseph F. Sohm. Scottdale: Herald P. 984–987. n.d. Web. 29 January 2014. <http://www.homecomers.org/mirror/martyrs144.htm>.

Nightingale, Florence. *Cassandra*. *The Broadview Anthology of British Literature: The Victorian Era*. 2nd ed. Eds. Joseph Black et al. Peterborough, ON: Broadview Press, 2012.

"The Passion of Perpetua and Felicity." *Mystics, Visionaries & Prophets: A Historical Anthology of Women's Spiritual Writings*. Ed. Shawn Madigan. Minneapolis: Augsburg P, 1998. 13–25.

Procopius. *Secret History*. Trans. Richard Atwater. Ann Arbor: U Michigan P, 1963.

Rossetti, Christina. "Monna Innominata." *The Broadview Anthology of British Literature: The Victorian Era*. 2nd ed. Eds. Joseph Black et al. Peterborough, ON: Broadview Press, 2012. 558–561.

Who's Counting? Sexes, Genders, and Sexualities from Ancient Myths to Fin-de-Siècle and Twentieth-Century Literature and Theory

Katerina Kitsi-Mitakou

Well before our own time, the human sexes were not always considered two and distinct. In Plato's *Symposium,* for example, Aristophanes, the renowned comic playwright of ancient Athens, speaks of a third sex, the "androgynous," a combination of male and female. In his attempt to explain the power of *eros* in human lives, Aristophanes devises an entertaining myth, according to which human beings were originally round and had four legs, four arms, two faces, and two sets of genitals (two male, two female, or combination of the two). These creatures were so mighty and arrogant that they even threatened the gods and attempted to usurp their power. Zeus then, Aristophanes recounts, devised a scheme to weaken their strength and withhold their force: he cut them into two pieces. Since then, each human being has had only one face and one set of arms, legs and genitals and is destined to a lifelong search for its other severed half. "That's how long ago," Aristophanes claims, "the innate desire of human beings for each other started" (191, d). As far as preference is concerned, it is, of course, logical that those men who are cut from the male sex are only interested in men, those women who are slices of the female sex are attracted to women, while those that come from the androgynous go for the opposite sex.

Aristophanes insists that his speech be not treated as a comedy (193b, d), and indeed, it has serious implications that call for further attention. Despite it being an ancient myth, it reflects the modern skepticism about the fixity of the two sexes and sexual orientation, as it shatters the dominance of the two-sex model and explains same-sex desire. Moreover, if the sexual urge is nothing but the need to reconstruct—through physical love—the original "rounded whole" we once were, our desire for others then is not only predestined (sexual inclination is purely a matter of which sex we have been cut from), but also self-absorbed (the "other" we strive for is actually *our* "other half"). One need only bring to mind here Oscar Wilde's renowned announcement: "To love oneself is the beginning of a life-long romance" ("Phrases and Philosophies . . ." 6), or Virginia Woolf's "different though the sexes are, they intermix" (*Orlando* 181), in order to realize how past views on sex, gender, and sexuality are recycled.

What this essay aims to discuss, by focusing on discussions and theories of gender, sex, and sexuality in late-nineteenth- and early-twentieth-century Britain, is how the generally considered normative patterns of biology and sexual behavior are products of a socio-political time period and have always been contested in surprisingly intersecting ways. The dominance of the two-sex model, heterosexuality and the patriarchal nuclear family (consisting of husband, wife, and offspring) throughout the nineteenth century was serving the needs of a fast rising nation that depended on curbing and channelling desire towards reproductive ends. The development of sexology from the 1860s onwards marked what was normative behavior and codified deviations as disease. But as control always incites reaction, by the end of the nineteenth century, there had begun a proliferation of medical, psychoanalytic, and philosophical discourses that recognized sexuality as a force beyond control and separated it from procreation. The idea of a third sex returned, gender roles were upset, and the notions of sex, gender, and sexuality were dissociated. The late Victorians and early modernists were, on the one hand, caught in the swirl of an era that was coming to an end and that insisted on drawing men and women further and further apart by prescribing steadfast gender roles to them. On the other hand, they invented ways of escaping their restrictive past and headed towards more progressive modes of thinking, which, in many ways, anticipate late twentieth-century perceptions of gender and sex identities.

Oscar Wilde
Being "thoroughly in earnest"

Throughout the nineteenth century, England expanded into a territorial, economic, and industrial power that possessed almost a quarter of the earth and controlled the world markets and banks. The vigor of the British Empire rested primarily on two solid foundations: *steam power*, which enabled unparalleled technological inventions, and its metaphorical equivalent, *earnestness*, which guaranteed stability and permanence. It is expected that a thriving nation be obsessed with constancy and the wish to preserve its status quo of supremacy all over the world. Such an imperial force would consequently be very sensitive to any changes in the structure of society and its institutions; class and gender hierarchies were safeguarded and the need to populate the nation became more pressing than ever before. Marriage and family were perceived as pillars of morality and state order, and the two genders were, in earnest, assigned disparate and unwavering roles: while men were called to take an active part in the social happenings, women were restrained in the domestic sphere. "The sexes," Virginia Woolf writes in *Orlando*, "drew further and further apart" (219). What guaranteed the building of a world empire was, she claims half-jokingly half-seriously, the fact that "the life of the average woman was a succession of childbirths" (*Orlando* 219).

More importantly, however, the might of the empire depended on an infallible tactic: performing one's appointed tasks in thorough earnestness. The most popular imperial hero, Charles Dickens' David Copperfield, shares with us the secret of his success at the height of Britain's grandeur, in 1850: "whatever I have tried to do in life," David confesses, "I have tried with all my heart to do well; . . . whatever I have devoted myself to, I have devoted myself to completely; . . . in great aims and in small, *I have always been thoroughly in earnest*" (590, emphasis added). Being sincere, serious and determined, however, proves to be more complicated than David Copperfield, Charles Dickens' shadow in this autobiographical novel, pronounces it to be. For if David would never dare practice infidelity, his real-life double questioned the sanctity of marriage and shook the peacefulness of family life. All modern biographies of Dickens recount the surprising fact that, after two decades of living with his wife, Catherine, he accused her for the birth of their ten children, denounced her publicly as an incompetent mother, and deprived her of the right to live with her family. It is no secret today that the last thirteen years before his death, Dickens was divided between his life with his children in a house run by Georgina, his wife's sister, and his parallel life with the young actress Ellen Ternan. He took, of course, great pains to veil his passionate relationship with Ternan and protect his image of a "thoroughly in earnest," booming writer, as Victorian society was more dependent on outward show and less concerned with what lay beneath the surface veneer.

Despite the efforts of Victorian society to shield marriage, it was evidently in crisis even during the time its sacredness was supposedly beyond doubt. In that light, the notion of earnestness, which epitomized the Victorian obsession with seriousness, stability, morality, and domesticity, ironically reflected also the disintegration of all those values and marked the transition from the Victorian to the late modern period. At the turn of the twentieth century, the word strikes back with a vengeance in the title of Oscar Wilde's stage comedy *The Importance of Being Earnest*. The name "Ernest" is deliberately confused with the adjective "earnest" and the play's female leads, Gwendolen and Cecily, are adamant about marrying someone—anyone—with the name "Ernest." As everyone in the play agrees, what matters, after all, are names and appearances rather than personality traits for, as they claim, if one has nothing, but can look everything, this is all one can desire (1735). Wilde's flat and shockingly good-for-nothing characters are a faithful representation of Victorian fixation with decorum and an indirect caustic attack on the hypocrisy of Victorian society. The mirror, which Wilde raises to his supposedly respectable audience, very cunningly insinuates that their exertion to silence sexuality (which went as far as even covering piano legs) was all in vain.

By the late Victorian period, as the highly stratified class and gender system became seriously impaired, the masks of respectability were beginning to fall. Britain's losses in actual ground that eventually led to the decline of the British Empire, ran parallel with social turmoil at home caused partially by the Reform Act of 1867 (which granted the male working class population the right to vote for the first time) and a few years later by the rise of women's suffrage. Meanwhile, Queen Victoria, the emblem of domestic propriety and moral responsibility, was unsettled when scandals with women and card games marred the name of Prince Edward, one of her nine children and heir to the throne. Victorian earnestness had clearly degenerated into etiquette and was in urgent need of revision.

"The only way to get rid of a temptation is to yield to it"
The above quote from "Phrases and Philosophies for the Use of the Young" reflects Wilde's subversive mode in *The Importance of Being Earnest*. There were not many people in the audience, when the play was first performed in 1895, who could grasp the undertones in Gwendolen's comment about the name Ernest "produc[ing] vibrations" (1707). To a closed group of Oxonians, however, who were publishing in the Oxford undergraduate magazine, suggestively called *Chameleon*, "Ernest" was a name alluding to same-sex desire. The one and only 1894 issue of this magazine contained, among others, Wilde's "Phrases and Philosophies for the Use of the Young," and two poems by Wilde's lover, Lord Alfred Douglas, tellingly titled "The Love that Dare not Speak Its Name" and "In Praise of Shame." "Ernest" was associated with the idea of Uranian love, a sexual variation conceived by the German activist Karl Heinrich Ulrichs (1825–95), who had also coined the term "Urning," Uranian in English, to describe a female psyche trapped in a male body. Ulrichs built his "third sex" theory, borrowing from Pausanias' speech in Plato's *Symposium* and the myth of the Greek goddess Aphrodite Urania, who was created out of god Uranus' genitals; he, in turn, inspired the English socialist and poet Edward Carpenter, another ardent advocate of the theory of the third sex and same-sex attraction. Carpenter's *The Intermediate Sex* (1908) is a work that reflects the culmination of a strong reaction to the binary sexual model that had begun in the 1860s and which also became a

seminal text of the LGBT movements of the twentieth century (see Bristow 20–25).

Among the writers of *Chameleon*, was also the Uranian poet John Gambril Nicholson, who, in his 1892 collection of poems, *Love in Earnest*, concluded one of his homoerotic ballads with a line that probably was Wilde's inspiration for his play: "Ernest sets my heart aflame" (Raby 217). While Wilde's play makes no overt remarks on sexuality, let alone deviant behavior, it is based on a series of witty inversions that disrupt all prevailing principles of marriage, family life, gender stereotypes, and sexuality. In his radical reassessment of marriage, Wilde exposes its dullness ("in married households the champagne is rarely of a first-rate brand" [1699]) and degeneration into a mere business transaction (a woman flirting with her husband across the dinner table is characterized as unethical [1703]). He spices the monotony of lifeless couples with extra members ("in married life three is a company and two is none" [1704]), introduces the idea of invented friends (like the "invaluable permanent invalid called Bunbury" [1703]), and rekindles the Victorian habit of leading a double life ("my name is Ernest in town and Jack in the country" [1702]). In Wilde's theater, moreover, his emasculated dandies (the fin-de-siècle version of today's metrosexual men) and feisty women (a caricature of the image of the autonomous and hardy New Woman) invert gender stereotypes and make a farce of traditional gender roles. "The home seems to me," Gwendolen announces, "to be the proper sphere for the man. And," she continues: "certainly once a man begins to neglect his domestic duties he becomes painfully effeminate" (1725).

What is more striking, though, is the fact that pleasure is equated with, or rather replaces, morality—Wilde is, after all, the most acclaimed representative of the aesthetic movement that preached art for art's sake and aimed solely at offering aesthetic pleasure—while it is made clear that desire is unpredictable, unimpeded, and largely monitored by style. The play's subtext is steaming with indirect references to odd cravings, which are filtered through the discourse of food. We are told, for example, that "Gwendolen is devoted to bread and butter" (1701) and Cecily has a "capital appetite" (1711), that eating muffins is an act of repentance (1731), that only the shallow are not serious about their meals (1704), or that sugar and cake are "not fashionable anymore" (1727). Such pronouncements may, at first, appear to simply reinforce the comic element of the play, they are, however, cryptic remarks on the key role desire plays in our lives and the fact that normative sexuality is constructed by social standards. As he was writing at a time when any digression from regular behavioral paths was medicalized and in extreme cases criminalized, Wilde relied on alternative modes of expressing his unorthodox views on sexuality. Wilde himself was tried for and convicted of sodomy and sentenced to two years' hard labor when his intimate relationship with Lord Alfred Douglas was made public.

Wilde's references to literal hunger in lieu of sexual desire foreshadow the psychoanalytic theories of the 1900s as formulated by Austrian psychologist Sigmund Freud. Freud was the first to officially disengage sexuality from the reproductive function, introduce the concept of infantile eroticism, and record three stages in human sexual behavior: the oral, the anal, and the genital. Hunger was thus legitimized as the most befitting metaphor for the sexual drive, as our lips are our first erotogenic zone and our initial sexual activity is associated with the satisfaction of the need for nourishment (*Sexuality* 98). "No one who has seen a baby sinking back satiated from the breast and falling asleep with flushed cheeks and a blissful smile," Freud argues, "can escape the reflection that this picture persists as a prototype of the expression of sexual satisfaction in later life" ("Some Physical Consequences" 98). The characters' pious and unswerving addiction to food in *The Importance of Being Earnest*, as well as the fact that their appetite must always be à la mode implicitly reinforce the idea that sexuality, desire, or "temptation" (in Wilde's terms) are both impossible to evade and basically directed by external, arbitrary, and inconstant forces, like style or etiquette. Wilde was not alone in relying on diet in order to tackle issues of sex. In 1919, Katherine Mansfield's "Bliss," for example, narrates the story of a "modern" marriage through recurrent allusions to food. Bertha Young's scrambled life is associated with her cook's "superb omelettes," her husband's infidelity is complemented with his "shameless passion for the white flesh of lobster," while their crème de la crème friends publish works with titles like: "*Love in False Teeth*," "Stomach Trouble," "*Table d'Hote*," and hint at the urgent need for variety in one's love life with lines like: "Tomato soup is *so dreadfully* eternal."

Virginia Woolf
"He was a woman"

The fin de siècle was a period of "sexual anarchy" (see Showalter's homonymous book). The theory of the third sex was revisited and Uranian love was devised, as we have seen, and homosexual desire was first defined as such. The term "homosexual" first appeared in English in 1892, in C. G. Chaddock's translation of Richard von Krafft-Ebing's foundational work *Psychopathia Sexualis*. It was devised much earlier, however, in 1869 by the now forgotten Hungarian writer Karl-Maria Kertbeny (1824–82) as an alternative for the derogatory words "sodomite" and "pederast" (Bristow 4, 179) and had also been used by the Victorian poet and scholar John Addington Symonds in 1873 in his study on ancient love, *A Problem in Greek Ethics*. It is important to observe, moreover, that all those bold and groundbreaking ideas about sex and sexuality were expressed, welcomed, and widely espoused by male authors who either overtly or covertly deviated (to varying degrees) from Victorian norms. Edward Carpenter, John Addington Symonds, Oscar Wilde, and later, writers, poets, or critics like E. M. Foster, Rupert Brooke, and Lytton Strachey could, in some way or another, identify with a model largely based on Plato's idealized view of same-sex love, as it was love involving men exclusively. A female writer, however, who attempted to tell the truth about her own experiences as a body, as Woolf says ("Professions for Women" 2217), could hardly find a voice of her own in any of the aforementioned alternatives to heterosexual bipolarity.

According to Woolf, there had always been *one* canonical sex and gender throughout history. Invoking popular Renaissance symbolism, whereby men were identified with the sun and women with the moon, she argues in her lengthy essay *A Room of One's Own*, that women have been nothing but pale reflections of men, mere moons orbiting around bright suns. All these centuries, she observes, women have been playing the role of magnifying mirrors "possessing the magic and delicious power of reflecting the figure of man at twice its natural size" (*Room* 35). No glorious wars would have been fought, no supermen would have existed, and our civilization would have never come to a zenith, Woolf reasons with a generous dose of irony, if women had not agreed to diminish themselves into mere props, against which men could measure their superiority. For power is, of course, a relative value: it may increase or decrease according to whom one is compared to. It is women's lowliness and obscurity, their yielding to domesticity and anonymity that have served as vitality boosters for men: "the looking glass vision," she concludes, "stimulates the nervous system. Take it away and man may die, like the drug fiend deprived of his cocaine" (36).

But it is not only in terms of gender that women shrink to extinction; their conspicuous "physical inferiority," attested through the endless list of books on the subject in the catalog of the British Museum (*Room* 28–30), renders them an endangered species in terms of biology as well. In Woolf's famous passage on Shakespeare's sister, the hypothetical, equally-talented as her brother William and eager-to-explore-human-nature Judith Shakespeare can never achieve a victorious career like him, not only because women were not allowed to act on the Elizabethan stage, or even enter a public house unescorted, but also because they are trapped in their own physiology. "[W]ho shall measure the heat and violence of the poet's heart when caught and tangled in a woman's body?" (47), Woolf wonders, when Judith, rejected as an actress and pregnant with the actor-manager's child, puts an end to her life one winter's night at the end of the sixteenth century and is no more remembered.

Woolf's *A Room of One's Own* has been considered a feminist manifesto and spawned feminist criticism after the 1970s. Gilbert and Gubar's major critical work, *The Madwoman in the Attic: The Woman Writer and the Nineteenth-Century Literary Imagination*, for instance, is an analogous attempt to acknowledge the presence of women throughout the history of literature. Their feminist poetics are inspired by Woolf's conviction that the first step towards female creativity is inextricably linked with the violent killing of the Victorian angel haunting the lives of women and forcing them to subservience to men. It is Woolf's resurrection of Shakespeare's sister that motivates Gilbert and Gubar's radical quest for all those stifled female voices and exiled female presences in past literary texts, like the Victorian Bertha Mason, Mr. Rochester's mad Creole wife, locked up in the attic in Charlotte Brontë's *Jane Eyre*.

If history has obliterated woman both as an active participant and as physical presence, in her fictional account of the woman writer, Woolf invents witty and amusing ways of reinscribing the female and reintegrating women into history. The main character in her mock-biography, *Orlando,* is born male in Renaissance England because only as a man does he have the right to own property, think, and act freely. Orlando's sex, gender, and sexuality, however, are so perplexed that they annul any preset notions around them. Despite his being indubitably pronounced male in the very first sentence of the book, Orlando's sex is both disguised by the fashion of the time and relies entirely on his ability to simulate a series of actions performed in the past by his male ancestors. As he is slicing at the head of a Moor, already slaughtered by his father or grandfather and now gently swinging from the rafters (13), Orlando defines masculinity as an imitation of valiance rather than a genuine expression of bravery. And despite his broad taste for court ladies or serving maids, Orlando's heart beats only for the Russian princess Sasha, who, like Orlando, flees all conventional sexual demarcations.

In a passage that defies all reason, even more perhaps than the fact that the character's lifespan covers over 350 years, Orlando wakes up after a seven-day trance and discovers, "he was a woman" (132), an act "accomplished [so] painlessly and completely" that he "showed no surprise at it" (133). It is not by accident that this "change of sex"—which, by the way, "did nothing whatever to alter their identity" (133)—occurs in the eighteenth century, a key point in time as far as sex is concerned. His being a woman coincides both with the birth of the female writer—for the first time "the middle-class woman began to write" (*Room* 63) and make money out of it—and the birth of the female sex, as it was then that the model of anatomic isomorphism was abandoned by scientists and physicians. As historian Thomas Laqueur has shown, "the one-sex/one-flesh model dominated thinking about sexual difference from classical antiquity to the end of the seventeenth century" (*Making Sex* 25). From the writings of Galen, the Roman physician of the second century CE, to sixteenth- and seventeenth-century anatomical drawings, male and female reproductive organs have been represented as identical. The only difference was that women's genitalia were inverted, something which consequently established woman as a colder, weaker, and veiled version of man. By the late eighteenth century, though, writers and doctors emphasized difference and initiated the new concept of "radical dimorphism" or "biological divergence" (Laqueur, *Making Sex* 6), which reached its apex, as we saw, in the nineteenth century.

What do women want?

As a woman in the eighteenth century, Orlando soon realizes that adopting a gender identity can be more agonizing than adopting a sex identity, for it entails carrying out a number of prescribed acts, which may be utterly detestable to her; like, for example, lacing one's corset, powdering one's nose and pouring tea for men. Gender in the novel is reduced to the repetition of a series of stylized acts—in exactly the manner gender theorist Judith Butler spoke of it in her 1990 seminal work *Gender Trouble*—which Orlando is called upon to perform. According to Butler, "gender is an identity strenuously constituted in time, instituted in an exterior space through a *stylized repetition of acts*" (*Gender Trouble* 140), what she terms "gender performativity"; moreover, gender "is a norm," Butler concludes, that can never be fully internalized" and "gender norms are finally phantasmatic, impossible to embody" (*Gender Trouble* 141). This is evident when Orlando fails to perform some of the roles that are compatible with her feminine identity, a fact that makes Orlando an uncategorizable hybrid; she very perplexingly, for instance, "never takes more than ten minutes to dress," loathes household matters

(181) and is "bold and active as a man" (182). But as she can't be an eternal floating signifier, she lets her clothes decide for her, and "wears" her gender according to the spur of the moment. The narrator's declaration that "In every human being a vacillation from one sex to the other takes place, and often it is only clothes that keep the male or the female likeness, while underneath the sex is the very opposite of what is above" (181) is a fascinating preview of Butler's definition of gender as "a construction that one puts on, as one puts on clothes in the morning." "[T]here is a 'one,'" Butler argues, "who is prior to this gender, a one who goes to the wardrobe of gender and decides with deliberation which gender it will be today" ("Critically Queer" 21).

Clothes, of course, can be fun to change and roles fun to play, and as long as Orlando can match the right gender with the right clothes, she can both have her cake and eat it, too. The hysterical twitch in the second finger of her right hand, for example, is a clear manifestation of how well she can play her role as woman in the nineteenth century who feels she won't be part of history unless married. So married she was. But if Wilde rejoiced in trios in marriage, Woolf invented the solos, when she draws her character in a marriage that isn't exactly a marriage. Orlando's gallant husband is also unclassifiable as far as sex/gender is concerned ("You're a woman, Shel!" she cries to him shortly after their wedding; "You're a man, Orlando!" he replies [240]), and he is conveniently forever absent from home, as a sailor always sailing around Cape Horn. Orlando's *mariage blanc* saves her from the eternal dullness of heteronormativity (represented in the novel through a revolting Archduchess/Archduke, whose sex alternates into the opposite of Orlando's in her/his effort to capture him/her) and grants her space and freedom to act as she likes.

What does Orlando want though? The question haunts the book and resonates with Freud's foremost concern in his essays on female sexuality composed almost simultaneously with Woolf's novel. Although Freud's contribution to the field is momentous—he was the first, after all, to attempt a systematic analysis of it—his theories sound like a comeback to the pre-Enlightenment era, as they seem to eliminate woman once again. Freud bases his model of the development of female sexuality on that of male sexuality and sums up with the epic assertion, "we are now obliged to recognize that the little girl is a little man" ("Femininity" 151). Disregarding common medical knowledge about the "abundance of specialized nerve endings in the clitoris and the relative impoverishment of the vagina" (Laqueur, *Amor Veneris* 94), he dichotomizes female sexuality into a masculine and feminine phase. The first stage is characterized by "phallic" activities and the girl's focusing on her "virile" clitoris, which is "analogous to the male organ" ("Female Sexuality" 374); during the second phase, the woman realizes she (like her mother) is only a "castrated" version of man, and so "renounces her masturbatory satisfaction from her clitoris, repudiates her love for her mother" ("Femininity" 157) and, finally, aims at regaining the phallus by giving birth to a male child. What every "mature" woman wants, according to Freud, is heterosexual procreative sex.

Although this view was challenged by psychoanalysts contemporary to Freud, like Ernest Jones and Karen Horney, the urge to equate normative sexuality with heterosexual activity and reproduction persisted. Woolf's Orlando, however, dares defy Freud's assumptions, as she makes a farce of heterosexual marriage, is indifferent to the birth of her son, and connects her sexual climax with the solitary pleasure of writing poetry. Her ecstasy coincides with her discovering a cypher language she can share with her circumnavigating husband and her completing the poem she had been carrying in her breast throughout the ages. In a patriarchal phallogocentric world, Woolf's Orlando can be a woman only if she can be a poet; not only when science differentiates her from man, that is, but also when she is able to explore the potential of male-centered language and invent new spaces and modes in order to speak of her own experiences as a body. This principal thesis expressed in the book became a top issue after the 1970s in the agendas of the French feminists Hélène Cixous, Luce Irigaray and Julia Kristeva. "There is no room for her if she is not a he," Cixous asserts in her 1975 essay "The Laugh of the Medusa" (258), in which she urges women to break the "psychoanalytic closure" (263), regain their lost, muffled bodies and pleasures (250) and write in white ink" (251). In a similar vein, Irigaray in *This Sex Which Is Not One* rejects what Cixous termed as "glorious phallic monosexuality" (254), celebrates woman's multiple sexuality, and insists on *l'ecriture feminine*, a writing related to the rhythms of the female body and sexual pleasure (*jouissance*). Kristeva, in turn, maintains that language is the key to repositioning women in history, and presents Woolf as an example of a writer who has discovered the rhythms and tones of what she terms a "semiotic" language that crosses the borders of the patriarchal "symbolic." Although Woolf is by no means always compatible with the French feminists, her challenge of psychoanalysis and her destabilizing of sex and gender fixities have established her as a source of inspiration and pivotal figure in feminist thought.

Conclusion

What our close examination of two significant texts of the fin de siècle and early twentieth century has shown is that numbers are unstable as far as sexes and sexualities are concerned, and they are always dependent on who's doing the counting. Taking diverse paths, Wilde and Woolf converged in deconstructing some of the most rigid notions around gender and sexual behavior, dissociating the terms 'sex,' 'gender,' and 'sexuality,' and disclosing their constructedness. While borrowing from past discourses around sex, they also point towards new ways of rethinking it and pave the way for feminist criticism and queer studies of the second half of the twentieth century.

Works Cited

Bristow, Joseph. *Sexuality*. London: Routledge, 1997. The New Critical Idiom Ser.

Butler Judith. *Gender Trouble: Feminism and the Subversion of Identity*. New York/London: Routledge, 1990.

_____. "Critically Queer." *GLQ: A Journal of Lesbian and Gay Studies* 1.1 (1993): 17–32.

Cixous, Hélène. "The Laugh of the Medusa." In *New French Feminisms: An Anthology*. Eds. Elaine Marks and Isabelle de Courtivron. Brighton: Harvester, 1981. 245–264.

Dickens, Charles. *David Copperfield*. 1850. Ed. Nina Burgis. Oxford: Oxford UP, 1999. Oxford World's Classics Ser.

Foucault, Michel. *The History of Sexuality. Vol 1: An Introduction*. Trans. Robert Hurly. Harmondsworth, UK: Penguin, 1984.

Freud, Sigmund. "Infantile Sexuality." *On Sexuality*. Ed. and Trans. James Strachey. Harmondsworth, UK: Penguin, 1986. 88–126.

_____. "Some Physical Consequences of the Anatomical Distinction between the Sexes." 1925. *On Sexuality*. Ed. and Trans. James Strachey. Harmondsworth, UK: Penguin, 1986. 323–392.

_____. "Female Sexuality." 1931. *On Sexuality*. Ed. and Trans. James Strachey. Harmondsworth, UK: Penguin, 1986. 367–392.

_____. "Femininity." 1933. *New Introductory Lectures on Psychoanalysis*. Ed. and Trans. James Strachey. Harmondsworth, UK: Penguin, 1986. 145–169.

Gilbert, Sandra M., & Susan Gubar. *The Madwoman in the Attic: The Woman Writer and the Nineteenth-Century Literary Imagination*. New Haven: Yale UP, 1989.

Irigaray, Luce. *This Sex Which Is Not One*. Trans. Catherine Porter. Ithaca: Cornell UP, 1985.

Kitsi-Mitakou, Katerina. "'Which Is the Greater Ecstasy?': Desiring the Body's Text and Writing the Body's Desire in Virginia Woolf's *Orlando.*" *Yearbook of English Studies*, 3 (1991–92): 215–52.

Kristeva, Julia. *Revolution in Poetic Language*. 1974. Trans. Margaret Waller. Columbia UP, 1984.

Laqueur, Thomas. "Amor Veneris, vel Dulcedo Appeletur." *Fragments for a History of the Human Body, Part I*. Ed. Michel Feher. New York: Zone, 1989. 90–131.

_____. *Making Sex. Body and Gender from the Greeks to Freud*. Harvard UP, 1990.

Mansfield, Katherine. "Bliss." n.d. Web. 20 January 2014. <http://www.katherinemansfieldsociety.org/assets/KM-Stories/BLISS1918.pdf>

Nye, Robert A., ed. *Sexuality*. Oxford UP, 1999. Oxford Readers Ser.

Plato. *The Symposium*. Ed. and Trans. Christopher Gill. London: Penguin, 1999.

Raby, Peter. *The Cambridge Companion to Oscar Wilde*. Cambridge UP, 1997.

Showalter, Elaine. *Sexual Anarchy: Gender and Culture at the Fin de Siècle*. New York: Viking, 1990.

Wilde, Oscar. "Phrases and Philosophies for the Use of the Young." 1894. *Shorter Prose Pieces by Oscar Wilde*. 5–6. 2006. Web. 20 January 2014. <http://www2.hn.psu.edu/faculty/jmanis/oscar-wilde/Shorter-Prose-Pieces6x9.pdf>.

_____. *The Importance of Being Earnest*. In *The Norton Anthology of English Literature*. Vol. 2. Ed. M.H. Abrams. Eighth ed. New York: W.W. Norton, 2006. 1699–1740.

Woolf, Virginia. *Orlando*. Ed. Rachel Bowlby. Oxford: Oxford UP, 1998.

_____. *A Room of One's Own*. 1929. London: Triad Grafton, 1987.

A Queer Time for Sex in Matthew Lewis' *The Monk*

Lisa Blansett

The murder and madness, sex and sorcery of Matthew Lewis' *The Monk* (1795) makes its world familiar to twenty-first century readers of Stephen King or audiences of television shows like *The Walking Dead*. The righteous are tempted and fall, the innocent are manipulated and slain, women are imprisoned in crypts, men are seduced, heirs are lost, young love is frustrated, marriages are thwarted, demons are exorcised; we find blood on nun's habits, a burning cross on a stranger's head, vipers, wands, poison draughts, and daggers in this eighteenth-century Gothic novel. What makes the novel "Gothic" and different from other types of novels at the time are the horrors wreaked on its pages—horrors whose effects are meant to incite readers' fear and disgust. At the same time, the Gothic novel was very popular in eighteenth-century Britain; its overwhelmingly terrorizing images did not drive audiences away. One critic contemporary to Lewis notes that *The Monk* "has neither originality, morals, nor probability to recommend it," and yet "it has excited and will still continue to excite, the curiosity of the public. Such is the irresistible energy of genius" (*The European Magazine* 110). Against the normative rules, then, the novel entices the reader to partake of its energy and ponder the apparent contradiction between wanting to read about murder and taking pleasure in its telling. In a way, the reader leads a textual double life, in which his or her desire to know overcomes any concern about the morality the reviewer mentions. The desire to know is not abated by believable explanations or neat resolutions, and yet, despite the lack of "probability to recommend it," *The Monk*'s critic recommends it.

Lewis' work disrupts the very narrative form that might unfold in sequence the rationales behind mysterious motivations and outrageous actions. This formal rupture echoes the failures in family lineages that undo the sequence of aristocratic genealogy at the heart of the novel, leaving procreation an exercise in heterosexual futility. In short, the novel challenges the limits of categories to contain textual and bodily forms, and, by reveling in a full range of human and supernatural behaviors, it gestures toward alternative forms of both. *The Monk* is a rather queer novel if we take queer to mean "the open mesh of possibilities, overlaps, dissonances and resonances, lapses and excesses of meaning when the constituent elements of anyone's gender, anyone's sexuality aren't made (or can't be made to) signify monolithically" (Sedgwick, *Tendencies* 8).

Alongside the many horrors of Matthew Lewis' *The Monk* (1796), we find the ostensibly less-horrible Romance plot elements. In such Romance plots—also called courtship or marriage plots—authors fashioned their one true pair from a young man and a young woman. As a convention of the novel, the courtship plot stretches back to novelist Samuel Richardson, who labeled it "a new species of writing" (Richardson lii). Although the Aristotelian definition of comedy includes a culminating marriage, the novel's emphasis on psychological particulars of desire and domesticity transforms the comic form into a study that represents falling in love and getting married as the most ordinary course of human events. As conflict drives narrative, the many obstacles the young lovers must overcome shape the action until they can be united in such a story. Whereas a Romance plot might include distressing separations or letters gone astray, the Gothic novel conjures for the couple hyperbolic difficulties that are always presented as supernatural, sometimes unraveled as the natural misperceived. The Gothic takes Romance conventions and weds them to horrors resolved only when the terror is ended and social order is restored: closeted skeletons are cleared, evil is vanquished, and a marriage arranged. In *The Monk*, the obstacle to love is not just the concerned family members represented as "ordinary" in a plot; instead, *The Monk* introduces an extraordinary evil to be vanquished in the form of a nun and a monk, each of whom intervenes in the two different courting couples. An eighteenth-century novel reader might expect a friar to perform the rites of marriage, not to destroy it. Yet this monk, Ambrosio, emerges as the secretly noble foundling who is represented as a sex-obsessed rapist and murderer. Early in the novel, the young couples endeavor to make their way to the altar. The evil and the marriageable converge to crowd into a chapel for the famous monk's sermon. They assemble not "from motives of piety or thirst of information" (Lewis 7). Instead, "the Women came to show themselves, the men to see the Women" (7). The world of this novel is immediately organized into two opposing categories based on a definition of sex that indicates anatomy identifies and differentiates one group of bodies from another. Further, anatomical sex becomes a function of sexuality by allying these bodies with particular behaviors. At the same time, that sexuality is defined by the subject and object—"men to see the women"—effectively channeling desire into a particular form of sexuality. Church attendance in the Capuchin chapel is a heterosexual affair. Moreover, by referring to "*the* women" and "*the* men," the ritual appears to represent a universal practice and, as such, represents these bodies and these practices as the norm. To be in this space, characters are both appropriated by and identify with these categories in order to perform the rituals and recognize the roles each is to play. Lewis' characters make sense of each other in terms of differences figured as prior to their participation in the ritual. A very few words create a system of intelligibility that sets in motion a narrative of normative desires and heterosexual relations assembled in the church.

The public inscription of heterosexuality becomes individualized desire when two "young, and richly habited" noblemen hear a female voice complaining about the crowd; they turn momentarily to see a woman who does not hold their attention, but focus their energy to behold her quiet young niece, Antonia (8). The young woman warrants a full-bodied description detailing the whiteness of her skin and her dress, the color of her hair, the length of her neck, continuing all the way down to her feet, where they spy "a little foot of the most delicate proportions" (9). The men appreciate each part of her body in turn, first for its aesthetic merit (her "symmetry and beauty might have vied with the Medicean Venus" [9]), and then for her likeness to the mythological Hamadryad, a figure of nature destined to live and die with the tree it was born in. The narrated details of her body serve "to materialize the body's sex, to materialize sexual difference in the service of the consolidation of the heterosexual imperative" (Butler, *Bodies* 2). This heterosexual imperative is embedded in a complex matrix, the elements of which do not establish a causal narrative; in other words, the body is gendered, but without gendering, there isn't a way to sex and sexualize a body. The moves that identify what is masculine and what is feminine do not have a visible beginning or end; nor is there a fixed direction of the multi-directional flow. As part of the matrix in this two-body system of knowledge, Antonia is described by adjectives indicating a set of traits that accrue to the female form. Antonia is *delicate and elegant*, her foot is *small*, her bosom, skin, and dress are *white*. Such adjectives flow back to her body: her delicacy and elegance indicate that she does not have the sword-wielding strength that her admirers will shortly demonstrate in the narrative; her tiny feet (adorned in silk shoes, given the fashion of the late eighteenth-century) would not be able to break into a run; her pale skin means that she spends much of her time confined inside, away from the sun; her white dress symbolizes purity, in other words, virginity. Antonia's difference is marked as a material difference, made so through the words chosen to describe it—her body recalls Venus rather than Apollo—but there "is never simply a function of material differences which are not in some way both marked and formed by discursive practices" (Butler, *Bodies* 1). Antonia demurely resists participating in their discourse—which of course makes her the perfect object of it—but the two men press on, marking their own characters as active—curious and insistent—and signifying that hers enacts the passive spectacle the men come to see. The active and passive behaviors leverage the cataloged physical traits into a gender assignment that makes two differences seem complementary and desirable one to the other and so produces a narrative that is heteronormative—what appears to be the normal course of human events is heterosexuality.

The careful choreography of the heteronormative couple emerges from a complex continuous and continual staging of "normal" visibly defined by what it is not. If Antonia appears appealing set next to her middle-aged aunt Leonella, who, with her feline name is a kind of early modern "cougar," she is defined by her difference from the flirtatious aggression her aunt indulges in with Don Christoval. The comic function Leonella performs is a faint, but important, assertion of a sexuality beyond the pale. That the comparison is comic means that it is a familiar enough situation that readers would laugh at it. So naturalized is the comparison, that it seems inconsequential to the dossier of desirability and heterosexuality assembled, and yet it inaugurates the extraordinary interplay of sexual identifications that must be, to use Judith Butler's vocabulary, foreclosed and/or disavowed to produce the normative subject. Antonia represents a normative position within the circumscribed space in which gender operates as "the social significance that sex assumes within a given culture" (Butler, *Bodies* 5). Her chastity is frequently referenced, but her identification as the "chaste, and gentle, young and fair" woman "who would be some good Man's blessing" becomes vexed when the reader encounters her first reaction to Ambrosio during his sermon (Lewis 38). In a description suggesting orgasm, Antonia "felt a pleasure fluttering in her bosom which till then had been unknown to her, and for which She in vain endeavored to account" (8). This fantasy-driven auto-eroticism was not among the activities recommended for young women in the eighteenth century; forty-six editions of *A Guide to Old Age, or a Cure for the Indiscretions of Youth* (1799), warn that young women will "have their minds as well as their bodies frequently enervated by shameful practices" (Brodum 212–13). "By these filthy activities," argues the doctor, their bodies are rendered:

> not only so weak and emaciated, that they are often rendered barren, and thereby greatly prejudice society and posterity; but they at length contract an unconquerable habit of this kind of gratification, which is always so ready at hand, and which they fancy an indulgence, without the danger of childbearing, the loss of reputation, or of health (213).

The warnings that begin by establishing the "natural" desire of men for the "tender sex" suggest, too, that masturbation will provoke women's "unnatural distaste for the male part of the creation, for whom they were by Providence destined" (213). In short, women would find such an experience so pleasurable that they would have been in danger of spending too much time masturbating and not enough time making themselves available to appropriate husbands. The written description of Antonia's blushes and flutters would have been as titillating to its readers as it is obvious to us. For all, it functions as a textual transgression that problematizes the gendered "chastity" attached to Antonia. If the "construction of gender operates through exclusionary means," then "woman" excludes age and sexual appetite, and "chastity" excludes church-pew orgasms.

Antonia's pleasurable indulgences continue after her exit from the sacred confines of the church. In the street she discovers a very different sort of homily delivered by a "gypsy." There, Antonia beseeches Leonella to "indulge [her] this once! Let me have my fortune told!" (36). In the "Gypsy's Song," the fortune-teller first erases Leonella's sexuality by admonishing her to "Lay aside Your paint and patches, lust and pride" because:

> Believe me, Dame, when all is done,
> Your age will still be fifty one;
> And Men will rarely take a hint
> Of love, from two grey eyes that squint (37).

As the "gypsy" circumscribes Leonella's role, her song establishes the perimeter around her desire, foreclosing any opportunity for post-menopausal sexual practice by making it laughable in a sing-songy tetrameter (it still upholds the male-female pairing, however). While Leonella is identified as pathetically transgressive, the "gypsy" subsequently predicts how Antonia's sexual future will be foreclosed. The prophesy, coming on the heels of Antonia's physical episode, first establishes her value in a normative economy: "You would be some good Man's blessing" (38). At the same time, the gypsy ends any possibility of continuing auto-eroticism or "that unnatural distaste for the male part of creation" (Brodum 213). This "Gypsy's Song" episode indicates that the normative is intensely regulated: the episode shuts down Antonia's orgasmic micro-transgressions, even as it indicates how unstable the definitions that accrue to her are. Antonia's satisfying experience plays along the line dividing the normative/non-normative, in part because her ignorance of the sensations proves her sexual naiveté. Simultaneously, it adds a titillating (and, therefore, complicating) detail to the language of purity built around her in this "highly gendered regulatory schema" (Butler xi). The line between the sanctioned and the transgressive is blurred at best, and yet, at the same time, enforced to a character's grave peril. As such, the line becomes the site where the gendered subject must be continually and continuously performed as a matter of life and death. The "performative" compulsion of gender and sexuality does not mean "perus[ing] the closet or some more open space for the gender of choice, donn[ing] that gender for the day, and then restor[ing] the garment to its place at night" (Butler, "Preface" x). Rather, the social regulation of norms plays almost like an actor directed to "keep doing this until we get it right," even though getting it right is never a possibility, except that there are no actors that exist before the play; or, put another way, the performance of gender is the "forced reiteration of its norms" as a way to prove the stability of the norms, while at the same time making visible how unstable those norms are (Butler x).

Challenges to the norms move beyond the micro-transgression of a heterosexualized identity in rather spectacular ways. Consider the activities of many other characters who roam the narrative, including the second core couple, the unhappy apparition of a murdered woman, and Antonia's mother: Agnes has sex with Raymond while she's a nun; Beatrice wanders through a castle destined to play the post-mortem role of the Bleeding Nun for her part in a love triangle that ends in double murder; Elivira, Antonia's mother, is slain for cock-blocking Ambrosio, whose sexual thirst would only be slaked by the young virgin (who turns out to be his sister); and Matilda begins the narrative as the young monk Rosario, but reveals him- / herself to be a sexually potent woman, who serves the demon-leading Ambrosio to his damnation. At this juncture, the reader encounters how "the mobilization of the categories of sex within political discourse will be *haunted* in some ways by the very instabilities that the categories effectively produce and foreclose" (Butler 4; my emphasis). At the heart of *The Monk* is an enactment of this haunting, as Lewis makes visible not only where the line is apparently fixed, but also what settles on both sides of that line. For a novel that many argue represents a cautionary tale in the service of reinforcing normative sexuality, *The Monk* seems oriented toward haunting those boundaries through both the characters' identifications and the social practices, particularly those around the marriage plot. Wendy Jones contends that:

> *The Monk* abounds in marriages and, as we have seen, marriage is constitutive of both good desire and the conventional happy ending. But as *The Monk* differentiates desire itself, so it also investigates the possibility of different types of marriages. And as it valorizes good desire, it endorses a relatively recent marital ideal, the marriage for love, and concomitantly, a new definition of love itself (139).

Through its parsing of desire, Jones proposes, *The Monk* defines the necessary complement, bad desire, which is represented as "repressed desire, which can never know its true object and therefore incapable of satisfaction . . . the violence of repression both perverts it and adds fury to its pent-up force . . . and represses natural instincts" (238). Good desire, following this line of argument, is the desire that ends in the plot driven to a marital ideal and love itself. Yet, to my mind, what Jones identifies as the "good desire" delineated in *The Monk* includes precious little happily-ever-after and more coupling that ends with death, destruction, and familial as well as eternal damnation. Glimpses of a post-marital state reveal family dysfunction predicated on unauthorized marriages, pre-marital relations, jealous rages, and incestuous desires. A novel in which the characters are, as Kate Ellis asserts, "rewarded with domestic happiness at the end of their respective stories" just never materializes (Ellis 131). Antonia never experiences domestic happiness, and any promise of that ends brutally, as Ambrosio spirits her away to a crypt to rape her. Lorenzo, her professed love, ends debilitatingly sickened by Antonia's death and ends up in an arranged marriage by acceding to his Uncle's desires. The only thing to recommend that engagement is "when the Duke proposed to him the match [with Virginia] . . . his Nephew did not reject the offer" (419). The only marriage performed is mentioned on the heels of the disturbing death of Raymond and Agnes' infant, who expires while its mother is chained deep in the crypts beneath the abbey and monastery properties. The nuptials of Raymond and Agnes receive a single, perfunctory sentence, recording that "the marriage was therefore celebrated as soon as the needful preparations had been made" (418). The next phrase, "This being over. . . ," ends any mention of marriage (418). Little in *The Monk* recommends marriage or heterosexual relations, which are very often represented as ridiculous, misguided, and even violent.

Yet, marriage was expected to produce new generations for aristocratic families to enlarge the family tree and to ensure the smooth transfer of property and prestige from one generation to the next. Among the heirs apparent to their respective aristocratic families are Antonia and Ambrosio, but Antonia does not have an as-yet legitimated claim to her genealogy, and Ambrosio was kidnapped and left as a foundling at the Capuchin Monastery door. Missing heirs and lost children were recognizable complications to Lewis' first readers, and the stories of how characters were lost and then found become part of establishing the mandate of genealogical succession and proper social order. Less recognizable to Lewis' readers would be narratives that included scenes of insemination, pregnant bodies, and the post-partum maternal body. The bodies that perform those acts would have been assumed (a body has to produce a baby and heir) but excluded from the narratives as readers expected bodies to enter the narrative fully formed and sexed. Lewis' work unsettles those expectations by making these bodies visible as suffering and wretched, pushing the story of aristocratic succession beyond the pale it had erected for itself. Facts of heterosexual life that had been unwritten in popular romance novels of the time become legible in *The Monk* to reveal the paradoxes of a domain that excludes the very acts that make it possible.

Although a necessity for the whole undertaking of genealogy, pregnancies are not fruitful here. No infants survive and no heirs are produced, making *The Monk* a sterile recommendation for either companionate or arranged marriages. Noble blood is tainted and spilled by imprudent or unsanctioned marriages, as well as by the "unbridled debauchery" of heterosexual liaisons (173). The noble blood of two families spills when, pregnant out of wedlock, Beatrice murders her lover to run off with his brother, who in turn slays his gravid paramour out of shame for his part in the conspiracy. Antonia is penetrated, but genealogy is disrupted by both Ambrosio's status as brother and because he murders her before any outcome of the ejaculate is established. In this novel, Spanish society organized around genealogy is in shambles. As actors in what would have been positioned as cautionary heterosexual tales, these characters can be said to promote the dominant narrative: that one must find a class-appropriate opposite sex, marry primarily to continue the family line, and avoid any pleasurable debauchery in sexual relations. The examples might, in fact, serve to prohibit certain behaviors and foreground "the setting apart of the 'unnatural' as a specific dimension in the field of sexuality" (Foucault 39).

Other narratives emerge, however, that challenge how the normative has become "the natural" and, at the same time, showcase for readers everything that they fear (and want to know) about the foreclosed territory. Wendy Jones argues that the novel "shows that disastrous consequences, including the intervention of the supernatural, are incurred only when characters respond to oppressive forms of authority" (144). Organizing social relations around a heterosexual genealogy and the procreative acts required to reproduce it is represented as oppressive and unnatural. For Agnes, the process of childbirth and post-partum maternity is written as unnatural, given that labor and delivery take place in a dungeon, and she has no idea how to care for the infant. Despite being described as possessing the requisite anatomy, she does not intuitively (that is, naturally, essentially) know how to offer her breast to it, and so the infant expires. Because no birth referenced in the novel produces any "natural" subject, the procreative dictate is neutered. As a framework for the un-sanctioned marriages and the gruesome outcomes of childbearing, the genealogical model starts to look bankrupt. If genealogy acts as historical goal, then the telos, or endpoint, of that history does not coincide with the end of the novel. A long chapter on Ambrosio's Inquisition interrogation, his deal with the demon, and eventual torture closes off the novel, supplanting any happy ending. Lewis' novel does not simply offer a gentle reproval for marriageable youths or propose any happy resolution to smooth over the trials and tribulations. While it produces in spectacularly graphic detail a study in what not to do, the novel also supplies negative models far beyond any human experience that make the tale ridiculous: Don't run off with a lover or you'll end up a bloody zombie; don't marry the wrong woman or you will produce a monk who turns rapist and murderer.

That space opened by the ridiculous creates an opportunity to investigate and challenge the line drawn between who is socially valued and who should be rejected. Lewis' novel makes it:

> possible to raise the critical question of how . . . constraints not only produce the domain of intelligible bodies, but produce as well a domain of unthinkable, abject, unlivable bodies. . . . This latter domain is not the opposite of the former, for oppositions are, after all, part of the intelligibility; the latter is the excluded and illegible domain that haunts the former domain as the specter of its own impossibility, the very limit of intelligibility, its constitutive outside (Butler xi).

Marrying for love, bearing children, consolidating aristocratic power, and producing particular forms of sexuality constitute legible domains, and yet, at the same time, they represent "unthinkable and un-livable" experiences, too. What appears livable in one context emerges as unthinkable in another: sexual relations inside the abbey compared to such relations outside the abbey, as well as heterosexual sex between Agnes and Raymond versus Ambrosio's rape of Antonia, all work to position normative in non-normative territory and vice versa. A space designated as the site of assumed celibacy, the convent and monastery, becomes a hotbed of desiring bodies and sexual assignations. Ambrosio "abandoned himself to his passions in full security" with the "feigned Rosario" while "the honour of Agnes was sacrificed to [Raymond's] passion" (234–35; 186). The processes by which the non-normative produces the normative through negation is a vexed business: if heteronormativity is the valued practice, then fixing heteronormativity in a place where it is not normal muddies the values. In particular, the hetero/homo opposition is unsettled by a character who claims she is a woman, yet dresses as a man so that s/he might have sex with a man in a monastery.

The complex arrangements of gender play and performance between Ambrosio and Rosario/Matilda make legible new configurations even as those relationships are represented as not-the-norm. George Haggerty argues that "the monastery is a precursor of the sexual laboratory, and in a sense it functions as the controlled environment in which the habits of an unfamiliar species can be studied" and where "Male-male relations are being examined, even if they are held up as a sign of horror and disgust" (Haggerty, *Queer Gothic* 71). To vivify heteronormativity, then, the homoerotic plays the spectre that haunts it. In a genre defined by hauntings and muddied identifications, the ghostly "Bloody Nun" is but one of many (and she was written as heterosexual). Among those spectral figures is Rosario, whose dual gender identities and relation to Ambrosio do not precisely enact a heteronormative logic that holds it up as a sign of horror and disgust. Rather, the descriptions of Ambrosio's desire for Rosario are represented in terms that suggest gentleness, mutual affection, generosity, and reciprocity; instead, it is Ambrosio's relationship with Matilda that incites horror and disgust for its coercive dynamic and the couple's relentless drive toward rape and murder. The reader is introduced to Rosario when he enters Ambrosio's room with a small gift, "A few of those flowers, reverend Father, which I have observed to be most acceptable to you" (43). Just prior to Rosario's entrance, Ambrosio engages in verbal self-flagellation over his erotic reaction to a painting of the Madonna in his cell. He assures himself that "what charms me, when ideal and considered as a superior Being, would disgust me, become Woman and tainted with all the failings of Mortality. It is not the Woman's beauty that fills me with such enthusiasm; It is the Painter's skill that I admire, it is the Divinity that I adore!" (41). Ambrosio's rejection of the "Woman tainted" is answered by the gentle knock of the novice monk, Rosario, who brings flowers for Ambrosio's room. When together, each changes the other for the better: Rosario assumes "an air of gaiety" which is reciprocated in "a tone milder that was usual" for "no voice sounded so sweet to him as did Rosario's" (42). For all the disgust Ambrosio expresses at the painted face of the Madonna, "he could not help sometimes indulging a desire secretly to see the face of his Pupil" (42–43). After Rosario reveals that he is a woman (and the pronoun remains "he" until the word "woman" is spoken), s/he conspires to remain at the monastery by continuing to cross dress as a man. The sexed body ostensibly remains female, while the public gender identity is performed as masculine.

The link forged between gender identity and sexed body made in the opening scenes of the novel is uncoupled in Rosario/Matilda's relationship with Ambrosio. When at the height of her powers, Matilda is described as forceful and aggressive, while Ambrosio vacillates between ardent physical desire and abject self-reproach for his newly developed habits. At a moment of weakness in his resolve, Ambrosio is chided for its being "weaker than a Woman's" (268). Sorting through the complex relations of sex to gender and Rosario/Matilda to Ambrosio results in a panoply of configurations, including male body to male body; female body to male body; feminine behaviors to masculine behaviors, but transposed onto the male and then female body; masculine to masculinized character; feminine body and femininized character. The dizzying array of subject positions begs the question of whether desire between these two characters is heterosexual, homosexual, bisexual, lesbian, *ad infinitum*. The "phantasmic abundance" of pleasure written through Rosario/Matilda seems the better choice than what we might call the "heteronormativized" relationship of Ambrosio to Matilda (Butler 98). The identifications here are "multiple and contested" and appear to "reflect in a dense or saturated way the possibilities of multiple and simultaneous substitutions" (Butler 99). Not even our own contemporary binarized categories of "butch" and "femme," "top" and "bottom" account for the fluidity. Ultimately, according to Judith Butler, "Insofar as a number of fantasies can come to constitute and saturate a site of desire, it follows that we are not in the position of either identifying with a given sex or desiring someone else of that sex; indeed, we are not, more generally, in a position of finding identification and desire to be mutually exclusive phenomena" (99).

The desire to explore the relation of identification and desire, as well as to make legible the multiple and contested gender and sex roles in Gothic novels has yielded many new studies of the genre. Among those who have written extensively on the Gothic and sexuality, George Haggerty, notes that Lewis' novel "can be seen as an attempt to come to terms with the kinds of inner conflict that the emerging crisis of homosexuality made inevitable" (Haggerty, "Literature and Homosexuality" 343). The Gothic novel makes visible those conflicts in behaviors, identities, and sexualities that function as the *ne plus ultra* that delimited heteronormativity by excluding other forms of gender and sex. By making legible that which has been foreclosed, "these works are liberating—not only because they were able to bring such issues—if not the issue—out into the open, but also because they challenge conservative opinion about both the nature of literary expression and the terms of 'private' experience" (Haggerty 350). The critical moves to make this salient and important point have often pointed toward Lewis and other "male Gothic" novelists, like Horace Walpole and William Beckford, as forbearers who opened up the possibility of critique and liberation. The genealogy of a discourse of difference plays an important part in untangling the social and political history of categories cast not as categories at all, but as natural facts of life, and the novelists who produced that discourse are important figures to identify with. Haggerty recovers Lewis from a lukewarm "attempt to evaluate the long-standing tradition that Lewis was homosexual" undertaken by Lewis' biographer, Louis F. Peck (348). In response to Peck's argument for "insufficient evidence either way," Haggerty ponders whether we might "accept the implications of Lewis' extravagant and long-term financial and emotional commitment to the young William Kelly as a sign of sexual attachment," adding that Byron described Lewis as "'a middle-aged man who fills up his table with young ensigns, and has looking-glass panels to his bookcases'" as suggestive of "the nature of Lewis' taste" (348). The history of queer identity can emerge from a discourse that works by insinuation, or "that which can only come into being indirectly, through allusion, secrecy, theatricality, etc." (Roulston 761). By identifying novelists whose gender and sexual identifications were previously unspoken means that the history of sexuality is not just a history of (re)productive sexual relationships between opposite sexes. Reimagining the historical record is an inclusive move that gives human shape to the phantasmagorical figures of non-normativity for a community that needs recuperation.

At the same time, assembling a literary genealogy such as this has its drawbacks, as it attempts to establish origins and lineages. This kind of legitimating project gives Lee Edelman occasion to ask, "What if that very framing repeats the structuring of social reality that establishes heteronormativity as the guardian of temporal (re)production?" (181). He argues that "the pattern of the logic of repetition . . . projectively mapped onto those read as queers, informs as well the insistence on history and on reproductive futurism that's posited over and against them" (181). Instead:

> rather than affirming identities through the lens of continuity, queer history has sought to destabilize, to question, and to challenge the ways in which we look backwards. For queer history, all identities are historically contingent and are defined by ruptures or breaks rather than any kind of progress narrative moving seamlessly from oppression to liberation (Roulston 762).

Situating Lewis on a (linear) timeline from oppression to liberation is enticing, but it is also fraught as a critical move. The very temporality invoked by recuperating the author for queer history works by the same logic it seeks to undo. The logic of genealogy is, as noted above, a logic of heteronormativity that relies on oppositions of normal and hetero- against not-normal and not-hetero, on a smooth succession from one generation to the next. In order to disrupt such a logic, the terms of investigation have to be changed from "queerness-as-being" to "queerness-as-method" (Doan viii-ix, Roulston 762). *The Monk* provides some of the evidence we might use to embrace queerness-as-method: the novel unmoors sexual behavior from sexual identity and gestures toward an unacknowledged non-normativity of heteronormativity. While the non-normative defines the normative from without, the normative is not a unified by either practice or population in the novel.

Temporality itself is challenged, as the narrative moves back and forth from story to story, many of which cross each other's time lines. The reader must jump from one historical moment and geographical space to follow, for example, Raymond's story, which he relates in retrospect, and within which the reader is given the story of the Bleeding Nun, set generations before Raymond's explanation of his relationship with Agnes. The historical record for the Bleeding Nun is characterized by its temporal gap (and its specter) as Agnes comments "in all the Chronicles of past times, this remarkable Personage is never once mentioned" as she begins her tale "in a tone of burlesqued gravity" (139). Tales within retrospective accounts merge and then are disturbed by a teller's present moment as Raymond's stories of past trials are punctuated with comments directed at his present listener, Leonardo, to regale the cleverness of his servant Theodor in his pursuit of Agnes. The novel moves to scenes of Ambrosio and Matilda that seem to have occurred during the time that Raymond was relating the story. A straight, linear narrative would reflect some of the same structural qualities that a genealogy might, and the novel's queerness can be seen in its method of story-telling. Genre itself is unsettled as the work includes several poems both lyrical and narrative, making clear that fixed, unified categories can't be strictly applied to Lewis' work either.

The Monk provides little in terms of form or content from which an "ancestral genealogy" might be reconstructed. Tracking a subject to identify with assumes that a stable identity is out there awaiting our recuperation and that a continuity of subjects and experiences exists prior to the search for it. Yet, Lewis' novel itself disturbs the terms of identity, questions normative histories and challenges the narrative moves that produce and maintain normative identities and linear histories. The hyperbolic pressure applied to the two-body system of desire, and the slippage between desires and practices points toward the failure of constitutive categories to make sense of the myriad gender and sexual configurations the novel's represented bodies inhabit. Lewis articulates what could not be stated, describes what has been made invisible and excluded, and offers sexuality as indecipherable and desire as incoherent. As if to foreshadow the broken frames in the hall of family portraits, Lewis breaks the narrative frame in the novel's "Dedication." There he claims that he makes visible all plagiarisms "of which he is aware," but suggests that others may yet lurk unbeknownst to him. In other words, the knowledge is and will always be incomplete. Between what has been intentionally copied and what has been unwittingly (or unacknowledged wittingly) reproduced, Lewis intimates that there are some things that cannot be made visible. The line of textual ownership for the reader is fuzzy— it is unclear how a reader might negotiate the conundrum of recognizing based on their reading and knowledge, and trying to figure out if Lewis knew about that or not. If we see it and think that we know it, does that make it so? Using the logic here, how does one "read" behaviors and assemble them into a dossier of "sexuality"? Where is the line drawn that would inscribe the difference between one type of unspoken desire and another? Does an act define an identity? Does an unacknowledged desire dictate an identity that one would not make public? Lewis' addition to the Gothic canon takes the reader into an imagined world where gender and sex slip into shifting configurations. In this world, narratives do not account for the practices of desire, chronology does produce or represent a genealogical imperative, and all bodies are queer.

Works Cited

Brodum, William, MD. *A Guide to Old Age, or a Cure for the Indiscretions of Youth.* 46th ed. London, 1799. *Gale.* Web. 16 Dec. 2013.

Butler, Judith. *Bodies That Matter: On the Discursive Limits of "Sex."* New York: Routledge, 1993.

Ellis, Kate Ferguson. *The Contested Castle: Gothic Novels and the Subversion of Domestic Ideology.* Champaign, IL: U of Illinois P, 1989.

European Magazine, and London Review; Containing the Literature, History, Politics, Arts, Manners and Amusements of the Age, The. The Philological Society of London. Volume 31. London [England]: n. p., 1782. 86 vols. *Gale.* Web. 26 Feb. 2014.

Foucault, Michel. *The History of Sexuality, Vol. 1: An Introduction.* New York: Random House, 1978.

Haggerty, George E. "Literature and Homosexuality in the Late Eighteenth Century: Walpole, Beckford, and Lewis." *Studies in the Novel* 18.4 (1986): 341–352.

_____. *Queer Gothic.* Champaign, IL: U of Illinois P, 2006.

Lewis, Matthew. *The Monk.* London: Oxford UP, 2008.

Richardson, Samuel. *The Correspondence of Samuel Richardson ...: Selected from the Original Manuscripts, Bequeathed by Him to His Family, to Which Are Prefixed, a Biographical Account of That Author, and Observations on His Writings.* London: R. Phillips, 1804. 6 vols.

Roulston, Chris. "New Approaches to the Queer 18th Century." *Literature Compass* 10.10 (2013): 761–770.

Sedgwick, Eve Kosofsky. *Tendencies.* Durham: Duke U P, 1993.

"What to Become?" Religion, Masculinity, and Self-Determination in *A Visitation of Spirits*, *Parable of the Sower*, and *Parable of the Talents*

Marlon Rachquel Moore

The topic of religion has a long, historical thread in African American literature. What is generally understood about it is that black writers have served as representatives of their community and used their platforms to express the belief that God is on the side of the oppressed in liberation struggle, from the anti-slavery movement to the modern Civil Rights Movement. While this perspective is certainly correct, there is an equally time-honored parallel tradition of critique and repudiation that has existed alongside such expressions of faith. The question at the heart of this oppositional discourse is whether organized religion in general, and Christianity in particular, is the proper worldview for black people. (Christianity refers to a belief in the teachings, life, death, and resurrection of Jesus, as they are rendered in the Bible, and the belief in the Bible as a sacred instructional text.) Writers in what I will call the anti-Christian tradition (which is different from anti-religion) make the observation that the Christian message of spiritual liberty is undermined because the Bible corroborates slavery (examples include Deut. 20:14; Lev. 25: 44–5; and Eph. 6). Their work asks, if the Bible serves the interests of our oppressors, how can it also serve us? Other religions, such as Islam, Rastafarianism, Santería, and Voodoo are often considered more fitting for various cultural and historical reasons (see Curtis; Coleman; and Pinn, *Varieties*). Another point of contention is the belief in an afterlife because, the argument goes, the focus on attaining entrance into Heaven discourages most believers from working on humanity's problems in the present moment. Writers who take this position ask audiences to expand their social consciousness, in order to improve society and their own lives (see Allen; and Pinn, *End*).

Another argument, made as often in fictional depictions as in prose and scholarly writing, is that the standards of religious behavior can impose a level of self-denial that results in its own kind of captivity (Jackson 626–7; Neal 2040–2041; see also Larsen; Wright; and Baldwin, *Go Tell*). The intellectuals and artists who take this position question the self-denial advocated in Bible verses, such as Luke 9:23–24 and 14:26; Rom. 8:7–8; 2 Tim. 3:1–5; Titus 2:11–12. From this perspective, the repression of one's innate desires as an expression of faith, or the sacrificing of secular pleasures for spiritual gain is the opposite of spiritual liberty. If it were a form of religious captivity, why would people with a history of slavery not consider such restrictions in conflict with their quest for self-determination? Who or what is served when people compartmentalize "the sacred" away from the rest of their life experiences? Why does sexual restraint, for example, appear to be valued over sexual intimacy? When author, activist, and ex-Pentecostal minister, James Baldwin, pondered these ideas in his prose work, *The Fire Next Time* (1962), he surmised, "If the concept of God has any validity or any use, it can only be to make us larger, freer, and more loving. If God cannot do this, then it is time we got rid of Him" (47). This essay will compare works by two modern writers with representations of the African American experience that are on this spectrum of critique and repudiation of Christian practices. At times, it seems their characters also question the validity of "the concept of God."

Randall Kenan's *A Visitation of Spirits* (1989) and Octavia Butler's *Parable of the Sower* (1993) and its sequel, *Parables of the Talents* (1999), which will be discussed together as the *Parable Series*, participate in anti-Christian discourse through depictions of the tension between religious tradition and the quest for individual self-determination. These texts have in common highly intelligent teenage protagonists with middle-class backgrounds and strong family ties to the Baptist church. An important part of each story is how the central character seeks to transform his/her life on his/her own terms. In both stories, gender and sexuality are key axes for understanding the protagonists' outcomes, particularly regarding masculinity: *Visitation* is about a teenaged boy, and the *Parable*

Series concerns a young woman who, for a time, passes for a man. For the male protagonist, the concerns and demands of masculinity produce negative experiences that undermine his self-esteem. By contrast, the female protagonist finds protection and self-revelation in the act of passing as a man. Guiding questions in this analysis are: what are the possibilities for individual self-determination in the characters' religious paradigm, and what roles do concerns about gender and sexual norms play in their outcomes?

The Limitations of Belief in *A Visitation of Spirits*

Christian beliefs, which are tied to family legacy, severely limit the possibility of self-determination in *A Visitation of Spirits*. Set in a small North Carolina town in the 1980s, the novel concerns the life of sixteen-year-old Horace Cross, a high-achieving student who excels in his science courses. There is a wide gap between the person he is becoming and the person he is expected to become. The explanation for this is two-fold: First, he has experienced same-sex erotic attractions and participated in sexual acts, which, according to his religious perspective, are unacceptable. Second, he is being groomed for a leadership role in his family's fundamentalist Baptist church.

Who is he expected to become? The answer is a "good" Cross man. The Cross family's involvement in their church reaches back to 1875, when Horace's great-great grandfather, Ezra Cross, donated a parcel of his land so that the physical structure could be built. Ezra's son had served as chairman of the deacon board and, ever since then, the Cross family has acted on the belief that their legacy of church leadership would continue as long as they produced male offspring. Ezra set this standard and passed down his deep desire that, among them, a preacher would emerge and serve as pastor. So every boy child, as he came of age, was observed for signs of the calling; many of them disappointed the watchers. Yet, not every one of them was a disappointment: Horace's second cousin, Jimmy, the "chosen one" of his generation, declined to seek a career in college-level teaching in order to return to his small hometown; he is principal of the high school and current pastor of the family church. Then, there is Horace's grandfather, Ezekiel, the current and highly esteemed president of the deacon board. All of these factors weighed heavily on how Horace is seen by others:

> As it was explained to him, his grandfather was the center, the source of the church's memory, the link to the terrible past they all had to remember. [Ezekiel's] father and his father's father before him were church leaders, and it had fallen upon [Ezekiel] to lead, to guide, to counse l his people, their people. A chief, a great elder. His place was higher than the pastor's, and to Horace this seemed so very close to God that he realized one day that his grandfather was something of a [biblical] David. He was the grandson of a shaman (71–72).

What a burdensome responsibility. In her study of representations of the south in African American literature, *The Scary Mason-Dixon Line*, Trudier Harris calls this cultural milieu "the slavery of religion" (128) and explains that Kenan assigns the surname "Cross" to this family exactly because they are all laboring to uphold the family's middle-class respectability. "They not only burden their family members and force them to make tremendous sacrifices," Harris writes. "[B]ut they do so under the ironic banner of Christian goodwill. The largest cross they construct, however, [is the one] they plop onto Horace's shoulders" (125). Indeed, Horace is treated with deference in the black community and his intellectual acumen qualifies him as a successor to the family's Baptist legacy. Yet, this is not how Horace sees himself.

Who or what is Horace actually becoming? He is becoming a man apart from his family's expectations. At his lowest emotional point, he is "overwhelmed with sadness . . . [because he] could never be *like* his grandfather, never *be* his grandfather, and most painfully . . . *did not really want* to be his grandfather after all" (Kenan 86; emphasis mine). This realization is tied to the moral doctrine that the Cross legacy represents. As Harris explains, "Through the prism of the Christianity that he has been taught, Horace recognizes his family as being as willing to consign him to hell as the Old Testament God would be" (128). This interpretation of doctrine severely limits Horace's ability to imagine a future that can successfully integrate his family's wish that he become a church leader and his own realization of his emerging self as a gay or bisexual man—and survive. His sense of responsibility to the family name and his queer desires are irreconcilable for the teenager, so he sets out to transform himself into an acceptable man.

The milestones in Horace's journey are marked by his attempts to disavow his attractions to boys, to seek religious counsel, and then to escape altogether the "human laws and human rules that he had constantly tripped over and frowned at" (Kenan 12). This search for an acceptable manhood triggers his psychotic break, the depiction of which suggests that the rigidity of his belief system is unhealthy, and aligns with the critique that the dictates of religious behavior is a form of captivity that undermines notions of self-determination. Through Horace's failed attempts to determine his own destiny, the author argues that fundamentalist, inflexible interpretations of the Bible, coupled with the general homophobic norms around masculinity, are incompatible with the black gay or bisexual person's sense of freedom.

The religious pressure to conform to heterosexual masculinity is a form of captivity for Horace. It imprisons him in silence and self-loathing. In his church, he receives homophobic messages that define unsanctioned sexuality as spiritual weakness. Gendered in its effect, this kind of equation potentially demeans male recipients in a different way than it does girls/women. From boyhood, men are socialized to deny weakness in themselves, and to equate all things feminine with weakness and inferiority. Erotic desire for the male body, even before any sex act occurs, is interpreted as "acting like a girl" and is, therefore, a sign of inferiority in a boy/man. In flashback scenes, Horace recalls a sermon in which a preacher recites Romans 1, a letter written by Paul that argues that God abandons believers who lose sight of the true God or His message. Paul alludes to the story in Genesis of God's destruction of the sinful cities of Sodom and Gomorrah. In Paul's interpretation (Rom. 1:25), God eradicates the cities in a blaze of burning sulphur because their people began to believe their own stories and "changed the truth of God into a lie" (KJV). Among other unethical deeds, such as backbiting, fornicating, disrespecting their parents, and gossiping, the Sodomites engaged in homosexuality and the pagan belief that the image of God could be found in mankind, as well as "birds, and four-footed beasts, and creeping things" (Rom. 1:23). For this turn down the wrong path, the Sodomites prove irredeemable and must be destroyed. The preacher in Horace's church uses the text as a springboard for a critique of contemporary culture and those Christians who think the church should adopt a more liberal attitude toward sexuality. In sum, the preacher advises such people to remember the misguided sinners of old because only "weak-willed people" would fall for that line of thinking (Kenan 77–79). These teachings tell Horace that he is "unclean" and "excluded" (82) from God's grace and mercy.

His school peers reinforce the church's upholding of gender and sexual norms. They stigmatize and bully Gideon, another exceptionally intelligent student, for his "soft" and "sweet" masculinity. Gideon is referred to, insultingly, as "pretty," and described as dainty, delicate, and girl-like (98). For these qualities, he is routinely picked on by the boys whose masculinity is more conventional and spurned as a "sissy" by the girls (97). In order to align himself with the homophobic norm, Horace participates by spewing the word "faggot" at Gideon during one of these encounters, even though, he admits to himself later, he was "aware, even [at that moment with Gideon], of his true mind" (100). This acknowledgement reveals that Horace's actions are as much about self-loathing as they are about the desire to feel included. Participating in this violent ritual of masculinity only deepens his self-contempt and denial. To further overcome his "true mind," Horace labors to actively embrace heterosexuality and traditional masculinity.

In order to counteract his failed masculinity, as he sees it, his first act of self-making is to refashion himself into an athlete and a heterosexual. He joins the track team and finds a sexually active girlfriend. None of this staves off the fantasies, attractions, or sexual behavior with men; so, he seeks religious counsel from Jimmy, his cousin and pastor. To Horace's inquiry into the possibility of accepting his sexuality as it is, Jimmy stumbles through a response: "Trust me. These . . . feelings . . . will go away. Just don't give in to them. Pray"

(114). When, in desperate frustration, Horace asks, again, what he is to do if he cannot change, Jimmy responds with contradictory advice: "Search your heart. Take it to the Lord. But don't dwell on it too much" (114). Frustrated, Horace sinks into depression and resigns himself to the paradox that is his existence: He absolutely cannot change, and this inability to change is unacceptable to his family, peers, and God. His experience of the irreconcilability of his own understanding of his gender and sexuality with that of his family is so overwhelming that it sets him on the final, supernatural leg of his journey of (attempted) self-determination: a plan to fly above the fray of humanity, literally, as a bird. The impossibility of this undertaking is a large part of the point Kenan makes in *Visitation*.

Since his religious doctrine condemns him and heterosexual acts fail to change the object of his desire, Horace desperately turns to witchcraft as a path to freedom. His seriousness about the decision signifies his break with reality. The decision itself signifies his deep sense of confinement within family expectations and religious ideology. He seeks escape. "There are no moral laws that say: you must remain human," he deduced. "And [so] he would not" (12). With renewed optimism, he considers his options for a new existence through supernatural forces:

> What to become? At first Horace was sure he would turn himself into a rabbit. But then, no. Though they were swift as pebbles skipping across a pond, they were vulnerable, liable to be snatched up in a fox's jaws or a hawk's talons. Squirrels fell too easily into traps. And though mice and wood rats had a magical smallness, in the end they were much smaller than he wished to be. Snakes' heads were too easily crushed, and he didn't like the idea of his entire body slithering across all those twigs and feces and spit. Dogs lacked the physical grace he needed. More than anything else, he wanted to have grace. If he was going to the trouble of transforming himself, he might as well get exactly that . . . No, truth to tell, what he wanted more than anything, he now realized was to fly. A bird (11).

Through this plotline, *Visitation* indicates that self-denial and self-loathing can lead to madness. So impossible are the gender and sexual dictates of his religious heritage and societal norms that Horace resigns himself to the belief that the only reasonable response is his transformation into another species. "What to become?" he asks himself, as if he were selecting a costume for a masquerade party. Indeed, under these circumstances, what is he to become in a society that will not let him be as he is? What is the possibility for self-determination—for leading a livable life—when one is gay/bisexual/queer in a family whose deep investment in the mastery of a normative masculinity brings *them* so much respect and authority, even as it exacts the devastating price of an ultimately unlivable life? Horace's outcome suggests that this conflict of interests is irresolvable, for he commits suicide.

Through Horace's tragic life, *A Visitation of Spirits* participates in anti-Christian discourse with a resounding rejection of the notion that it can be compatible with gay/bisexual/queer subjectivity or that it is dynamic enough for gender and sexual minorities' full inclusion in the faith community. Instead, the novel argues that Christian dogma demands that such expressions or identities be muted, overcome, or otherwise made invisible.

The Possibilities within Belief in the *Parable Series*

While Randall Kenan constructs the Bible as a dead-end doctrine, Octavia Butler's futuristic *Parable Series* creates the possibility for self-determination by formulating an alternative, open-ended religious paradigm. Set in the mid-to-late twenty-first century, the tale put forth in *Parable of the Sower* and its sequel, *Parable of the Talents*, fuses a critique of theism with a concern for humanity and the ecological environment. In it, the United States is on an unalterable path of destruction for itself and the planet, and government entities are more concerned with maintaining Christian cultural hegemony and protecting the wealthiest class of citizens than serving the greater social good. Lawlessness and unchecked global climate change have created a society wherein no public space is safe from the threat of human or animal violence, or from extremely destructive and unpredictable weather patterns. So those who can afford to have already moved to Earth's twin planet to begin anew, while those left behind must fend for themselves and risk falling deeper into despair and desperation.

The *Parable Series* uses this setting in order to propose adaptability as an expression of self-possession, and social awareness as an alternative to doctrinal rigidity. Specifically, protagonist Lauren Olamina portrays adaptability as an expression of self-determination through her religious writings and successful male impersonation. The impersonation, or gender passing, serves as a vehicle for escape from oppressive conditions that can be contrasted with Horace's tragic failure to transform or escape alive. In the final aspect of this comparison, this essay shows that homoeroticism also figures into the *Parables* and allows readers to see where sexuality fits into Lauren's faith practice.

Like Horace's, Lauren's story begins with a crisis of faith. It is her fifteenth birthday and her father, a college professor and pastor of a Baptist church, is planning to baptize her. The impending ceremony troubles her because, not only does she not believe in the doctrine of salvation taught by her father's religious denomination, she also has, for three years, been cultivating her own theological worldview, one that has been culled from multiple sources. Lauren knows that she is only participating in the water ritual because her father takes it very seriously as an outward expression of faith and because she wants to please him. Ultimately, it would be a false expression, made only because it is what is expected of a preacher's daughter. Lauren responds to the dilemma not by beginning, as Horace does, with the question of what to become in order to avoid exile from community or from God. Instead, Lauren's starting point is a review of the competing definitions of God that the people in her life hold:

> The idea of God is much on my mind these days. I've been paying attention to what other people believe—whether they believe, and if so what kind of God they believe in. Keith says God is just the adults' way of trying to scare you into doing what they want. He doesn't say that around Dad, but he says it. . . . A lot of people seem to believe in big-daddy-God or a big-cop-God. They believe in a kind of super person. A few believe God is another word for nature. And nature

turns out to mean just about anything they happen not to understand or feel in control of (Butler, *Sower* 14–15).

This spectrum of perspectives allows Lauren to see her inability to become a "good" Christian woman not as a tragic end point but, rather, as a point of departure. The answer to the question "what is God" is already numerous in her small circle of believers. From this, she gathers that He must be whatever you need Him to be—and she will reinvent Him for her own purposes. She composes a doctrine, "Earthseed: The Book of the Living," which aims to empower people to seek to control of their destiny in a chaotic world and to see themselves as part of the solution to social problems.

Some literary critics construe Earthseed as progressive Christianity emptied of traditional intolerance and misogyny. Donna Andreolle, for example, describes it as a "newfound Christianity"; she makes the case that Butler's rhetorical project, accordingly, "reflects the validity of Judeo-Christian values as the necessary ideological foundation of American social order" (116). Meanwhile, Jim Miller reads Lauren, somewhat contradictorily, as a Christ figure whose religion "lacks pious self-sacrifice" (355, 356). It is not surprising that readers recognize that the *Parable Series* is biblically based, since the respective titles in it invoke the stories Jesus tells his disciples in order to instill in them the importance of ministry (Matt. 13 and 25). And like Jesus, Lauren is a storyteller, teacher, and philosopher whose radical break from the family's faith tradition will elevate her into the status of a deity in the minds of future generations. Furthermore, Butler closes each novel with the recitation of its biblical namesake; so, the last words readers encounter in each *Parable* novel is a direct quote from its corresponding Christian parable.

Even so, Earthseed, it seems, makes a dramatic shift away from Christian theology. Arguably, it presents atheism cloaked in religious language because the doctrine invests the sanctity usually reserved for God with the concepts of human cooperation and malleability. In Earthseed theology, the nature of God, is directly tied to known and visible aspects of the environment and universe; so, in order to understand humanity's relationship to God, one should study God's behavior in nature and respond accordingly. One of Lauren's Earthseed verses instructs followers to understand that "All successful life is adaptable, opportunistic, tenacious, interconnected, and fecund. [We are to] Understand this. Use it [and] Shape God" (*Sower* 124–125). Importantly, no part of the theology renders God an interactive, anthropomorphic being who must be worshipped or who answers prayers or who rewards strict obedience. Instead, believers are rewarded with the positive consequences of an "adapt, survive, and grow as you go" mentality. Regardless of how it is interpreted, this approach to life and, especially, the insistence that God's reflection is found in the natural environment inevitably create space for a spectrum of sexual and gender expressions, including fluidity or bisexuality (see Roughgarden; and Bagemill).

Lauren embodies the principles of adaptation and growth (and adaptation *as* growth) when she passes for a man and, in doing so, reveals to herself her capacity for same-sex attraction. Lauren's life on the streets teaches her that, although it is dangerous for everyone, women's bodies are preyed upon differently than men's. As a result, she realizes that she must adapt her appearance to her masculinist surroundings in order to increase her chances of survival. In contrast to Horace's experience, the norms and perceptions of masculinity—dominance, hardness, and impenetrability—serve Lauren's need for self-determination. The power associated with men's bodies is a welcome alternative to being perceived as a vulnerable woman.

The threat of rape notwithstanding, Lauren's body is not depicted as vulnerable. From the beginning, her gender expression is conveyed as masculine by several references to her size, strength, and hardness. As a teenager, she brags of her bone-breaking ability in fistfights (*Sower* 11–12). Her body is tall and broad, and she "towers" over her stepmother (*Sower* 104); and, in a crowd of women, her height distinguishes her (*Talents* 317). The transition to a male presentation requires that she enhance her already masculine aesthetic by cutting her hair and wearing baggy men's clothes. And she never sheds her female masculinity. By the end of *Talents*, when she is fifty-eight years old and long past her gender-passing years, Lauren is still "big and strong [as though she could] be hard with just the smallest change of expression" (398). The narrative does not go into further detail about how or if she changes her gait and voice to successfully pass. Instead, it provides evidence that her transformation is convincing to the people that she, as Cory, encounters. Lauren describes how men and women find this male persona alternately desirable and threatening when she hires herself out as a day laborer in exchange for food and boarding. Eventually, she realizes that this newfound magnetism might also serve her religious ends. When she tests it, she discovers her capacity for sexual fluidity.

As Cory, Lauren meets Nia, a woman who responds to "him" on intellectual, emotional, and erotic levels. Cory and a traveling companion spend the day weeding Nia's enormous vegetable garden and, after the compensatory meal, the three converse while Cory draws a sketch of Nia's face. Cory glances back and forth to the sketchpad, and poetic Earthseed verses fall gently from 'his' lips. The verses intrigue Nia and she inquires into their origins. Cory waxes philosophical, and "his" oratory skill and flattering sketch coax Nia into allowing the traveling couple to stay on for the night. The opportunity for more intimacy is important, as the minister has decided that Nia's property ownership and background as a teacher could serve Earthseed. After establishing Nia's trustworthiness, Cory reveals himself as a biological female. Nia stares intently at Cory/Lauren's face, but, because the performance of male masculinity is so well executed, none of the familiar cues and traits of conventional femininity are detectable:

> "But you . . . " she said. "I can't get over it. I still feel . . . I still feel as though you were a man. I mean . . . "
>
> [Cory:] "It's all right."
>
> [Nia] sighed, put her head back and looked at me with a sad smile. "No, it isn't."
>
> [Cory:] No, it wasn't. But I went to her and hugged her and held her (*Talents* 371).

Throughout the scene, Lauren brags about how she stimulates and channels the erotic energy into a commitment to the religion. Yet, Lauren's desires are also stirred by this intimacy: "To my own surprise, I realized that under other circumstances, I might have taken her to bed. . . . And I had never been tempted to want to make love with a woman. Now, I found myself almost wanting to. And she almost wanted me to. But that wasn't the relationship that I needed between us" (*Talents* 371). Although the urgency of Lauren's religious mission hinders her from exploring these same-sex desires further, it is important that her reaction to discovering them is not about gender taboos, shame, self-loathing, or denial. As a heretofore-heterosexual woman who values the lessons gained from lived experience, she simply marvels at her newfound capacity for sexual fluidity. It is the Earthseed way.

Still, for all of its insightful commentary on how religious belief can be used to facilitate gender and sexual nonconformity, the formula for self-determination in the *Parable Series* elicits other concerns. Lauren's inspired (as opposed to inherited) religion is a source of empowerment because it provides her with a framework for subverting gender-based social and sexual constraints. It is through—and not in spite of—her religious belief that she is able to forge a livable life of imagination and openness. This is a more desirable outcome than suicide, of course, but is the implication that, in order to live autonomously and with fewer physical threats, women's best recourse is to suppress (under the guise of "to protect") their femininity while they work for societal change? If, as Lauren says, God is revealed through the facts of the circumstances, is the "shape" of the Earthseed God as masculine as the Christian Jesus and His Heavenly Father? If Lauren is a role model for black female self-determination, would not this limitation on gender expression also be considered a form of misogynistic, sex-deprived captivity? The nebulous relationship between religion, masculinity, and self-determination in the *Parable Series* raises more questions than it answers.

Conclusion

What we find when we juxtapose *A Visitation of Spirits* with the *Parable Series* is that, although one story is, arguably, more tragic than the other, both Kenan and Butler present a problematic Christian-inflected perspective and propose a tenuous alternative to it. Horace and Lauren overlap in their experiences because the Bible, on its own fails, to serve either character's needs. The religious conservatives in *Visitation of Spirits,* who led Horace to such desperate ends, move on with little self-reflection about their impact on the boy they lost. Presumably, this is the point Kenan wants to make: Keeping one's eyes focused on Heaven creates blind spots in human relations. But the sorcery and witchcraft he turns to are also shown to be unreliable alternative traditions. They, too, fail Horace in his time of deepest need. As for Lauren, she survives, and Earthseed gains a worldwide following; membership grows to include many wealthy people who donate land, material, and financial support; and they are able to successfully relocate poorer community members to Earth's twin planet (this was always the Earthseed goal). What remains unknown is whether the Earthseed philosophy will take root outside of the poorer populations.

This outcome of mass outer-space migration suggests that "Save the Earth" and other social/ecological justice movements that currently exist will never be a match for the individualism bred by unethical, unbridled capitalism. Consequently, individualism will continue to exacerbate social inequities and increase violence against women and girls. What is the role of religion in that scenario? To whom should the oppressed turn for guidance, protection, and inspiration? Operating in the long tradition of anti-Christian critique and repudiation in African American literature, Kenan and Butler inquire about where our faith truly lies in times of turmoil, and whether we are becoming larger, freer, and more loving people because of it.

Works Cited

Andreolle, Donna Spalding. "Utopias of Old, Solutions for the New Millennium: A Comparative Study of Christian Fundamentalism in M.K. Wren's A *Gift Upon the Shore* and Octavia Butler's *Parable of the Sower*." *Utopian Studies* 12.2 (2001): 114–123.

Allen, Norm, ed. *African-American Humanism: An Anthology.* Amherst, NY: Prometheus Books, 1991.

Bagemill, Bruce. *Biological Exuberance*: *Animal Homosexuality and Natural Diversity.* New York: St. Martin's, 1999.

Baldwin, James. *The Fire Next Time.* New York: Vintage, 1992.

_____. *Go Tell It On the Mountain.* New York: Vintage, 1952.

Butler, Octavia. *Parable of the Sower.* New York: Grand Central, 1993.

_____. *Parable of the Talents.* New York: Grand Central, 1998.

Coleman, James. *Faithful Vision: Treatments of the Sacred, Spiritual, and Supernatural in Twentieth-Century African American Fiction.* Baton Rouge: Louisiana State UP, 2005.

Curtis, Edward E. *Islam in Black America: Identity, Liberation, and Difference in African-American Islamic Thought.* Albany: State U of New York, 2002.

Harris, Trudier. *The Scary Mason-Dixon Line: African American Writers and the South.* Baton Rouge: Louisiana State UP, 2009.

Jackson, Agnes Moreland. "Religion." *The Oxford Companion to African American Literature.* Eds. William L. Andrews, et.al. New York: Oxford UP, 1997.

Kenan, Randall. *A Visitation of Spirits.* New York: Vintage Books, 1989.

Neal, Larry. "The Black Arts Movement." *The Norton Anthology of African American Literature.* 2nd edition. Eds. Henry Louis Gates, Jr. and Nellie McKay. New York: W.W. Norton & Company, Inc., 2004.

Larsen, Nella. *Quicksand.* Minneola, NY: Dover, 2006.

Miller, Jim. "Post-Apocalyptic Hoping: Octavia Butler's Dystopian/Utopian Vision." *Science Fiction Studies* 25.2 (July 1998): 336–360.

Pinn, Anthony. *The End of God-Talk: An African American Humanist Theology.* New York: Oxford UP, 2012.

———. *Varieties of Black Religious Experience.* Minneapolis: Augsburg Fortress, 1998.

Roughgarden, Jane. *Evolution's Rainbow: Diversity, Gender, and Sexuality in Nature and People.* Berkeley & Los Angeles: U of California P, 2004.

Wright, Richard. *Black Boy.* New York: HarperCollins, 2005.

CRITICAL READINGS

Whistling Past the Grave of the Phallus: Aristophanes' *Lysistrata*

Roger Travis

There is one fact that needs to be kept straight, or nothing else in my introduction of this strange comedy will make any sense at all: there were no female Athenians in the Theatre of Dionysus in Athens when Aristophanes' *Lysistrata* was performed because there was no such thing as a female Athenian (Loraux 1). While the dispute over the presence of biological human females at the theatrical festivals continues (see Henderson), what is not in dispute is that the *notional* audience of Aristophanic comedy was male. When I describe the comedy as nevertheless in an essential sense a feminist play, I ask the reader always to remember that that description must always come with a layer of irony: that layer of irony is what I call "whistling past the grave of the phallus."

By "whistling past the grave of the phallus" I mean (to put it less evocatively but perhaps also more clearly), cracking joke after joke in the theatre about how men aren't really all that great, when the tragic evidence that men aren't really all that great—in the form of blood and treasure lost to warlike masculine display—is visible within steps of the theatre. I mean to say that besides being a feminist play, *Lysistrata* (the reader should do him- or herself a favor and pronounce it with the emphasis on the second syllable, like the British) is also a tune that the Athenians—men, all, for there was no word for a female Athenian—whistle to themselves as they walk hurriedly by the evidence that the male dominance of Athenian culture has been rotting away for a very long time.

Of Sex-Strikes, Sex-Workers, and the Getting of Heirs

Lysistrata's claim to fame is the sex-strike that provides the engine for the comedy's plot. The title-character, an Athenian wife portrayed as typical (more on what "typical" means for an Athenian wife in a little bit), convinces all the other Athenian wives (some with more difficulty and different results than others) to refuse sex to their husbands. When this unusual rebellion spreads throughout Greece—including, above all, to Athens' main opponent in the Peloponnesian War, Sparta—the formulation and ratification of a peace treaty takes only a few hours.

The plot of *Lysistrata* has made it one of the few Aristophanic comedies that can be successfully mounted today.[1] The timelessness of the basic idea of creating power directly out of sex, which inhabits a central place in human psychology, turned to a comic purpose, makes for a theatrical experience that continues to satisfy audiences where other Aristophanic comedies, revolving as they do around cultural dynamics that don't fit our modern context as well, have tended to languish.

The very intuitiveness of the sex-strike as a comic plot-device blinds us, however, to certain very important facets of the Athenian context that alone can make sense of what happened in the imaginations of the Athenian men who played and watched each other playing in the 411 BCE Theatre of Dionysus.[2]

For starters, our idea of sex-deprivation comedy (compare, for example, Shakespeare's *Measure for Measure*) revolves around a simple version of male sexual frustration, in that our expectation from the Middle Ages on—at least where our fictions are concerned—has been that if a married man is not having sex with his wife, he is having sex with nobody. Much of the comedy of these more recent examples comes as a result of the sympathetic reaction of the audience to the plight of the deprived men, in a cultural context where prostitution is considered unacceptable and is usually also illegal, and where much of the modern period's same-sex eroticism is similarly (notionally) forbidden.

In the Athenian context, however, married men had available to them at very low monetary cost and without the disapproval of their community slaves and sex-workers of both sexes, of whom, we can say on the evidence above all of Aristophanic comedy itself, Athenian men availed themselves with great frequency. Also, and much more unfortunately (as exploitative as even a legal sex-trade must always be), marital rape cannot but have been very common, again above all on the evidence of comedy—and *Lysistrata* itself most, where the strong possibility is acknowledged by Lysistrata saying that if their husbands should rape them, the rebellious wives should refuse to look happy that they are being raped[3]:

> It's necessary to provide yourself as an evil, evilly.
> For there's no pleasure for them to do it by force (163-4).[4]

Thus, when we try to understand how *Lysistrata* (like, indeed, more than one of Aristophanes' other comedies, ones that are regrettably less known to modern audiences, notably *The Assemblywomen* and *The Women at the Thesmophoria*) can seem so feminist to us in certain important ways, but nevertheless be, at its heart, just as misogynistic as the rest of Athenian culture, we must look first to the difference between the way we approach the comedy's central dynamic and the way the Athenian men watching in the theatre did. The Athenians at the dramatic festival in 411 BCE (we do not know which festival it was, but it must have been one of the two annual dramatic festivals of Dionysus), where *Lysistrata* was first performed, could laugh at the enormous, aching erections of the male characters in the *orkhēstra* (the space where the comedy was performed—think: stage) in large part because they knew that if their wives should ever refuse them their sexual favors, they would easily find other means of gratification. *Lysistrata*, whatever else it may be, is by no means a romantic comedy.

We must add to the ease with which real Athenian men could find bodies to penetrate another important difference in the social context of Athenian marriage, this one presenting the actual difficulty for Athenian men that lurks behind the false, humorous difficulty of sexual frustration: the getting of heirs. The easiest way to grasp the problem here is to consider the plight of Pericles, who had two sons by a famous sex-worker named Aspasia, who was a metic—that is, not an Athenian woman but a resident alien, who, according to a law backed by Pericles himself, was unable to confer Athenian citizenship on her sons. Towards the end of his life, without a son by his Athenian wife, Pericles was forced to spend what amounted to all his political capital in begging the Athenian assembly to make those sons citizens.

Only the daughters of Athenian citizens—remember again that there was no word for a female Athenian—could give birth to Athenian citizens. As I will detail below, the life of an Athenian woman was so circumscribed that the only way she could give birth to a citizen was through marriage to an Athenian citizen. This fact presented Athenian men with the difficulty that if they wanted heirs, having sex with their wives was a necessity. This problem, never mentioned in *Lysistrata*, nevertheless lies behind every line of the comedy, and provides a sort of backstop to the comedy: things are funny, after all, because they are unreal versions of real threats— the sex-strike in *Lysistrata* is no exception, in that the enormous erections of the frustrated husbands present an unreal transformation of the real threat of dying without an heir.

The above comes to a quick and dirty summary of how *Lysistrata* can whistle past the graveyard of the phallus—that is, one can joke about a real weakness in masculine power as if that weakness did not exist. What follows lends texture to that basic outline. This essay explores the context of the comedy in three different areas: the history of Aristophanic comedy and its genre-conventions, our evidence about the lives of real Athenian women, and the immediate politico-historical context of the comedy in the Peloponnesian War.

Context: Comedy

Old comedy, also called Aristophanic comedy because Aristophanes is the only comic playwright of the period whose comedies survive, seems to have developed into the form in which we have it, from the reed (think: pen) of Aristophanes, by a combination of some of the oldest forms of ritual poetry (such things as the *kōmos* [a revel] and processional *aiskhrologia* [festival-participants yelling bawdy insults at one another]) with the dramatic possibilities of the relatively recent (in those days) poetic form of what an Athenian would have heard as "goat-song"—that is, *tragōidia*—tragedy.[5] I introduce tragedy this way in order to keep the reader from thinking that an Athenian would have had the associations of sadness that modern English speakers do; for an Athenian, tragedy was an exciting new dramatic genre, in which practically anything could happen to traditional mythic figures, as long as nothing was really very different from the familiar version of the story. Similarly, in Aristophanic comedy, practically anything could happen to realistic-looking characters, as long as Athens was still basically Athens at the end of the story.

Three conventions of Aristophanic comedy, out of a great many that have a bearing on our understanding of *Lysistrata,* demand particular mention: the maleness of all the actors and all the audience, the large role of the chorus (and, in particular, their participation in the comic forms called the *agōn*—that is, "contest"— and the *parabasis,* a choral section in which the chorus addresses the audience directly), and the standard comic costume item of an oversized, erect phallus for every male character.

Like tragedy, and perhaps like the *kōmos,* from which comedy took its name (though our evidence is severely lacking where *kōmos* is concerned), comedy's active players—actors and chorus—were all men. The heavy preponderance of evidence also suggests that they played their comedies for an entirely male audience, as I mentioned at the outset of this chapter. Lysistrata, as noble as she seems to us, was to the Athenian audience first and foremost a comic, not a heroic, figure, played as she was by a man using a falsetto voice and wearing a mask that probably did not conceal his beard.

When Lysistrata says, "We bear the war to the full, or even double it, first bearing and then sending away our sons as hoplites" (588–590), then, as poignant as the words seem to us, they would certainly have been taken by the audience as sounding like the sort of thing they heard from their own wives and found not poignant but irritating. That fact in and of itself tells us a great deal about the position of women in Athens, and indeed strengthens the central argument made in this chapter—that Aristophanes is taking his cast and audience in a sort of whistling procession by the graveyard of the phallus, pretending to themselves that their masculine self-assurance does not rest on a foundation of exploiting the women of Athens, above all in the realm of sexual reproduction—because such jokes always belie an essential insecurity in the position of the jester and his laughing audience. Things can't be funny unless they make the one laughing uncomfortable to some degree.

The chorus was a central feature of Athenian life, and indeed life in all the *poleis* of Greece. Not only in tragedy and comedy, but also as a constant feature of a huge range of religious festivals (of which there were many, many more than feature in modern life—the reader wouldn't go far wrong to think of it in terms of two festivals a week, with a more or less monthly, multi-day festival to boot, nearly all of them involving a chorus), the song-and-dance group, with a heavy emphasis not on the song but on the dance, made up an important part of every young person's education—girls included. As they got older, Athenians would participate in different sorts of chorus, like the famous dithyrambic choruses of the most important festivals, re-telling mythic stories in innovative forms, which Aristotle tells us (though there is reason to doubt his word) were the origin of tragedy, and like the tragic and comic choruses themselves.

For that reason, the chorus could be said always to set the tone of an Athenian drama, whether comic or tragic, and so when we try to determine what sort of gender power-relations exist in *Lysistrata*, we must look to the chorus of women, and the way Aristophanes portrays them, above all in contradistinction to the strawman chorus of men.

Two important facets of choral practice in comedy merit particular notice and explanation: the *agōn* (contest) and the *parabasis* (address to the audience).

In the *agōn,* which rather unusually and quite significantly, given the nature of the comedy, begins with the very entrance of the dueling choruses. Two parts of a comic chorus, sometimes portraying the same sort of thing (clouds or birds, for example) and sometimes portraying different sorts of things (men and women, for example), face off in a verbal contest that goes back and forth between speech and song, and generally also involves the main characters of the comedy.

The *agōn* of *Lysistrata* unfolds among the chorus of old men, the chorus of women, a (male) magistrate, and Lysistrata herself.

Some of our most precious witness to the real lives of Athenian women comes in these passages, as Lysistrata protests the injustices done her by her husband, and, by extension, the injustices visited upon all Athenian women by the men of Athens. In fact, the *agōn* cannot truly be said to end until the choruses unite in the brief *parabasis* (see below): this comedy really being all about the eternal contest between men and women (or so it seemed to the Athenians, based on their traditional literature, like the works of the Homeric and Hesiodic traditions).

Hopefully, the foregoing sketch of the play's comic background indicates that, for Lysistrata to accuse her husband of real, actionable injustice—for not telling her what was happening in the assembly—would have seemed absurd, and his threat to strike her if she did not return to her weaving would have been a justified threat for henpecking, if not perhaps a just reward (slaves are beaten in old comedy, but wives never are, despite several threats, at least in the existing plays). But, by the same token, the presentation of Lysistrata's point-of-view in a comic *agōn* means that Athens, with Aristophanes, is once again whistling past the grave of the phallus, just as Jackie Gleason would do some two-thousand-three-hundred years later on *The Honeymooners* when his character Ralph Kramden threatened his wife Alice with a journey "right to the moon." In both cases, a bluff version of violent hyper-masculinity comically puts to rest the threat of the feminine ability to maintain order. To laugh at such threats both denies and exposes the problematic nature of masculine phallic dominance—or, in the terms of this chapter, it whistles past the grave of the phallus.

The comic *agōn* in the case of *Lysistrata* provides the perfect conventional vehicle for the oppositional humor that drives the sex-strike dynamic, and Aristophanes' decision to place that *agōn* so early in the play seems likely to have been made to highlight the opposition as much as possible. The most fundamental purpose of comedy being to make its audience laugh, we can surely trust that Aristophanes wanted to set the humorous tone of this comedy in relation to the serious matter of the council Lysistrata has called of sex-striking women from the other warring *poleis*: having a contest between Lysistrata and a male representative of state authority, played out against a parallel contest between the old men of Athens and the rebellious, sex-striking women. This then metamorphoses as the dramatic action continues, growing more and more pointed about the mismanagement of the state until finally the choruses unite and offer Aristophanes' own surprising advice to Athens. This lets the audience in for a great deal of humor, even as the real problem—the eternal problem—is laughed off over and over. However, it is the mere fact of the raising of that problem that makes *Lysistrata*, in its own limited way, ineluctably feminist. If we consider a feminist text to be a text that makes male, phallic dominance seem problematic, *Lysistrata* must be feminist.

It is usually said that *Lysistrata* has no *parabasis* because, at the usual location of the comic *parabasis*, the chorus is not yet united. Certainly, the comedy does not have a proper *parabasis*, but there is a moment that accomplishes the usual generic function of the *parabasis* in that the chorus, as a body, addresses the audience, thus:

> We are not preparing
> o men of the citizens, at all,
> to say anything mean—not a single thing.
> But on the contrary to say everything good—
> and to do it: for the evils are hand are sufficient!
> But let every man and woman say it out,
> if any needs a bit of cash
> to take two or three minas
> as there's much around
> and we're holding out our purses.
> And if peace is made,
> whoever borrows now from us,
> if he takes, he doesn't have to pay it back.
> And we're going to have a party for some
> Carystian friends, good and fine men,
> and there's still some soup: and there's a suckling pig,
> going to be slaughtered, so you'll eat tender, fine meat.
> So come over to my house today! (1043–1063)

This address would have probably astonished the Athenians, for the moment when the chorus addresses the audience was typically the time for the comic playwright to come right out and say exactly what he thought was wrong with the political situation of the city.

From a generic point of view, this *parabasis* is strange and false. Instead of offering a critique of the Athenian war-effort, a critique that the *agōn* has, in fact, been effecting for the past hour and more of comedy, Aristophanes invites the audience for a light lunch after the play. This *parabasis* represents precisely the kind of whistling I am suggesting *Lysistrata* is all about. To say that Aristophanes and his chorus don't want to create controversy, specifically on the grounds that there has been too much of that recently (a notion that applies equally well to the comedy *Lysistrata* thus far and to the political situation of Athens), is to say that Lysistrata's rebellion has merit, and may not be dismissed as a comic absurdity the way one might dismiss the plots of most of Aristophanes' other comedies (the building of Cloudcuckooland, for example, in *Birds,* or the trip of Dionysus to the underworld in *Frogs*). There is a cutting irony in this false *parabasis*: what the Athenians might perceive as an absurdity—a sex-strike that brings the war-effort to its knees—should make them think of how intractable the conflict between men and women in a macho society, like that of Athens, truly is, where the only thing a group of men and women can agree upon is an invitation to lunch.

Context: Athenian Women

The matter of the male/female opposition on view in the *agōn* and then ironically "resolved" in the little false *parabasis* leads us to the matter of *Lysistrata*'s relation to the lives of real Athenian women. Those lives were circumscribed for women of all statuses, but perhaps most of all for "typical" Athenian wives of the kind Lysistrata's character is shaped after. Kept indoors almost continuously, clad in veils when they were allowed to go out at all (like, for example, to a festival such as Demeter's Thesmophoria, the subject of another of Aristophanes' gender comedies), given in marriage very young to men they did not know, the daughters, wives, sisters and mothers of Athenian citizens, from a linguistic standpoint, were not even Athenians themselves: the word that *should* mean "female Athenian" refers instead to the goddess Athena.

Of the many misogynistic things one might read that the men of Athens would have known by heart, or nearly so, perhaps the most famous is this passage from Hesiod's *Theogony* about Pandora, the first woman:

> For from her is the race of women and female kind: of her is the deadly race and tribe of women who live amongst mortal men to their great trouble, no helpmeets in hateful poverty, but only in wealth. And as in thatched hives bees feed the drones whose nature is to do mischief—by day and throughout the day until the sun goes down the bees are busy and lay the white combs, while the drones stay at home in the covered hives and reap the toil of others into their own bellies—even so Zeus who thunders on high made women to be an evil to mortal men, with a nature to do evil. And he gave them a second evil to be the price for the good they had: whoever avoids marriage and the sorrows that women cause, and will not wed, reaches deadly old age without anyone to tend his years, and though he at least has no lack of livelihood while he lives, yet, when he is dead, his kinsfolk divide his possessions amongst them (590–607, tr. Evelyn-White).

With such passages in mind, an Athenian might well laugh—uncomfortably, because really all laughter is to some degree uncomfortable laughter—when Lysistrata says, in the second part of the *agōn*, when she's facing off against the magistrate, "So I remained silent, inside. We heard some other worse decree from you," (516–7). Women's lives were indoors, and such jokes as the Magistrate's about the possibility of adultery with jewelers and cobblers sent to the house (403–420) only serve to demonstrate the fixity of that arrangement, while demonstrating the anxiety that both leads to it and cannot be laid to rest even by its draconian prevention of anything like a fully-actualized life for the women of Athens.

We must read the standard jokes about women's sexual desire and love for wine against that backdrop of the basic practical conditions of their lives. When we see lines like Lysistrata's despair at her comrades weak return to their homes, victims of the power of unquenchable feminine libido, if we are to understand not simply the humor of that day in 411 BCE, but also its more serious side—not just the whistling, but also the graveyard—we must set them against the silencing Lysistrata evokes so vividly, earlier, a silencing both women and men must have known very well, women receiving and men commanding it:

> Why do you call on Zeus? This is the way it is.
> So I say that it's no longer possible for them to hold themselves
> apart from men, for they are running away.
> I caught the first picking out the hole
> where there is the house of Pan;
> another was wriggling down from a block-and-tackle;
> another deserting like a soldier; another on a sparrow. . .
> They drag out every excuse to go away homeward (717–727).

To put such realistic words in the mouth of an Athenian wife as Lysistrata speaks when she says:

> We endured through the men's war until now with our prudence whatever you were doing. For you didn't let us speak. And you didn't even apologize. But we were perceiving you well, and many time though we were inside we heard you making decrees badly in some big matter (507–511).

and then to hedge with the canard of insatiable female sexuality is mere whistling past the graveyard: playing with that which you know will doom you in the end.

Context: War

The final piece of context we must add is that of the terrible war that had already gripped the *poleis* Greece for twenty years when *Lysistrata* was first performed and would continue to grip them for another seven before Athens would, at last, go down to an ignominious defeat. The principal part of this backdrop, as far as understanding the gender-dynamics of the comedy is concerned, is the ineffectuality of the Athenian war effort and, above all, the tragedy of the Sicilian Expedition of 413 BCE, two years before.

Launched with great fanfare in 415 BCE, expected to revive the Athenian cause entirely with the plundered riches of the Greek *poleis* of Sicily, led by Alcibiades, the most brilliant-seeming young politician and general of Athens, the expedition had been plagued by trouble from the start. In its final, disastrous resolution in the loss of all the blood and treasure invested in it, it had demonstrated to Athens that something was seriously wrong with the Athenian state. In the decade afterward, the constitution of Athens would change several times into more than one form of oligarchy, back to democracy, back to a harsh oligarchy imposed by Sparta, and then finally, after the war, back into a more stable, less radical democracy.

In that context, things Lysistrata and her chorus say carry a great deal of weight at least on their negative side. The solutions they propose are, of course, played for laughs, but those jokes cannot but constitute yet more whistling—this of a very obvious kind, for it is in this regard that I can finally pull the phallus (or, rabbit, I suppose, if you like) out of my critical hat and refer to the famous incident of the mutilation of the herms that occurred in 415 BCE, on the eve of the Sicilian expedition (Hamel has written an excellent, very readable book about the incident).

A herm is a very-strange-looking-to-modern eyes statue, with the head of Hermes atop a square pillar bearing, as an inscription, the Athenian equivalent, more or less, of an address, and then, below the inscription, an erect phallus. The night before the expedition was to leave, parties unknown—though Alcibiades was blamed—went through the city, mutilating the herms. Though we have no direct evidence of how exactly they were mutilated, and our principal witness Thucydides decorously tells us that they were cut about the face, other sources make it seem likely that there was a more obvious target for mutilation on a herm—that is, the phallus was in fact the principal victim of this vandalism.

Two aspects of the incident are arguably of crucial importance in understanding *Lysistrata*'s attitude towards gender in Athens and towards gender more generally. First, the symbolic castration of the city; second, the strange, massive over-reaction to the event on the part of the Athenian assembly, which launched an investigation and finally recalled Alcibiades from the expedition, at which he defected to Sparta. Thucydides, no admirer of Alcibiades, would strongly imply that it was the fault of the assembly in recalling him that caused the disaster.

To put it succinctly: there was, in the Athenian imagination, a graveyard of the phallus. When Lysistrata says, "We bear the war to the full, or even double it, first bearing and then sending away our sons as hoplites," then, although, as already discussed, it would not have seemed poignant to the Athenian audience, nevertheless it must at least have posed, in a feminine voice, the age-old challenge of the war cemetery: "Mistakes were made."

Conclusion: The Limited Triumph of the Women's Voice

Argued here is that the feminism of *Lysistrata* arises despite a bluff overlay of misogyny in the comedy. That overlay is located in the broad humor of calling women insatiable and wine-loving. We also find it in the more sinister way Lysistrata's valid concerns are dismissed through the fantastic resolution of the war in a few hours by a sex-strike, when every Athenian man in the audience in the Theatre of Dionysus would have known himself perfectly capable of finding a sexual partner should he feel deprived. That feminism, I suggest, is to be found 1) in the real threat of the lack of heirs, 2) in the ineluctability of the conflict between men and women embodied in the choral *agōn* and the false *parabasis*, 3) in the seeping of women's real silencing around the edges of mundane domestic strife played for laughs, and 4) in the evocation of Athenian masculinity's defeat in the Sicilian expedition. To those can be added, finally, the simple fact of Lysistrata, comic version of a real Athenian, succeeding in putting an end to the war through the power of her words: a limited, laughable triumph, but a triumph nonetheless.

Notes

1. For the performance history of Aristophanes, see Van Steen.

2. On the gender-play aspects of *Lysistrata* and other Aristophanic comedy, see Zeitlin.
3. On domestic abuse in classical Athens, see Cohn-Haft.
4. Except where noted, all translations are my own.
5. See Rusten for a discussion of the evidence.

Works Cited

Cohn-Haft, Louis. "Divorce in Classical Athens." *Journal of Hellenic Studies* 115 (1995): 1–14.

Hamel, Debra. *The Mutilation of the Herms: Unpacking an Ancient Mystery*. CreateSpace, 2012.

Henderson, Jeffrey. "Women and the Athenian Dramatic Festivals." *Transactions of the American Philological Association* 121 (1991): 133–147.

Loraux, Nicole. *The Children of Athena: Athenian Ideas about Citizenship and the Division Between the Sexes*. Princeton, NJ: Princeton UP, 1993.

Rusten, Jeffrey. "Who 'Invented' Comedy? The Ancient Candidates for the Origins of Comedy and the Visual Evidence." *The American Journal of Philology* 127 (2006): 37–66.

Varley, H. Paul. *Venom in Verse: Aristophanes in Modern Greece*. Princeton, NJ: Princeton UP, 2000.

Zeitlin, Froma. "Playing the Other: Theater, Theatricality, and the Feminine in Greek Drama." *Nothing To Do with Dionysos? Athenian Drama in Its Social Context*. Eds. J. Winkler & F. Zeitlin (Princeton: Princeton UP, 1990). 63–96.

Shining Genji and the Women of the Heian Court in the *Genji Monogatari*

Sara R. Johnson

It is often said that the novel was first invented in early modern Europe, with the publication of Cervantes' *Don Quixote* in 1605 being the first clear example of the form (Hägg 2). While this may be true of the modern European novel, it is also at least occasionally acknowledged that earlier examples of the form exist in both European and non-European contexts. In particular, novels were written in both Greek and Latin in the early centuries of the Roman Empire, and the text that is still considered a masterpiece of the Japanese novel form, *Genji Monogatari* (*Tale of Genji*), was produced at the Heian imperial court of Kyoto shortly after 1000 CE. The *Tale of Genji* is the subject of this essay.

To do full justice to the complexity of the subject of sex and gender in relation to the world's first novel written by a named woman author, running over one thousand pages in most translations, featuring over five hundred characters, and taking for its primary focus the life of women in the Heian imperial court, is an impossibility, and this essay does not pretend to provide that. The main purpose of this essay is threefold. Drawing upon my background as a scholar of Greek and Latin literature, this essay tries to make some comparative connections between the classical world of Heian Japan (794–1185) and the production of novels in Greek under the Roman Empire (during the first and fourth centuries). Drawing upon Japanese history, culture, and language scholarship, this essay also seeks to provide a context within which a student, who may not be familiar with either modern or ancient Japan, can better understand the *Tale of Genji*. And finally, drawing upon modern *Tale of Genji* scholarship, the following essay attempts to identify some of the most important relevant themes and points students in the direction of far more detailed studies that can better do justice to the novel's complexity.

The *Tale of Genji* is traditionally ascribed to a female author, known to later generations as Murasaki Shikibu, who, according to the account preserved in her own diary, served as a lady-in-waiting upon an empress at the Heian court. Although far from being free of male-dominated preconceptions about the role of the ideal woman, the narrative reflects, to an extraordinary degree, the perspective of a noblewoman in a world where the roles of both women and men were highly scripted and regulated by an elaborate code of cultural norms. Moreover, readers will see that the emergence of the written Japanese language and vernacular Japanese prose itself took place within an explicitly gendered context, a context that the novel both embodies (in its prose) and reflects (in its representations).

Genji and the Greek Novel

My acquaintance with the novels that precede the emergence of the modern European form began with the Greek novels of the early Roman Empire. Although there was no direct contact between the cultures that produced these works, a brief comparison of the two can be illuminating. The comparison helps to highlight what makes the *Tale of Genji* unique—not least the fact that it, unlike the Greek novels, was written by a woman.

The Greek sentimental novel focuses on love, marriage, and domestic harmony to a degree unparalleled in earlier Greek and Roman literature, thus provoking in scholars a discussion of the relationship between the rise of the novel and changes in the position of women in society at the time (Hägg 81–108). Although (anonymous) female authorship of the Greek novels has sometimes been suspected (Hägg 96), all of the named authors are men, and it is more likely that women were rather an important part of the intended audience (Egger 113). Earlier scholars suggested that the popularity of the Greek novel reflects a shift in social mores away from the civic and the mythic, and toward a more bourgeois and domestic outlook, characteristic of a growing educated upper-middle class (Hägg 90–101). While not denying the appeal of the novel to an educated middle class, more recent commentators have tended to stress the concerns of the Greek elite under Roman rule to redefine the ideal roles of both men and women within the altered civic context of the Roman Empire (Whitmarsh 5–6, along with the essays of Bowie and Morales in the same volume). Whereas Konstan once argued that what is idealized in the novel is a reciprocal relationship, a type of "sexual symmetry" (7), recent work shows how the narratives, in fact, serve to reinforce a male-dominated standard of idealized female behavior, in the context of reconstructing Greek civic identity under Roman imperial rule (Egger 136; Haynes 18).

Likewise, we find in the *Tale of Genji* a preoccupation with the idealized roles of men and women within an elite context. There is, however, a distinct difference in point of view, which this essay will attempt to expand on more fully.

Murasaki Shikibu

The question of authorship should be dealt with at the outset. Murasaki Shikibu was born in the late tenth century (the date of 973 is traditional) and, according to the account in her literary diary (*Murasaki Shikibu Nikki*), served after her husband's death as a lady-in-waiting (*nyoubou*) at the court of the Empress Shoushi, the daughter of the greatest of all Fujiwara statesmen, Fujiwara no Michinaga, and was the consort of Emperor Ichijou (986–1011). The name by which the author is known to posterity, not unlike that of her characters (see below), is a nickname. She came from a remote branch of the Fujiwara family, but her branch of the family had since declined in status (her great-grandfather was the last to hold office above the middle rank). She was the daughter of a provincial governor and was married to a provincial governor in turn. However, "Shikibu" is the name of an office that was formerly held by her father, and "Murasaki" is a nickname taken from her most famous female character. What her given name was, we do not know (Tyler xvii; Shirane 215–223). She is generally called Murasaki in English.

That she is the principal author of the *Genji Monogatari* has never been doubted. At most, scholarly controversy has centered around whether she is responsible for all fifty-four chapters, or whether some chapters (typically some or all of the chapters from 42–54, most often chapters 42–44) may have been composed by a later editor, perhaps her own daughter (Tyler xviii). In any case, external evidence attests to the existence of over fifty chapters (thus, presumably, the whole) of the *Genji Monogatari* as early as 1021 (Tyler xviii; Shirane 222). It is not known when exactly the novel was written, but it appears that some of earliest chapters were written before Murasaki was summoned to court in 1006 (her growing literary reputation being the cause of that summons), and the last may have been written not long before her death, presumed to be around 1014 (Shirane 222). The chapters do not seem to have been written in the order that they now appear, but it is generally accepted that their present order matches up with the author's ultimate intention (Shirane 224).

Translations

The undergraduate may encounter one of several widely used translations of the *Tale of Genji*, and the translation used can have a substantial impact upon the student's understanding of the work. There have been three major translations of the *Genji Monogatari* into English in the last century: Arthur Waley's (1933), Edward Seidensticker's (1976), and Royall Tyler's (2001). All three remain in print and are commonly consulted. Each has its own strengths and weaknesses, but the differences in translation become apparent with the most casual comparison of the opening sentence of the novel (as cited in Nimura):

> **Arthur Waley**: "At the Court of an Emperor (he lived it matters not when) there was among the many gentlewomen of the Wardrobe and Chamber one, who though she was not of very high rank was favored far beyond all the rest."
>
> **Edward Seidensticker**: "In a certain reign there was a lady not of the first rank whom the emperor loved more than any of the others."
>
> **Royall Tyler**: "In a certain reign (whose can it have been?) someone of no very great rank, among all His Majesty's Consorts and Intimates, enjoyed exceptional favor."

Waley translated freely, making a particular effort to convey the spirit above the letter of the text, and many report finding his translation the most enjoyable to read, but it takes liberties that may obscure the original Japanese context by importing Western cultural allusions. Seidensticker's translation is terse, favoring short, spare sentences. It is closer to the original Japanese in its brevity, but because Japanese relies heavily on the use of context to convey implied meaning, sticking to the barest translation risks losing much of the feeling of the original (and, indeed, Seidensticker is more likely to leave out words that were in the Japanese altogether; he omits the reference to *nyougo* and *koui* in the citation above). Tyler seeks to strike a balance between the two, following the text as literally as possible while not shying away from interpretation and commentary where it helps us to understand what the reader might have understood when reading between the lines. In Nimura's apt phrase, "As guides, Waley is the most entertaining, Seidensticker the most unobtrusive, and Tyler the most instructive."

In this essay, I have chosen to follow Tyler, not least because of his effort to be precise in using the terminology and conventions of the original, even when they are less accessible to an English reader. A student using any of the three translations may find very valuable the *Reader's Guide* written by Puette, which was published before the release of Tyler's translation, but which serves as a reference guide, enabling the student to readily compare elements that differ between Waley and Seidensticker. In particular, Puette provides a list of the titles given to each chapter in Japanese, as translated by Waley and Seidensticker (7–10), and a cross-indexed list of names by which individual characters are known (149–167). This may be compared with the detailed information about both chapter title and the nomenclature of characters that Tyler provides at the head of each chapter throughout his translation. Finally, while few undergraduates will have a comfortable command of classical Japanese, a reader with even minimal or no Japanese can view the original text of the novel online, in three parallel columns, showing the original Japanese text, a modern Japanese translation, and a transcription (not a translation) of the original Japanese text into romaji (English transliterated text) ("Genji Monogatari").

Naturally, it goes without saying that every act of translation is an act of interpretation. However, an appreciation of the differences between translations is particularly important in the case of *Genji*, not only because the student is so likely to encounter a variety of translations that can differ dramatically from one another, but because the specific choices made by the translator can significantly impact the reader's understanding of the social role and identity of both male and female characters throughout the narrative, a factor which can be crucial when discussing matters of sex and gender.

What's in a Name?

The most important example of this is the use of names throughout the text. Classical Japanese shares with modern Japanese a heavy reliance upon context as understood by the reader to inform meaning. An aesthetic preference for that which is hinted or glimpsed over that which is explicitly stated is everywhere apparent throughout the *Tale of Genji*, and it reflects a fundamental linguistic characteristic of Japanese. As most eloquently expressed by Rubin (11–21), Japanese is often believed by speakers of English to be inherently vague, but it is not. A sentence may be written without explicitly stating a grammatical subject, but when read in context by a native speaker, the subject is as plainly apparent to the reader as if it had been explicitly stated. The danger of confusion arises only when a reader encounters a text without being able to supply the proper context. To this, one may add the view (which also survives in modern Japanese culture) that it is more polite to refer to a person, and even to address them, using their social role or title rather than a personal name. It was considered particularly rude at the Heian court either to directly address or indirectly refer to a person by their personal or family name. These two factors, when combined, produce in the *Tale of Genji* a system of nomenclature that far exceeds in complexity the tables found at the back of most nineteenth-century Russian novels.

The world of *Genji* is occupied by a voluminous cast of characters, most of whom appear over multiple chapters, spanning years or even decades. Classical Japanese nomenclature of the Heian period employed both family and personal names, with the family name taking precedence, as in modern Japanese (Fujiwara no Michinaga = Michinaga of the Fujiwara clan). However, the vast majority of the characters in the novel are never identified by either a family or a personal name. Most characters are alluded to by honorific titles (for example, the reigning Emperor is called "His Majesty"), or the text avoids naming them at all. This is easier to do in a language that does not require subjects or objects to be stated when the person referred to can be inferred from context (Rubin 25–31). Characters are instead described elliptically, by their relationship to another character; by some salient characteristic, such as the place where the character lives; or by a certain social rank. And, to complicate matters further, these relationships, and especially ranks, change over time.

Although the original author, and presumably her audience, may have been comfortable keeping this sprawling cast straight using only indirect allusions and titles that change over the course of the narrative, it soon became a problem for subsequent readers who had less in-depth knowledge of the Heian court. Already in the medieval Kamakura period (1185–1333), we find handbooks compiling a list of sobriquets (nicknames) that can be used consistently throughout the text to identify a given character, even when the text itself never once uses that name to refer directly to the person in question, and these sobriquets continue to be used in modern discussions of *Genji*.

To take a few examples from the earlier chapters, Genji's father, the first reigning emperor in the narrative, has come to be called Kiritsubo no Mikado, the "lord/husband of Kiritsubo." Throughout the narrative, however, he is always referred to by the honorific appropriate to his rank at the time. Kiritsubo, in turn, refers not to Genji's mother's personal name, which we do not know, but to the place where she lived, the "paulownia pavilion" (*kiritsubo*) within the palace enclosure. One of Genji's earlier lovers is known to readers as the Rokujou Haven (a combination of her place of residence on Rokujou, meaning Sixth Avenue, and her status at court, "Haven" (a type of *nyougo*, or imperial consort). Genji's first wife, the daughter of the Minister of the Left, is called Aoi because of the flower with which she is associated in a poem in chapter nine, "Aoi." Genji's brother-in-law and confidant, later to become his rival at court, appears first with the rank of Chamberlain Lieutenant (*tou no chuujou*), which subsequently becomes his sobriquet (Tou no Chuujou), although he holds many other ranks over the course of his life. Genji (源氏) himself bears a sobriquet that means "one of the Gen" (another pronunciation for the family name 源, Minamoto, the clan to which he is assigned by his father), and the personal name by which he is sometimes called by commentators, Hikaru, means "Shining." Genji Hikaru is a nickname ("shining member of the Minamoto clan"), not a personal name.

A reader should then always be aware, whenever reading either a given name or a title/rank within the narrative, that the usage of certain terms to identify characters is a delicate choice made by the translator. In most cases, there is no dispute among commentators who is meant by a certain designation in the text, but sensitivity to the ever-shifting world of roles and titles can be lost when a translator consistently uses sobriquets (Fujitsubo, Aoi, Murasaki, etc.) to explicitly identify characters throughout the narrative. Tyler's choice to use English translations of honorific titles within the narrative, combined with a list at the head of each chapter matching the character's title, age, and relationships to the traditional sobriquet, is more challenging to the reader but closer to the spirit of the original.

The Women of Genji's World

The *Tale of Genji* is fundamentally the story of Genji and his many loves. Indeed, some have argued that the story is more about the women than it is about Genji, and in some ways, that might be true, but it should be kept in mind that Genji's life is the strand that ties the narrative together and provides its structure (Tyler xiii). Even his successors, Niou and Kaoru, are best understood in terms of their relation to the hero (Tyler xii).

The first Japanese novel, like the Greek novel, shows a deep preoccupation with love both inside and outside of marriage. Of course, the social setting and the moral values associated with it differ from those found in the Greek city-state under Roman rule. Both the emperor and other high-ranking (male) members of the court were expected to form multiple marriages. Marriage itself could be consummated simply by the formal witnessing of three successive nights spent together, so that even participants and witnesses might not be certain of the formal intent until the third encounter is achieved. Liaisons outside of marriage were frowned upon for men, principally if they involved affairs with another man's wife, or if they otherwise were the cause of public scandal. As long as scandal does not result, however, the narrative rarely expresses any disapproval of Genji's many liaisons. Indeed, at times, it seems to celebrate Genji's extraordinary ability to charm women, to form connections beyond those normally encouraged by social convention, and ultimately to function as a husband, father, and patron to numerous women as the virtual emperor of his own private court within the four quarters of his Rokujou estate. The narrator is at pains to tell us, on several occasions, that Genji never forgot any woman in whom he ever took an interest (Tyler xiv). However, the narrative also reveals an extraordinary sensitivity to the complicated reality of love, courtship and marriage for aristocratic women. The author rarely condemns anything Genji does outright, but she quietly allows us to see the complicated and sometimes painful results of the choices he makes—both for the aristocratic women with whom he forms relationships and for the principally female attendants who surround these noble women.

In the *Bridge of Dreams*, Shirane analyzes Genji's relationships through three lenses which may be of help: the political, the social, and the religious. In the political sphere, the narrative becomes a sometimes detached, sometimes ironic or critical mirror held up to the political dynamics of the Heian court. In this era, the emperors were largely dominated and controlled by the Fujiwara clan through a complicated network of marriage-alliances, but in the novel, Genji rises through this power structure and triumphs over it despite his status as a commoner. Both in the person of the emperors themselves, and in Genji's unconventional position at court, the author explores an idealized image of imperial rule that would have been impossible in her own early eleventh-century world.

In social terms, close attention is paid to the difficulties created by distinctions in status among the elite. For the inhabitants of the Heian court in Kyoto, the court was a rarefied world, outside which normal people almost literally did not exist (when allusion is made to ordinary people outside the world of the court in the narrative of *Genji*, they are described in terms that suggest that they are not quite human). For those who did occupy this world, social stratification was elaborately constructed in terms of relationship to the imperial and noble families. In the notorious "discussion of women on a rainy night" that takes place in the second chapter (*Hahakigi*, "The Broom Tree"), Genji's brother-in-law Tou no Chuujou makes a distinction between women of the upper rank, middle rank, and lower rank. He means not what many social historians might expect—the three estates of nobility, merchants, and peasants (or some similar variant)—but the differing ranks to be found among the elite at court (Shirane 51). There were a total of eight court ranks. Earlier in the Heian period, any of the top five ranks would have been considered high-ranking, but by the later Heian period, the upper rank comprised only the immediate imperial family and the top three court ranks; those in the fourth and fifth ranks were now relegated to an increasingly marginal status, with the men frequently serving as provincial governors who had little hope of ever rising above that position, and their daughters often obliged to seek service as cultured ladies-in-waiting to higher-ranking noblewomen, as an alternative to making marriages that were far below their self-perceived social status. Murasaki Shikibu, the author, was herself a daughter of a provincial governor of the middle rank, and the circumstances of her life are echoed in the lives of several of her characters (particularly the Akashi lady, Utsusemi, and the Uji sisters).

Genji as a young man characteristically pursues and enjoys happy relationships with women of the middle rank more than those of upper rank. He is unhappily married to a lady of upper rank (Aoi), and prefers to pursue affairs with women of the middle rank such as Yugao. (The rainy-night conversation in chapter two, as is well known, becomes a template for many of the relationships that Genji subsequently seeks out.) At first, this might seem to embody the fairy tale of the "social romance," featuring a high-ranking noble who rescues a woman from relative social obscurity and makes her his principal wife; Genji's cultivation of and marriage to his principal wife Murasaki initially seems to fit this model. Throughout the narrative, however, attention is paid to the painful reality of limited social status for women of the middle rank, and as youth gives way to middle age for both Genji and his wife Murasaki, it becomes increasingly apparent through the narrative that life for aristocratic women of any rank in Genji's world was no fairy tale.

An early warning of the dangers that Genji is risking by his unconventional choices comes in the form of political scandal. Genji longs for women who are beyond his reach (particularly Fujitsubo and Oborozukiyo, both of whom are or become the consorts of emperors, members of Genji's own family), but even when consummated, such relationships cause only scandal. In the case of Fujitsubo, Genji seems to metaphorically get away with murder. He enjoys an illicit affair with his father's favorite consort, which produces an illegitimate child, a baby who bears a startling resemblance to Genji himself (Reizei, the future emperor). In a stroke of extraordinary good fortune for all concerned, however, the fraud is not discovered. The emperor, Genji's father, believes to the end of his life that Reizei is his own son, and Reizei discovers his true parentage only much later in life; the truth is never revealed to the public. Fujitsubo retires to take religious orders, and Genji himself finds happiness with Murasaki, who is Fujitsubo's niece and bears an uncanny resemblance to her.

This good fortune is, however, subtly undermined by a less fortunate episode of Genji's love life. In spite of his happy marriage to Murasaki, Genji cannot resist pursuing a target that has often rejected him, known to readers as Oborozukiyo, even after she becomes the consort of the currently reigning emperor, his own half-brother, Suzaku. Eventually he is successful in seducing her, but this time, he does not get away with it; he is discovered in the act by his political enemies—Oborozukiyo's father, the Minister of the

Right, and her sister, the Kokiden consort (Empress Mother). With Genji's father, the previous emperor, now deceased, and the party of the Minster of the Right (who represents the dominant influence of the Fujiwara over a young and passive emperor Suzaku) in the ascendant, Genji must withdraw into self-imposed exile at Suma and Akashi, a crucial turning-point in both his political fortunes and his own personal maturation.

Miraculously (literally, with the aid of divine intervention), Genji is enabled to return from exile and, ultimately, to regain a position of political ascendancy. The pinnacle of his political career is reached when the now-emperor Reizei discovers his father's true identity. Reizei conveys upon Genji the ultimate mark of status, the unheard of (indeed, invented—the only invented rank in the novel) rank of *jun daijou tennou* (chapter thirty-three, *Fuji no uraba*, "Wisteria Leaves"; Shirane 27). Effectively, Genji is honored as retired emperor when he has never actually held the position of emperor.

The pinnacle of Genji's domestic good fortune is reached in chapter twenty-one (*Otome*), when he is able to establish a private estate at Rokujou, where he installs several of the women in his life. The four quarters of Rokujou, a virtual representation of the natural world and, by extension, the imperial court, are named according to the four seasons. Spring is the quarter of Genji's principal wife, Murasaki, and the daughter whom he persuades her to adopt, the daughter of the Akashi lady. Autumn (with the quadrants of Spring and Autumn being given the highest precedence [Shirane 29]) is occupied by Akikonomu, the daughter of the Rokujou Haven, who will one day become Reizei's principal consort (making Genji both the secret biological father of an emperor and the adoptive father of an emperor's consort, that position most coveted by all Fujiwara nobles). Summer is occupied by Tamakazura, Genji's adopted daughter whom he, for some time, passes off as his own daughter (she is in truth the lost daughter of Tou no Chuujou by Yugao), and Winter by the tragic figure of the Akashi lady, the middle-ranking mother who gives up her daughter by Genji to be raised by Murasaki. In the end, the daughter of the Akashi lady will become the consort of the emperor who succeeds Reizei, making Genji both father and grandfather to an emperor's consort. No Fujiwara could aspire for more.

Genji's great good fortune, however, is undermined in later life, and this sheds light on the religious as well as the social aspect of the narrative. He succumbs to pressure from his half-brother, the retired emperor Suzaku, to take Suzaku's daughter (The Third Princess) in marriage. Suzaku is worried about his daughter's fate if she does not marry; the painful situation of imperial daughters, who were effectively too high-ranking to ever make a suitable marriage as long as the Fujiwara made it their priority to marry their own female relatives to every eligible imperial candidate, is one of the social realities depicted in sharp relief by the author (Shirane 133–140). The marriage is, however, an unmitigated disaster: the couple is not well suited. Genji neglects his new wife when his favored wife, Murasaki, falls ill out of jealousy, and in the end, the Third Princess succumbs to the seduction of another man (Kashiwagi) and bears an illegitimate child, Kaoru. Genji is thus, in karmic fashion, obliged to enact the role of victim, where he was once the offender; he knows of the adultery, but has no choice but to accept Kaoru as his own (unlike his father, who never knew that Reizei was not his own child). In the end, Murasaki dies of her illness, and Genji does not long survive her.

Shirane points out that, while so many earlier Japanese *monogatari*—particularly the social romances—end with the happily-ever-after marriage, in *Genji*, marriage is only the beginning (107–119). The life of Genji's principal wife Murasaki is, in one sense, exceptionally blessed, since she is rescued from a life of obscurity and enjoys her husband's greatest favor throughout her life, being honored at one late stage with tributes equal to those of an Empress (*chuugu*). Her middle-rank social origin should have ensured that she was not eligible even for marriage to Genji, let alone such privileged status among his wives and among other women of the court. But her married life is not entirely a happy one, and the author acutely reflects upon the painful limitations that women faced, whether they, like Murasaki, were lucky enough to grasp the brass ring of a high-ranking marriage, or whether, like the Akashi lady (and later Oigimi, who commits suicide rather than accept a marriage that she thinks will surely end in humiliation), they were obliged to go through life facing painful reminders of the impossibility of ever rising to a higher status.

It is in this area that the contrast with the Greek novel emerges most forcefully. While the question of gender identity in the various Greek novels is, by no means, a simple one, the ideal that is upheld throughout is that of noble woman's chastity, which ultimately ensures marriage to a noble husband and (one assumes) subsequent felicity. Unlike *Genji*, the story ends with the moment of the happy union/reunion (that is, marriage) rather than beginning with it. Never does one find articulated so clearly in the Greek novel the plight of the aristocratic woman, who must grapple with personal disappointment and the limiting reality of social conventions even as she seeks to live up to the standards of ideal womanhood set by the society around her (as, for instance, the young Murasaki not only fulfills all of the cultural ideals set out for her by her education, but strives throughout her later life not to trouble her husband with her jealousy, willingly embracing and adopting a daughter by another woman and supporting Genji's marriage to the Third Princess). It may be that, at least in the early days of the novel, only a woman author, who was herself of the middle aristocratic rank, was able to represent the reality she inhabited so clearly.

Gender and Language

When considering the *Tale of Genji* within a gendered perspective, it is important to understand the literary context from which the novel emerged. *Genji* is written in classical Japanese prose, which shares with modern Japanese the use of a hiragana syllabary, many common kanji (Chinese characters), and common word-roots, but differs substantially from modern Japanese in that it is highly inflected (modern Japanese, much like modern English, has only minimal inflection; the degree of inflection in classical Japanese is very similar to that found in Latin) and makes use of many grammatical forms and word-endings, which are as alien to the modern Japanese reader as Latin is to a speaker of English. Although a certain amount of classical Japanese is a compulsory subject in Japanese high schools, the modern Japanese reader will experience *Genji* through a modern Japanese translation, just as even advanced students of high school Latin typically read the bulk of Virgil's *Aeneid* in English.

The comparison with Virgil can be deceiving, however. Despite the enormous literary prestige that *Genji* now holds, at the time when it was written, Japanese (*kana*) prose was not highly regarded. The highest value was attached to works written by members of the Japanese elite in classical Chinese prose (*kanbun*), and to the native Japanese poetic form of the *waka*. Classical Chinese literature (biography, historical chronicle, and philosophical treatise) was considered the exclusive province of educated males. Women were normally excluded from the study of Chinese, and within the *Genji*, any pretention to Chinese learning in a woman is marked as distressingly unfeminine. (Interestingly, we learn from Murasaki's diary that she acquired Chinese learning by eavesdropping on her brother's studies; her own work reflects considerable knowledge of Chinese literature, but is careful to distinguish itself as *kana* rather than *kanbun* prose.) The leading practitioners of the *waka* as represented in the famous collection of the *Kokinshuu* were likewise men, although this form, being written in native Japanese, was also accessible to women. The ability to spontaneously compose poetry in Japanese is treated throughout the *Genji* as one of the essential qualifications of any educated woman, be she noblewoman or lady-in-waiting. Japanese *kana* prose, however, was, in this period, almost exclusively left to the province of women, so much so that some of the earliest male writers of Japanese prose either assumed a female pen-name (for example, the *Tosa Nikki*) or remained anonymous (the early *monogatari*, such as the *Taketori Monogatari*) (Varley 61–63).

This literary and linguistic divide reflects the unusual circumstances surrounding the emergence of Japanese as a written language. Japanese society became literate as a result of contact with the Buddhist scholars of China in the sixth and seventh centuries. As the Romans, a younger society growing up in the shadow of the older Greek civilization, first wrote their treaties and contracts and composed their histories and epic poems exclusively in Greek before beginning to cultivate Latin as a literary language, the earliest Japanese writers (seventh and eighth centuries) wrote almost exclusively in Chinese.

The adaptation of Chinese written characters for Japanese use proved even more challenging. The Roman alphabet modifies the Greek alphabet in relatively minor ways, thus producing a writing system that was well adapted to their own tongue when authors began to use it for higher literary purposes. Japanese, however, differs much more profoundly in linguistic structure from Chinese than Latin does from Greek. Chinese is a monosyllabic language, well adapted to the use of a rich vocabulary (many thousands) of Chinese ideographs, each representing a syllabic word with its own pronunciation and meaning. Japanese is a polysyllabic, inflected language (the classical form being even more inflected than the modern), heavily dependent upon particles and shifting word-endings to convey meaning.

After some failed experimentation, the modern Japanese writing system came into use in the late ninth century (scarcely a hundred years before the publication of *Genji*), by combining two interwoven writing systems, a syllabic *kana* alphabet, known as the hiragana, united with the use of Chinese characters (kanji) to represent word roots. Although a text could be written entirely in hiragana, mirroring the pronunciation of the spoken language, the existence of many homophones and the ubiquity of Chinese learning gradually led to the substitution of Chinese characters for word-roots. The earliest surviving manuscripts of *Genji* are written in this hybrid style. For an example, the opening sentence of the novel, quoted in three translations above, reads in classical Japanese thus:

いづれの御時にか、女御、更衣あまたさぶらひたまひけるなかに、いとやむごとなき際にはあらぬが、すぐれて時めきたまふありけり。

It is possible, then, to speak of the earliest production of written Japanese as a predominantly female art (Morris 12–13, 199–250), in contrast to the mastery of classical Chinese, which was the province of men. The production of prose Japanese literature in the Heian period thus belonged to women in a way that simply does not have an equivalent in most cultures in any period in history. The achievement of Murasaki Shikibu in producing her sprawling, masterfully complex psychological novel belongs to this period. Already in the later eleventh century, and even more so in the medieval Kamakura period, named male authors began to move into and monopolize the production of Japanese prose, but the female authorship of the *Genji Monogatari* has never been seriously questioned. This is striking when compared with the world of Greco-Roman antiquity, within which it is extremely difficult to establish even one major literary work—certainly any work of prose—that has been broadly credited to a woman's hand. Even in late medieval Europe, which featured a somewhat similar exclusion of educated women from the production of Latin literature, the production of vernacular literature (e.g., in English, French or Italian) nevertheless remained very much the province of men, with women authors representing a small minority. The value of Heian prose Japanese literature for a scholar who is interested in female authorship in the premodern world can scarcely be overestimated.

In this context, it is striking to note how much attention is given throughout the narrative to the production of writing by women. The pinnacle of a woman's literary art may have been the ability to compose poetry, but these poems were typically written down and conveyed in hand-carried letters, and particular attention is given to handwriting as a mark of both cultured education and feminine propriety. Murasaki's development from an artless child into a cultivated young woman, under Genji's close supervision, is paralleled by the development of her handwriting from the childish (Tyler 96, 100, 108) to the exquisite. Indeed, her attendants encourage her to use Genji's letters as a copybook model to develop her own style (Tyler 100). A more appropriate metaphor for Genji's cultivation of Murasaki, Pygmalion-fashion, into the ideal wife could hardly be found. By contrast, the miserable example of an awkward lady who attempts to produce Chinese-style poetry is held up as unattractively mannish, both in diction and in handwriting (Tyler 35).

Conclusion

Tenth- and eleventh-century Japan, in which, for a relatively brief time, the creation of an entire branch of prose literature was left almost exclusively in the hands of a small number of elite women at court, provides a unique window both into the development of one early masterpiece of the novel and into the social world of the Heian court, especially as it appeared through women's eyes. In the Heian world as in the Greek world, it seems that the most clear-eyed scrutiny came from those who were very close to, but not located in the highest positions of power. The author of the first fully preserved Greek novel (first and second centuries), Chariton's *Callirhoe*, identifies himself as the secretary of a *rhetor* in Aphrodisias, a city in Asia Minor (Reardon 21). Like Murasaki Shikibu, Chariton spent much of his life waiting upon one of the elite (a *rhetor* occupied the highest possible social and literary position in the world of the Greek city under Roman rule). Their perspectives upon the lives—in particular the courtship and marriage—of aristocratic women are far from identical, but they might have understood one another's life experience rather well.

Works Cited

"Genji Monogatari." *Genji Monogatari*. University of Virginia Library Electronic Text Center, 29 June 1999. Web. 11 Mar. 2014. <http://etext.lib.virginia.edu/japanese/genji/index.html>.

Egger, Brigitte. "The Role of Women in the Greek Novel: Women as Heroine and Reader." *Oxford Readings in the Greek Novel*. Ed. Simon Swain. Oxford: Oxford UP, 1999. 108–136.

Hägg, Tomas. *The Novel in Antiquity*. Berkeley: University of California, 1983.

Haynes, Katharine. *Fashioning the Feminine in the Greek Novel*. London: Routledge, 2003.

Konstan, David. *Sexual Symmetry: Love in the Ancient Novel and Related Genres*. Princeton, NJ: Princeton UP, 1994.

Morris, Ivan I. *The World of the Shining Prince: Court Life in Ancient Japan*. New York: Knopf, 1964.

Murasaki Shikibu. *The Tale of Genji*. 1921–1933. Trans. Arthur Waley. 6 vols. Tokyo: Tuttle, 2010.

———. *The Tale of Genji*. Trans. Edward G. Seidensticker. Vol. 1–2. New York: Knopf, 1976.

———. *The Tale of Genji*. Trans. Royall Tyler. Vol. 1–2. New York: Viking, 2001.

Nimura, J. P. "Courtly Lust: The Amatory Adventures of Genji in a New Translation." *New York Times*. 02 Dec 2001 Web. 1 Jul 2014. <http://ezproxy.lib.uconn.edu/login?url=http://search.proquest.com/docview/92047472?accountid=14518>.

Puette, William J. *The Tale of Genji: A Reader's Guide*. Tokyo: Tuttle, 1983.

Reardon, Bryan P. *Collected Ancient Greek Novels*. Berkeley: U of California P, 1989.

Rubin, Jay. *Making Sense of Japanese: What the Textbooks Don't Tell You*. Tokyo: Kodansha, 2002.

Shirane, Haruo. *The Bridge of Dreams: A Poetics of the Tale of Genji*. Stanford, CA: Stanford UP, 1987.

Varley, H. Paul. *Japanese Culture*. Honolulu: U of Hawaii P, 2000.

Whitmarsh, Tim, ed. *The Cambridge Companion to the Greek and Roman Novel*. Cambridge University Press, 2008. *Cambridge Companions Online*. Web. 12 March 2014.

Sexual Disgust and the Limits of Tolerance: Learning about Regulatory Regimes from Sanskrit Drama
Patrick Colm Hogan

Social tolerance across identity groups is clearly an important topic in many contemporary societies. However, the concern for defining the extent and limits of tolerance is not confined to the present time. Bhaṭṭa Jayánta's *Āgamaḍambara*, a tenth-century work from Kashmir, directly treats the topic. Moreover, in doing so, it particularly addresses the issue of non-normative sexuality. Beginning with Judith Butler's insight that "identity categories tend to be instruments of regulatory regimes" (13), the following essay first discusses different sorts of identity and their consequences for social tolerance. Drawing on research in social psychology and social neuroscience, the first section argues that there are complex ways in which identity categories may interact with emotional attitudes to produce different sorts of identity oppositions. Disgust seems especially important in defining the limits of tolerance. Moreover, it appears to have a particularly strong connection with sexuality. The essay then goes on to consider Jayánta's play. The play both illustrates and extends the analysis. Specifically, it suggests the profound importance of sexual liberation—not only for sexual minorities, but for a range of groups that might be subjected to social exclusion.

Sexuality and Identity

Judith Butler has influentially argued that the assertion of an identity—defined by, for example, sexual preference—commonly carries with it a *regulatory regime* (13), thus a set of norms and constraints, perhaps including formal or informal means of enforcing those regulations. Butler's analysis may be further clarified by isolating different sorts of identity and different relations into which these varieties of identity may enter. Specifically, it is important to distinguish categorial from practical identity.[1] Categorial identity is fundamentally a matter of labeling. It is the sorting of oneself or other people into putatively definitive or essential classes. These classes commonly include race, ethnicity, religion, and nationality, as well as sex and sexuality.

Identity categories define what social psychologists refer to as in-groups and out-groups. In-groups are simply the sets of individuals who share one's identity category in a particular domain (e.g., who share the category *white* in the domain of *race*). Identity categories may or may not have some relation to facts (e.g., regarding ancestry). However, they are profoundly socially consequential. Monroe and colleagues explain that "thousands of experiments . . . have consistently shown that individuals identify with the in-group, support group norms, and derogate out-group members along stereotypical lines, even when there is no individual gain at stake" (435). The biases turn up even when the division of the groups is explicitly arbitrary and the group members are not known to one another.[2] More recent, neurological work furthers these points. Barsalou explains that, "As participants view the faces of people from in-groups, their own faces adopt positive expressions; as participants view people from out-groups, their faces adopt negative expressions" (252). Fiske, Harris, and Cuddy note that "[c]ategorization of people as interchangeable members of an out-group promotes an amygdala response characteristic of vigilance and alarm and an insula response characteristic of disgust or arousal" (1482–83).

Identity group definition is often associated with norms for and constraints on in-group behavior. For example, in an Irish nationalist context, those with Irish national identity may be expected to know the Irish language. This is where Butler's regulatory regimes enter. This, in turn, brings us to practical identities. One's practical identity is one's set of competences and motivational propensities, particularly as these enable interaction with other people. For example, part of my practical identity is knowing English. This allows me to speak English with other people who know English. Note that practical identity is wholly individual. First, it is individual in its particular combination of competences and propensities. Second, it is individual in the particular components of that identity (e.g., no one has exactly the same vocabulary). The regulatory regimes spoken of by Butler may be taken as means of rendering practical identity more uniform for members of a category-de fined in-group.

Clearly, one thing that goes along with regulatory regimes for in-group members is a parallel set of regulatory regimes for out-group members. Thus straight people have, historically, sought to regulate not only what straight people do. They have sought to regulate what out-group members—gays and lesbians—do. In itself, the point is so obvious as to appear banal. However, it is not banal. After all, historically, there have been differences in the ways that in-groups have sought to regulate the behavior of out-group members. A key variable here is the degree to which the out-group and in-group are viewed as part of one society. The imposition of in-group norms becomes a pressing issue in a shared political community. Conversely, the question of "tolerance" arises in the context of such a community.

Today, most Westerners and many non-Westerners think of themselves as living in a tolerant, multicultural, multi-identity society. That is largely correct. However, it would be incorrect to assume that the tolerance is thoroughgoing and unique. It would be wrong to see tolerance as unbounded today or to imagine that there was no multi-identity tolerance in previous societies. In fact, all societies have, to some extent, been multicultural and all societies, including our own, in some ways limit that tolerance. For example, in the contemporary United States, straights are increasingly accepting of gays and lesbians. Straights, gays, and lesbians are able to join together, however, in opposition to pedophiles. That may seem all to the good. After all, who wants fifty-year-old lechers violating infants? But the strong opposition to pedophilia leads to sometimes severe regulatory regimes through inquisitions and witch hunts. Thus Alexander Cockburn notes that, "U.S. sex offender registries doom three-quarters of a million people—many of them convicted on trumpery charges—to pale simulacra of real life. Others endure castration and open-ended incarceration" (9). Moreover, there is a tendency to expand restrictions in one direction once tolerance arises in another direction. Everyone agrees that day care workers should not be sexually assaulting their charges. But what about the recent University of Connecticut regulation that forbids romantic relations between any faculty and undergraduate students, even when the faculty are not teachers, advisors, or former teachers or advisors of the students?

Here, we need to expand our account of identity categories. In any given society, some identity categories are affirmed; others are accepted more or less grudgingly; and some are rejected—often in a way that is crucial for defining overarching social in-groups (prominently, shared societies). What is the basis for this division? It is probably not, in the first place, cognitive. It seems much more likely that, to a great extent, we act on the basis of emotional responses, which we subsequently rationalize cognitively (see Slovic and colleagues on the "affect heuristic"). Thus, to understand tolerance and its limits, it is crucial to understand the different emotions that animate group definitions. The main emotions of in-group identification are pride and shame. More significantly for our purposes, the primary emotions involved in out-grouping appear to be fear, anger, and disgust. Fear is likely to express itself not only in flight but in efforts to restrain the target population (e.g., through the penal system). Anger tends to manifest itself in overt aggression, though it is likely to be limited in duration. Disgust tends to be far more prolonged than anger and perhaps less episodic than fear. Like fear, it first tends to manifest itself in avoidance, but its extension goes well beyond mere constraint of the out-group. Indeed, the far limit of tolerance appears to be defined largely by disgust. As Nussbaum and others have noted, invoking disgust is one of the main ways in which in-groups entirely dehumanize out-groups, thus enabling their brutal mistreatment (347–349).[3] In keeping with this, disgust is connected with the most severe forms of social bias and hatred, not mere control or aggression, but systematic, social "cleansing."

For our purposes, a key point is that disgust related to out-groups is often bound up with sexuality. The point is obvious in the case of pedophiles. Indeed, there is an expansive sense of sexual contamination that leads from worries over daycare centers to the outlawing of romance between faculty and students at a university. We see this relation to sexuality also in Nazi policies regarding gay sexuality. But the link between disgust and sexuality is not confined to sexual identities as such. It includes ethnic, religious, and other out-groups, who are often represented as in some way degenerate or disease-bearing in their sexuality. For example, Edward Said has famously described the Orientalist characterization of the East as sexually depraved (see, for example, 57 and 62). Even more strikingly, Sander Gilman has treated the anti-Semitic association of Jews with syphilis (96). These cases suggest that specifically sexual disgust is an important factor in many of the most severe types of out-group denigration. In other words, it may be recruited to ethnic or other domains of out-group definition. In consequence, it would seem that overcoming sexual disgust is a fundamental aspect of liberation from some particularly cruel forms of out-group discrimination, even in cases where the group in question is not sexually defined.

There are obviously historical differences in precisely what sexual practices are considered non-normative. However, the functionalizing of such differences in terms of identity groups and the processes of "cleansing" are not confined to Nazi Germany or the modern period. Moreover, they arise not only in the context of highly intolerant societies, but in the context of multicultural societies. Indeed, they have a complex relation to multiculturalism. A "tolerant" society is one in which some identity categories are able to co-exist, in part at the expense of whatever identity categories are excluded. In fostering the former, tolerant societies are, to some extent, forming another sort of regulatory regime. This is particularly true if tendencies toward out-group disgust are not undermined, but simply redirected.

Āgamaḍambara directly examines the problem of a multicultural society, illustrating the nature and limits of qualified tolerance. Moreover, it does so with particular attention to the role of sexuality and disgust in defining the limits of tolerance. Despite its distant provenance, the implications of the play remain deeply relevant to contemporary society.

A Lot of Noise about Tradition

Āgamaḍambara comprises a prologue and four acts. Acts one through three treat two topics—first, the specific differences between opposed traditions; second, which traditions should count as part of one society and which should be excluded from society. The fourth act concerns how one might reconcile the various traditions included within one society.

Before beginning the play, it is worth briefly considering the title. Dezső somewhat creatively translates it as *Much Ado About Religion*. "Āgama" is perhaps better understood as "tradition" (see Grimes 16–17). "Ḍambara" is "great noise" (Monier-Williams 430). Thus "Much Ado" is a reasonable translation. Both appear to suggest a somewhat ironic attitude toward the subject matter. This sense of irony is enhanced elsewhere in the play when characters poke fun at the author, who thus exists as an off-stage character in the story-world of the play. For example, on the first page, the assistant director worries that the play's director has been made sorrowful by associating with "the pupils of that Writer of the Commentary" (31), the "Writer of the Commentary" being Jayánta. The director later complains that Jayánta's play does not "follow the . . . rules" (33).

It is difficult to say just what the nature of this irony is. One obvious interpretation is that the differences in tradition are, in fact, trivial and that they simply result in a lot of (pointless) noise. This is not entirely inconsistent with one aspect of the play's final act, which asserts the validity of a wide range of traditions. On the other hand, that final act seems to take the traditions entirely seriously. In contrast, the title seems to suggest that the traditions themselves, and their reconciliation, are not really serious matters. They are perhaps the practices of overly self-regarding groups that demand aggrandizing deference.

Despite the apparent tone of the title, the play begins with the usual sort of invocation, a spiritual appeal, in keeping with Sanskrit tradition.[4] It characterizes brahman (or godhead) as the "destroyer of beginningless ignorance" (31). The ignorance at issue here is presumably the failure to recognize that (as Vedāntic doctrine would have it) all that truly exists is brahman and that any apparent differences are illusory. This is relevant in that a strict acceptance of the Vedāntic doctrine would seem to commit the believer to the rejection of all personal or egoistic investment—including all in-group investment—in a particular tradition. This clearly facilitates the multicultural tolerance advocated later in the play. Indeed, it is consistent with seeing religious difference as merely "a lot of noise," though now in a metaphysical, rather than cynical way.

Following the benediction, the play turns to the standard prologue material in which the director and assistant director introduce the main action. Though usually not developed to foster postmodern self-reflection and irony, in this case, the director immediately picks up on the topic of illusion and presents the play itself as illusion, "a ceaseless tumult of utter deception" (31). I do not take this to mean that the play is simply parody, a tongue-in-cheek representation of utopian reconciliation or perhaps simple diplomacy. But it does suggest that the reader should not take the philosophical arguments and reconciliations entirely at face value. The author seems to expect the viewer to respond to the play with a degree of philosophical skepticism.

The politics of the play are further complicated by the director's behavior. He actually quits the production and enters a monastery (37). This deprives the play of a director and may suggest a certain degree of disorder in the play, a certain inconsistency—even if this disorder is not, in fact, the result of a missing director, but the plotting of a careful author. At the same time, the director's decision more simply follows the usual practice in Sanskrit drama of providing a transition between the prologue and the main action of the play, since the first act of the play shifts to a Buddhist monastery. Perhaps most importantly, however, it hints at an issue that is present, but not foregrounded in the play—caste. According to the foundational, Sanskrit dramaturgical treatise, the *Nāṭya Śāstra*, actors are "sure to become mere Śūdras," members of the servant caste, who (within the orthodox system) were not allowed to study or even hear the sacred scriptures (Wolpert 42). In keeping with this, actors were viewed as low caste and subjected to caste taboos (e.g., Brahmins could not accept their food—a disgust-related restriction).[5] The director presumably chooses Buddhism because its anti-caste teachings allow him to pursue enlightenment.

The point is consistent with the conclusion of the play. There, the logician Dhairyarāśiḥ argues that different *āgamas*, or traditions, serve different sorts of people to help them achieve realization. This bears on the director's choice in the sense that Buddhism becomes an important alternative to orthodoxy, as it allows Śūdras a means of pursuing spiritual advancement. At the same time, it goes against the argument of the first act that Buddhism is doctrinally mistaken—perhaps further suggesting that such arguments are just "much ado."

The prelude to the first act introduces the "no soul" doctrine of Buddhism, the view that there is no "permanent Self" or Ātman (42, 43). The Buddhist monk goes on to maintain that the belief in an ego is the source of all suffering. The main body of the first act includes a putative refutation of this and related doctrines. However, it is presented with apparent sympathy in the prelude, and it is conceivable that few readers have any clear sense of the nature of the intellectual arguments on either side. Rather, if the critique of Buddhism is effective, it is effective because it portrays the Buddhist monastery as opulent, filled with wealth and luxury, thus marred by a type of self-indulgence. On the other hand, this condemns Buddhist practice rather than Buddhist principle.

Moreover, the Graduate who criticizes Buddhism returns us to the caste issue, identifying the practices of the Buddhists as "the same as that of Shudras" (57). The statement is, of course, a straightforward condemnation from his orthodox position. But the association of actors with the Śūdra caste—an association implicitly recalled by the director's embrace of Buddhism—at least complicates the simple acceptance of this criticism by the audience. Certainly, to a modern reader, the orthodox Graduate, arguing against Buddhism, appears arrogant and demeaning. Indeed, the monk later characterizes him as "abusive" (61). Perhaps the presentation of the Graduate as abusive is a critical representation of the Graduate's character flaws, just as the opulence of the Buddhists is a critical representation of the Buddhist's character flaws.

In sum, on the surface, the act presents a philosophical defense of a non-Buddhist, philosophically "orthodox" position. However, it may, in fact, suggest that the fixation on one's separate ego is a source of delusion and that both the Buddhist and the Graduate are ego-fixated, if in slightly different ways. In this respect, the opening act is less a critique of a particular āgama than a critique of egoism. Perhaps there is a hint that the attachment to a specific āgama is one key feature of such egoism. If so, the point is consistent with the title and opening invocation. For our purposes, this indicates that egoism is inseparable from categorial identity. It is not simply the personality of the Graduate that makes him arrogant, but rather his sense of the identity opposition between *orthodox* and *Buddhist*.

Act two continues the same general approach by introducing Jainism through a lecherous monk. This characterization obviously serves to bring sexuality into the play as well. The Jain doctrine of anekānta—non-onesidedness—is presented in a less sympathetic manner than it merits. The doctrine opposes the idea that any single point of view can capture the truth even about a single object.[6] Moreover, the act may parody the "maybe" doctrine—the view that all assertions should be prefaced by "maybe" in order to acknowledge incompleteness and uncertainty.[7] But the anekānta doctrine seems to be taken up at the end of the play with the assertion of the validity of all scriptures (245). Moreover, the "maybe" doctrine is suggested in the qualifications given to points on which the various āgamas do not agree (231).

Thus, here again, we may distinguish between what the text says and what it seems to show. It says that orthodoxy has defeated Jainism—the author's in-group has defeated an out-group. But it seems to show that āgamas are correct precisely to the degree that they criticize egoism and foster instead self-criticism. Act two, in particular, suggests the importance of a group's self-criticism regarding its own doctrinal certainties. Or, rather, this is what we may see the act as suggesting, once we have read the conclusion of the play, with its apparent adoption of the non-egoism of Buddhism and the non-onesidedness and "maybe" attitude of Jainism. Indeed, this now begins to make more sense of the self-deprecating humor of the author. It is a form of self-criticism, an acknowledgment that his own doctrines are not certain and absolute, and perhaps an attempt to free himself from egoism.

But here something changes. To this point, the author has, in effect, been preparing us for the "tolerance" of the play's final society. Now, he begins to prepare us for the limitations on tolerance. Specifically, he introduces the "Black Blankets"—or, more precisely, "Indigo Blankets" ("nīla" [116]).[8] The indigo of their name connects them with "indigo-throated" Śiva or Nīla-kaṇṭha, whose throat is filled with poison.[9] The Indigo Blankets are in effect a 1960s-like, counter-culture group that advocates non-standard sexual practices. Specifically, they are Śaivite (Śiva-worshiping) absolute monists, who accept the divinity of nature, including the divinity of the human body, affirming that "this world is a transformation of the Supreme Self" (119).[10] Their tantric sexual practice is aptly characterized as "steadily continued mutual arousal" (121). This group is implicitly opposed to the putatively legitimate Śaivites, led by the Abbot, who is linked with Śiva as "Śrīkakaṇṭha" (146), thus "beautiful throat," as opposed to "indigo throat."

The introduction of the Indigo Blankets ends act two. Act three introduces explicit Śaivites, who identify themselves with the Indigo Blankets (131). One of the Śaivites explains that the king's soldiers have "nabbed the mendicant indigo-blankets, beat them to jelly, and expelled them from the kingdom." He goes on to explain that similar mendicants, too, will "be beaten up, killed, thrown in jail, or slain" (131, altered). He and his companion therefore flee.

The suggestion of this part of the play is that there are some differences of tradition that bear not on metaphysical beliefs, but on moral—or, rather, putatively immoral—practices. These immoral practices require, not debate and tolerance, but suppression by force, so that "the kingdom belongs to the virtuous alone" (151). There are at least three aspects of this that are disturbing. First, the putative immorality is viewed as requiring the "cleansing" of society, either through killing the adherents of the tradition or expelling them. This view derives in part from moralizing a categorial identity division. But that moralizing merely rationalizes the brutality. Here, as elsewhere, such moralization must be connected with motivational systems in order to have practical consequences. In this case, the motivation system is just what current research would lead us to expect—disgust. Thus the Graduate refers to the absence of "purity" (121, "śuddhir" [120]) and bodies that "lack cleanness" (121; "śauc-" [120]).

The second problem here is the nature of the moral violations involved. As we will see, the mutual tolerance of the āgamas involves neutrality regarding the caste system (239). As such, it permits, for example, the enforcement of legal disabilities on Śūdras within the āgamas that accept caste. What it moralizes is very narrow—non-normative sexuality. This is, of course, fine if one's moral principles are opposed primarily to sex. But if one's moral principles are aimed at preventing cruelty, then this sex-denying morality is not only misguided, but positively harmful in that it tends to promote disgust and, thereby, cruelty. Obviously, sexuality may involve harm. But there is an important difference between condemning harmful sexuality because it is harmful (thus inspiring empathy) and condemning it because it is (disgust-provoking) sexuality. The former calls for responses of care and protection; the latter provokes "cleansing."

The third problem with this sort of moralized, disgust-based opposition is that it is so readily extended. It is very easy for members of one group to find the real or imagined practices of another group disgusting. This, in turn, may foster "cleansing."

Having established the moral and emotional limits of tolerance, Jayánta may now turn to the practical politics of establishing harmony among the different identity groups that remain. Specifically, the logician in act four maintains that all āgamas "are authoritative" (197). The argument is a peculiar one, and this writer, at least, finds the reasoning impossible to follow. The logician does make a valuable point in connection with one's evaluation of other identity groups, however. People have a strong tendency to be critical of out-groups, but not of in-groups.[11] One principle of a multicultural society should be the transfer of that criticism from others to oneself. The converse of this holds as well. One tends to give the benefit of the doubt to one's own group. That interprctive generosity should be extended to out-groups. As the logician puts it, "If you obviate the contradiction in . . . Vedic passages through" interpretive means, "the course of action must be the same . . . regarding the propositions of other religions" (227). Put differently, when it comes to the recognition of faults or errors, one should be particularly self-critical. In contrast, one should make a particular effort to give the best possible interpretation to the practices and doctrines of out-groups. This is as good a general ethical principle for a multicultural society as one is likely to come up with, whether one is referring to a period centuries in the past or to the present.

But this principle of generosity to out-groups is, again, qualified. Toward the end of the play, the logician returns to the limitations of tolerance. Even though he has maintained that all āgamas are legitimate, he does not accept every tradition as genuine. He maintains that some are excluded—specifically, a tradition is not legitimate if the Āryas, "honorable" men or those "faithful to the religion of [their] country" (Monier-Williams 152), are "*repulsed* by associating with it or discussing it" (247, emphasis added). The differentiation of permissible and impermissible identities is here directly a matter of disgust. (Jayánta's word, "vimukha" [246], refers to turning one's head away, as in disgust.)[12] The logician then goes on to explain just what promotes such disgust—again, it is not murder, cruelty, caste discrimination, or any other act that might be excluded by a Buddhist and Jain stress on ahiṃsā (non-harming). Morally heinous and disgust-provoking practices are, rather, "making love to" those "one must not have sex with, or eating impure things" (247).

One function of an emphasis on sexuality and food is that it readily promotes disgust across groups.[13] This fits with the need to denigrate and expel the potentially disruptive Indigo Blankets and tantricists. But the claim here is more general. It presents sexual and culinary propriety as the definitive principles for inclusion in the society. But sexual and culinary propriety are, at least in part, a function of group-based principles, not society-based principles. Commonly, marriages across key identity categories are discouraged, even forbidden. The elevation of such identity group restrictions to the level of restrictions across society would seem to have the function of insulating these groups, separating them off from one another, even as they are joined in a single society. Indeed, this enhanced insularity even within union is a standard feature of multiculturalism—and one that we find directly in the play. Specifically, the Graduate—now representing the king—announces that the tolerated "traditions . . . are not intermixed." He goes on to urge his audience, "you, gentlemen, must always pay attention to prevent their confusion" (251). Indeed, the necessity of insularity in practical identity and doctrine—an insularity defined by strict categorial identity—is arguably the main point of the entire play. This is indicated by the conclusion that "Each should adhere to his own religion according to the established customs." The only line that follows is, "Honorable Dhairya-rashi [the logician], come now, we shall report to [the king] the events as they have happened" (253), a line that suggests the convergence of reason (represented by Dhairyarāśiḥ), normative practice (represented by the Graduate), and social or political authority (represented by the king). It is almost as if the play were written to illustrate Butler's statement that "identity categories tend to be instruments of regulatory regimes" (13).

Conclusion: Against Purity

Jayánta's play illustrates nicely some key points made in the opening section regarding categorial identity, norms of practical identity, tolerance, and regulatory regimes. More significantly, it helps us to extend those points. It indicates, for example, that multicultural societies may operate in such a way as to insulate groups from one another, even as it integrates them into a single society. In connection with this, it suggests that the social centrality of disgust at non-normative sexuality is, in part, related to the crossing of identity categories. Indeed, the play is unusually explicit about the importance of keeping traditions separate. Finally, the play not only allows us to exemplify and develop the social psychological analyses discussed in the opening section. It also suggests some possible responses to the problems of qualified tolerance and its limitation in sexual disgust, largely of an ethical nature.

First, a humane, multicultural society should foster, not pride in one's in-groups, but self-criticism, both individual and group related. This may be furthered particularly by accepting some version of the Buddhist rejection of ego. Complementary to that, such a society should cultivate a *prima facie*, relative preference for the practices and achievements of out-groups. This is what I have elsewhere referred to as "politics of Otherness" (as opposed to politics of identity; see *Colonialism* 323–324). This may be enabled by self-application of the non-onesidedness and "maybe" principles of Jainism. The former indicates that no set of normative principles is adequate in all ways, while the latter indicates that no such principles are certain. In this context, the practices of other groups should be approached initially as ways of understanding the inadequacies of one's own group practices. Third, such a society should encourage social practices that minimize disgust across identity groups and indeed facilitate the development of cross-identity attachment bonds (attachment being the system most clearly opposed to disgust).

Finally, and perhaps most significantly, a humane society should work to overcome disgust over sexuality. Sexual disgust promotes cruelty against sexual minorities and, even in cases where objections to sexual practices are warranted, they encourage a violent expansion of regulatory regimes. Moreover, sexual disgust may be extended to non-sexual out-groups. Sexual liberation, then, becomes perhaps the most fundamental form of liberation, serving as a basis for other types of freedom from discriminatory out-grouping. Jayánta may not have approved of this conclusion. Despite his intentions, however, his play suggests the profound importance of violating many sexual taboos. Of course, we will still decide that some varieties of sexual practice are either imprudent or immoral. But even in those cases, we should try to make our response as little involved with disgust as possible—at least if we want a society that is not prone to witch hunts, Inquisitions, and ethnic or other forms of "cleansing."

Notes

1. See Hogan, *Understanding Nationalism: On Narrative, Cognitive Science, and Identity.*
2. See Duckitt, *The Social Psychology of Prejudice,* 68–69.
3. See also Harris and Fiske, "Perceiving Humanity or Not."
4. See Gitomer, "The Theater in Kālidāsa's Art," 66.
5. See Keith, *The Sanskrit Drama in Its Origin, Development Theory and Practice,* 363.
6. See Dezső's note for 2.67.
7. See Dezső's note for 2.113.
8. For more on "nīla," see Monier-Williams, *Sanskrit-English Dictionary,* 566.
9. See Daniélou's *The Myths and Gods of India,* 191.
10. On absolute monism, see Pandit, *Specific Principles of Kashmir Saivism.*
11. See Pronin, Puccio, and Ross, "Understanding Misunderstanding: Social Psychological Perspectives," 637.
12. For more on "vimukha," see Monier-Williams, *Sanskrit-English Dictionary,* 980.
13. On culinary differences and group divisions, see Pinker, *How the Mind Works,* 385.

Works Cited

Barsalou, Lawrence. "Situating Concepts." *The Cambridge Handbook of Situated Cognition.* Eds. Philip Robbins and Murat Aydede. Cambridge: Cambridge UP, 2009. 236–263.

Butler, Judith. "Imitation and Gender Insubordination." *Inside/Out: Lesbian Theories, Gay Theories.* Ed. Diana Fuss. New York: Routledge, 1991, 13–31.

Cockburn, Alexander. "So Who's the Fascist Here?" *The Nation* (21 May 2012): 9.

Daniélou, Alain. *The Myths and Gods of India.* Rochester, VT: Inner Traditions, 1985.

Duckitt, John H. *The Social Psychology of Prejudice.* New York: Praeger, 1992.

Fiske, Susan, Lasana Harris, and Amy Cuddy. "Why Ordinary People Torture Enemy Prisoners." *Science* 306.5701 (2004): 1482–83.

Gilman, Sander. *The Jew's Body*. New York: Routledge, 1991.

Gilovich, Thomas, Dale Griffin, and Daniel Kahneman, eds. *Heuristics and Biases: The Psychology of Intuitive Judgment*. Cambridge: Cambridge UP, 2002.

Gitomer, David. "The Theater in Kālidāsa's Art." *The Plays of Kālidāsa: Theater of Memory*. Ed. Barbara Miller. Delhi, India: Columbia UP, 1999, 63–84.

Grimes, John. *A Concise Dictionary of Indian Philosophy: Sanskrit Terms Defined in English*. Revised ed. Albany, NY: State U of New York P, 1996.

Harris, Lasana, and Susan Fiske. "Perceiving Humanity or Not: A Social Neuroscience Approach to Dehumanized Perception." *Social Neuroscience: Toward Understanding the Underpinnings of the Social Mind*. Eds. Alexander Todorov, Susan Fiske, and Deborah Prentice. Oxford: Oxford UP, 2011. 123–134.

Hogan, Patrick Colm. *Colonialism and Cultural Identity: Crises of Tradition in the Anglophone Literatures of India, Africa, and the Caribbean*. Albany, NY: State U of New York P, 2000.

_____. *Understanding Nationalism: On Narrative, Cognitive Science, and Identity*. Columbus, OH: Ohio State UP, 2009.

Jayánta, Bhatta. *Much Ado About Religion*. Ed. and trans. Dezső, Csaba. New York: New York UP, 2005.

Keith, Arthur B. *The Sanskrit Drama in Its Origin, Development Theory and Practice*. Delhi, India: Motilal Banarsidass, 1992.

Monier-Williams, Monier. *Sanskrit-English Dictionary*. New Edition. Delhi, India: Motilal Banarsidass, 1963.

Monroe, Kristen Renwick, James Hankin, and Renée van Vechten. "The Psychological Foundations of Identity Politics." *Annual Review of Political Science* 3 (2000): 419–47.

Muni, Bharata. *Nāṭya Śāstra*. Delhi, India: Sri Satguru, 1987.

Nussbaum, Martha. *Upheavals of Thought: The Intelligence of Emotions*. Cambridge: Cambridge UP, 2001.

Pandit, B. N. *Specific Principles of Kashmir Saivism*. New Delhi, India: Munshiram Manoharlal, 1997.

Pinker, Steven. *How the Mind Works.* New York: W. W. Norton, 1997.

Pronin, Emily, Carolyn Puccio, and Lee Ross. "Understanding Misunderstanding: Social Psychological Perspectives." *Heuristics and Biases: The Psychology of Intuitive Judgment.* Eds. Thomas Gilovich, Dale Griffin, and Daniel Kahneman. Cambridge: Cambridge UP, 2002. 636–665.

Robbins, Philip, and Murat Aydede, eds. *The Cambridge Handbook of Situated Cognition.* Cambridge: Cambridge UP, 2009.

Said, Edward. *Orientalism.* New York: Random House, 1978.

Slovic, Paul, Melissa Finucane, Ellen Peters, and Donald MacGregor. "The Affect Heuristic." In *Hueristics and Biases: The Psychology of Intuitive Judgment.* Eds. Thomas Gilovich, Dale Griffin, and Daniel Kahneman. Cambridge: Cambridge UP, 2002, 397–420.

Todorov, Alexander, Susan Fiske, and Deborah Prentice, eds. *Social Neuroscience: Toward Understanding the Underpinnings of the Social Mind.* Oxford: Oxford UP, 2011.

Wolpert, Stanley. *A New History of India.* 4th ed. Oxford: Oxford UP, 1993.

Unsexing Gender in Shakespeare's *Macbeth*

Greg Colón Semenza

In some ways, Shakespeare's feelings about sex and gender were as progressive as those of the average twenty-first-century American. When I try to explain this fact to my students, they often seem skeptical, as if yet another "liberal" English professor is simply making stuff up. I don't fault them for their skepticism. After all, in other ways, Shakespeare's feelings about sex and gender were appallingly narrow-minded (see *The Taming of the Shrew*). As a step towards investigating this contradictory fact, I make them read Shakespeare's memorable Sonnet 20:

> A woman's face with nature's own hand painted,
> Hast thou, the master mistress of my passion;
> A woman's gentle heart, but not acquainted
> With shifting change, as is false women's fashion:
> An eye more bright than theirs, less false in rolling,
> Gilding the object whereupon it gazeth;
> A man in hue, all "hues" in his controlling,
> Much steals men's eyes and women's souls amazeth.
> And for a woman wert thou first created;
> Till Nature, as she wrought thee, fell a-doting,
> And by addition me of thee defeated,
> By adding one thing to my purpose nothing.
> But since she prick'd thee out for women's pleasure,
> Mine be thy love and thy love's use their treasure (1–14).

The poem expresses the love of a male narrator for his beloved male "friend," whom scholars refer to as the "fair youth." The narrator weighs the advantages and disadvantages of the fact that the fair youth was born (i.e., crafted by nature) with a "prick" instead of a vagina. In the end, he decides that while he can't "use" his beloved sexually, the way that rival women are able to do, he still can enjoy a non-physical relationship with him. The poem, it is true, is sexist in places, suggesting that women are fickle ("with shifting change") and deceptive ("false"). It also says that women are more "gentle" and more beautiful than men. More important, the poem interrogates the male/female binary on which it plays by suggesting that the beloved's appeal lies precisely in his mixture of masculine and feminine qualities. The narrator's "passion" is inflamed for his "master mistress" because of the youth's feminine face, that "woman's . . . heart" complemented by a man's "hue." In fact, the master is so much like a mistress that the poet can only surmise that Mother Nature had intended to make him a woman; however, after she herself began desiring the girl, she selfishly decided to unsex her, to "prick" her out, to make the mistress a master, so that she too might "use" the youth sexually. And so the narrator is cheated of that one significant "pleasure" and forced to quell his physical "passion."

We can extrapolate at least four facts about gender and sexuality from this wonderful poetical puzzle:

1) Men and women are said to differ *sexually* based only on the presence or absence of a penis.
2) Men and women are said to differ *behaviorally* only in terms of degree; a male can possess characteristics usually labeled as "feminine" and, presumably, the reverse would be true as well. This fact further implies that the gendered behavioral differences—clearly recognized in the poem—must be culturally constructed rather than naturally prescribed.
3) Same-sex *desire* is presented as perfectly natural; it is not pathological, criminal, or sinful. Nature desires the mistress-in-progress. The narrator desires the fair youth.
4) Male and female same-sex *acts* are presented as off-limits, though the poem fails to say why this should be the case.[1]

I always experience a twinge of sadness at the end of this poem. Though tonally the narrator seems less than devastated about the concession he is forced to make, this fact alone seems no reason to dismiss the pathos of the situation—especially since he will continue to struggle with unsatisfied desire throughout much of the sonnet cycle. Just under the surface of the poem's clever playfulness, there lurks a kind of psycho-sexual trauma, the offspring of the narrator's attempt to play by certain societal rules whose intrinsic logicality is obviously flawed. Like most of Shakespeare's sonnets, number 20 is an extended meditation on the contradictions of desire, a subject to which the poet will return throughout his dramatic career as well—and in no play more directly than the powerful tragedy *Macbeth* (c. 1605).

The following essay offers a brief reading of *Macbeth*'s thematic preoccupation with socially constructed gender roles, focusing especially on their psychological impact on both male and female characters. In many ways, the play can be seen as a meditation on what happens when natural human desires are circumscribed by the arbitrary mores of early seventeenth-century society. These mores were informed pretty equally by the strictures of the decidedly homophobic and patriarchal dogma of Christianity, and the relentlessly masculinist ethos of the war-torn, eleventh-century Scotland depicted in the play. Is *Macbeth* an oppressively conservative fable about what happens to men and women who refuse to act their proper parts? Or is it the opposite: a radical exposure of the destructive sociological codes governing masculinity and femininity?

In the letter Macbeth sends his wife, describing the prophecy imparted by the three Weird Sisters—that he shall be king—he addresses her as "my dearest partner of greatness" (1.5.11–12). It's a remarkable appellation, stressing the unusual degree of intimacy and equality defining their relationship. Yet Lady Macbeth reveals, even in her first two lines, an aggravated conviction that sexual inequality will wind up preventing the prophecy's fulfillment: "Glamis thou art, and Cawdor, and shalt be / What thou art promised. Yet do I fear thy nature" (1.5.16–17). Moments later, she begs the spirits of darkness to "unsex me here" so that she might manage the assassination of King Duncan herself, which she believes her husband will prove too weak or conscientious to carry out (1.5.42). Lady Macbeth's words reveal several inter-related notions about sex and gender, which might remind us of Sonnet 20:

1) Femininity is associated with gentleness and, therefore, with weakness and passivity. Lady Macbeth fears her husband's "nature" precisely because he is "too full o' th' milk of human kindness" (1.5.18). Macbeth, in other words, possesses attributes his wife considers to be feminine; the "milk," which necessarily connotes the maternal realm, transforms plain human "kindness" into a specifically regrettable feminine trait. Lady Macbeth asks to be "unsexed" so that she might take the place of her husband, conjuring a fantasy of masculinity as cold-bloodedness, remorselessness, and unbounded determination. So that she might acquire the ruthlessness needed to murder the meek Duncan, she offers up for "gall" (i.e., boldness) the milk of her "woman's breasts" (1.5.48).
2) Masculinity is defined, then, in contradistinction to feminine passivity and gentleness, as a kind of conscience-less and single-minded savagery.
3) The differences between men and women have seemingly more to do with what's on the outside—the prick in Sonnet 20, say, or the breasts in *Macbeth*—than what's on the inside. This is true not merely because the speakers in each respective work imagine the simple removal of body parts as keys to their own happiness and fulfillment, but because their own desires are shown to far exceed the proper boundaries of their supposedly prescriptive gender roles. In the wonderfully paradoxical case of Lady Macbeth, she longs to be a man so that she won't have to rely on her too-feminine husband to complete an act that her own too-masculine personality is better suited to perform.

Whereas items one and two above describe how sexuality and gender are viewed by a character within the play, item three describes a dynamic revealed by the play itself. Somewhere in the interstice between Lady Macbeth's vision of sex and gender, on the one hand, and the play's examination of her psyche, on the other, the nurture/nature dialectic is again dramatized. Lady Macbeth arbitrarily assigns to men and women certain traits, albeit ones she's inherited from the society she inhabits, that finally come to stand in for her as the natural markers of masculinity and femininity. She can't see the irony, but Shakespeare may be encouraging us to do so.

One of the best proofs of what Shakespeare wants us to see is in the massive gulf between Macbeth as he really is and as he is described by his wife. The notion that Macbeth is effeminate surely is meant to be viewed as absurd. The first description of him in the play, after all, is of a mighty warrior unparalleled in the field of battle:

> For brave Macbeth—well he deserves that name—
> Disdaining Fortune, with his brandished steel,
> Which smoked with bloody execution,
> Like valor's minion carved out his passage
> Till he faced the slave;
> Which nev'r shook hands, nor bade farewell to him,
> Till he unseamed him from the nave to the' chops,
> And fixed his head upon our battlements (1.2.16–23).

The image of Macbeth "carving" his way with a sword through human flesh until he is face to face with Macdonwald is gruesome enough; the subsequent image of Macbeth plunging his sword into Macdonwald's naval, and somehow slicing him in half through the organs and ribcage and all of the way up through his jawbone, suggests a sort of superhuman strength. Macbeth, we might argue, epitomizes the very definition of masculinity that Lady Macbeth herself advances throughout the play.

Perhaps it is because she is so self-conscious about her own gender identity—plagued, that is, by how poorly her desires match cultural definitions of proper femininity—that she is also so skillful manipulating the sexual anxieties of a husband whose masculinity seems unquestionable. After Macbeth reaches the castle, Lady Macbeth begins to convince him of the necessity of murdering Duncan. She does so precisely by "unsexing" him. Though Macbeth has decided earlier not to act but, rather, to allow fate to play itself out (1.3.146), he proves unable to withstand her assaults on his manhood. When she asks whether he is a "coward" in desire, he tellingly replies, "I dare do all that may become a man" (1.7.46). She challenges that claim directly, suggesting that the very definition of manhood has to do with one's willingness to act on one's desires:

"When you durst do it, then you were a man" (1.7.49). Macbeth, she suggests, has given up his claim on manhood by refusing to act on his desire to become king.

Then, in the most outrageous and perhaps most memorable passage in the play, Lady Macbeth seeks to illustrate the bottomlessness of her own pure will [to] power:

> I have given suck, and know
> How tender 'tis to love the babe that milks me;
> I would, while it was smiling in my face,
> Have plucked my nipple from his boneless gums,
> And dashed the brains out, had I so sworn as you
> Have done to this (1.7.54–57).

Again exploiting specifically maternal imagery, Lady Macbeth is able to denigrate her husband's masculinity by suggesting that if masculinity equals action unimpeded by conscience, she must be more the man than he. What can Macbeth say to *this*? Forgetting that he hadn't actually "sworn" to anything, he asks a simple question, "If we should fail?" (1.7.58). After she answers him, he demonstrates a semi-conscious awareness of what has just transpired: "Bring forth men-children only; / For thy undaunted mettle should compose / Nothing but males" (1.7.72–74). Missing the point that she had to first unsex him before she could "make" him a proper male, Macbeth seems almost willing to concede that she is more masculine than he.

We should find all of this utterly disturbing, especially in light of the historical consequences of associations between masculinity and violence. Were Lady Macbeth the mother and Macbeth the child, we would call this sort of manipulation a form of sexual abuse; it's no mistake that the image of a mother beating her child to death is the primary vehicle for her doling it out. As it is, Macbeth is a powerful man, and he alone is responsible for allowing himself to be swayed from his own half-conviction that murdering Duncan would constitute an unforgivable sin. If he is a victim, though, so too is Lady Macbeth, for they both are prisoners of arbitrary cultural definitions of gender. Readers focus *ad nauseum* on Macbeth as the manipulated victim of his diabolical wife; however, most are less willing to see her as an equally manipulated individual, one whose anxieties about her own femininity wind up destroying her. Something irrevocable is lost too, I think, in the reductive assertion that Shakespeare's portrait of Lady Macbeth reveals only the misogyny of the historical context in which the play was written. It reveals much beyond this, such as a commonly expressed discomfort in this increasingly relativist period with traditional binaries such as good and evil, masculine and feminine. Much is to be gained, in other words, from deeper consideration of the psychological crisis that precipitates Lady Macbeth's twisted ambition in the first place. Carolyn Asp convincingly sums up the character's dilemma when she writes, "In a society in which femininity is divorced from strength and womanliness is equated with weakness, . . . the strong woman finds herself hemmed in psychologically, forced to reject her own womanliness" (Asp 159). Since womanliness is directly associated with positive attributes or "humane virtues," the systematic rejection of it will have tragic implications for nearly everyone inhabiting this world.

If it feels like we're making sex and gender too much the focus of the play, then we might consider, first, the ways the topic ties into the larger supernatural events and, second, the way it extends well beyond the two major characters. Consider first those three master-mistresses who have so central a role in the play: the Weird Sisters. When Macbeth and Banquo first stumble upon them, Banquo marvels at their unearthly appearances, exclaiming, "You should be women, / And yet your beards forbid me to interpret / That you are so" (1.3.45–47). Marjorie Garber says, "I think we can say with justice that those unisex witches, with their women's forms and their confusingly masculine beards, are, among other things, dream images, metaphors, for Lady Macbeth herself: physically a woman but, as she claims, mentally and spiritually a man" (Garber 713). Certainly, the Weird Sisters' manipulation of Macbeth parallels Lady Macbeth's machinations. Although a reductive reading would again discover only misogyny in the fact that evil deeds spring from (predominantly) female sources, the larger point seems to be that the sources aren't female at all, especially considering the play's explicit, repeated associations of femininity with maternalism, mercy, and other humane virtues. These sources of evil are, instead, unidentifiable in simple binary terms of gender and sex. Especially if Garber's assertion is correct, all evil in the play can be said to result from a crisis of identity precipitated by culture, not nature.

The American historian Thomas Laqueur has written extensively on the popularity, prior to the eighteenth century, of what we call the "one-sex model" of human anatomy, which may offer a useful context for reading the play. Laqueur discusses the common belief prior to the Enlightenment—proposed by such venerable thinkers as Galen—that men and women were merely two different manifestations of a single sex. According to this theory, differences in the reproductive organs and other sexual characteristics could be explained through a simple logic of inversion, with the woman's parts typically figuring as internalized versions of the external male parts. For example, the uterus was viewed as an interior scrotum, the labia as foreskin, and so forth. By the eighteenth century, this model begins to give way to a "two-sex model," which argued that males and females were essentially different, even diametrically opposed. Whereas in the eighteenth and nineteenth centuries, then, two distinct sexes were theorized, "Sex before the seventeenth century . . . was still a sociological and not an ontological category" (Laqueur 8). Most important for our purposes would be the implications of such a fact for Renaissance views of gender, which easily could account for more "feminine" men and more "masculine" women.

Though scholars have rightly questioned Laqueur's insistence on the dominance of the "one-sex model" (competing theories certainly existed at different times), a general consensus continues to locate a major historical shift at just around the time that Shakespeare wrote *Macbeth*. We've already seen from Sonnet 20 that Shakespeare would appear to view gender as more a sociological than an ontological category. What we will see in *Macbeth*, though, is that sociological pressures on men and women cannot be assumed to have been less prescriptive or less traumatizing than assumed ontological ones.

Especially intriguing about *Macbeth* is the play's elaborate consideration of how such pressures impact men as well as women, and not merely the titular character. Consider Macduff, Macbeth's key foil. The most positively portrayed woman in the play, Lady Macduff, is a harsh critic of her husband's masculinity. When we first meet her, she is lambasting him for having escaped to England while leaving his family behind in Scotland. She says he lacks "the natural touch" (4.2.9), meaning the sort of nature that would cause him to act lovingly and protectively towards his wife and children. Note that masculinity is capable here of encompassing humane virtues, such as affection and love, precisely because Macduff, unlike Macbeth, is a father. What's natural for a man with children is said to be entirely different from what's natural for a man without children. The fact that he has abandoned his wife and children means not only that he is dead to Lady Macduff (4.2.30), but also that questions about his masculinity are made relevant for the reader. When Macduff's house is at last raided by Macbeth's cronies, his wife and children savagely murdered, Lady Macduff's prescience about the event seems a most damning indictment of Macduff's callousness and cowardice.

In the following scene, which takes place in England and includes Ross' communication of the massacre to Macduff, the play offers a most elaborate reflection on the subject of "proper" masculinity. It begins with a conversation between Malcolm, the future king of Scotland, and Macduff about what their next step should be in resisting Macbeth. When Malcolm says they should find a shady place to "weep" and bemoan their plight, Macduff says, "Let us rather / Hold fast the mortal sword, and *like good men*, / Bestride our down-fall'n birthdom" (4.3.3–4; italics mine). The fact that we've just witnessed his own family's massacre, because of his desertion of them, makes this argument for the men's protective role in Scotland almost laughable. Amazingly, Malcolm—uncertain whether he can trust Macduff as an ally—calls him out on his seemingly unforgivable desertion: "Why in that rawness left you wife and child, / Those precious motives, those strong knots of love / Without leave-taking?" (4.3.26–28). The men move on to discuss whether Malcolm is a good enough man to be king, meaning that Macduff, stunningly, fails even to acknowledge Malcom's question.

Worse, when Ross arrives, Macduff reveals his own suspicion that his family has been destroyed—erasing, in other words, any possibility that he had fled Scotland ignorant of the significant danger to his family:

>   Macduff. How's my wife?
>   Ross.   Why, well.
>   Macduff. And all my children?
>   Ross.   Well, too.
>   Macduff. The tyrant has not battered at their peace?
>   Ross.   No; they were well at peace when I did leave 'em.
>   Macduff. Be not a niggard of your speech: how goes't? (4.3.177–180)

How are we to read this exchange? Macduff asks after his family, Ross lies, and Macduff asks again, as if he can't believe that they really are safe. Now perhaps Ross pauses just long enough with each lie to make Macduff suspicious, but, either way, the dialogue forces us to recall Lady Macduff's and Malcolm's accusations against Macduff. When Ross finally announces that he will tell the truth, Macduff admits, "I guess at it" (4.3.203). When it's confirmed that "Wife, children, servants, all that could be found" have been slain (4.3.212), Macduff's first thought is of himself: "And I must be from thence!" (4.3.213)

If we are to find in Macduff any redeemable qualities, we must consider his more measured reaction to the news, which at least registers shock about what has occurred:

>   Macduff. My wife killed too?
>   Ross.   I have said.
>   Malcolm. Be comforted.
>   Let's make us med'cines of our great revenge,
>   To cure this deadly grief.
>   Macduff. He has no children. All my pretty ones?
>   Did you say all? O hell-kite! All?
>   What, all my pretty chickens and their dam

> At one fell swoop?
> Malcolm. Dispute it like a man.
> Macduff. I shall do so;
> But I must also feel it as a man.
>
> . . .
>
> Sinful Macduff,
> They were all struck for thee! Naught that I am,
> Not for their own demerits but for mine
> Fell slaughter on their souls (4.3.213–227).

I said above that this scene offers the play's most extended meditation on what masculinity really is, and the high point of the scene is Macduff's insistence that "I must also feel it as a man." When Malcolm urges him to "dispute" his feelings of grief, the future king attempts to reassert a model of masculinity which should remind us of Lady Macbeth—who also associated masculinity with remorselessness, murderous will, and the rejection of "gentle" emotions. Thus Macduff's words, "must also feel," serve as a crucial reminder that men are humans, and humans by necessity feel, and what they must feel is not only ambition and rage.

Though Janet Adelman is correct that "Macduff's response to the news of his family's destruction insists that humane feeling is central to the definition of manhood" (107), we should be careful not to see this moment as a turning point for the male characters in the play. It's probably wisest to see in Macduff's "must" a begrudging acknowledgment of what he cannot avoid feeling. The fact is that these men give all of a few seconds to "humane feeling" before they begin sounding exactly like Lady Macbeth again. Malcolm urges Macduff to "Let grief / Convert to anger; blunt not the heart, enrage it" (4.3.228–29), and Macduff's reaction clinches the point: "I could play the woman with mine eyes, . . . But . . ." (4.3.230–231). But instead I will stamp out all "womanly feelings." Instead I will pick up my sword. Instead I will hack Macbeth to pieces. Only after Macduff's testosterone has again begun to flow can Malcolm heartily declare, "This time goes manly" (4.3.235), and then the men are on their way back to Scotland.

In case it isn't obvious, I'll state in the clearest possible terms that my own doubts about Macduff's moral integrity are never allayed. While it may be unfair to judge a person's individual expression of grief as being adequate or inadequate, nothing Macduff does at any point in the play can convince me that he possesses "the natural touch." Worse, I cannot find a single male character in *Macbeth* who does possess it, if we mean by this phrase a possession of humane values, such as compassion, love, or gentleness. The shared fantasy of so many men in the play, as Adelman effectively points out, is of an "escape from the dangerous female . . . presences like Love, Nature, [and] Mother" (93). Macbeth's own desire to escape those female presences is so great that it will kill him in the end, in the most literal sense, when he fails to decipher the trick within the witches' riddle about an enemy not born of woman—an imagined enemy, that is, who has managed to escape the female presences altogether. Of course, no man can escape female presences like "Mother" in any literal sense. Through Macbeth's death at the hands of another man determined to repress his feminine qualities, the play suggests that the presence of the feminine might have prevented all of this bloodshed from occurring.

This is why Roman Polanski proved so insightful a critic of the play when he chose to end his infamous film, *Macbeth* (1971), not with Malcolm's triumphant acceptance of the crown, but with a made-up scene in which Donalbain seeks to know his own future from the Weird Sisters. In this reading, there is no restoration of an orderly society at the end of the play, but rather, a momentary pause before the blood will begin flowing again. And why shouldn't this be the case? The play proper ends, after all, back at the beginning, with a hyper-masculine warrior, who lacks the natural touch, chopping off the head of a traitor. Remember, too, that in the final lines, Ross can still compliment Siward for sacrificing his son in battle, according to the logic that one's military prowess reveals one's manliness: "Your son, my lord, has paid a soldier's debt: / He only lived but till he was a man; / . . . / But like a man he died" (5.8.39–43). Comforted by this nonsense, Siward says that he wishes he had more sons so that they, too, could die in battle and then declares that enough time has been spent grieving (fifteen seconds?). *These* are the men who close out the play, and no women are left to raise better ones. Could Shakespeare possibly have intended us to feel hopeful about this new society?

So what, ultimately, are we to make of sex and gender as *Macbeth* presents them? To begin, I think we can say that despite Lady Macbeth's immoral, manipulative personality, the problems of the play stem less from the presence of the feminine than from the absence of it. Flip the script slightly, and we might see how the problems stem from the sort of masculinity celebrated by this brutal culture. Yes, there are occasional glimmers of hope, and nearly all of them have to do with visions of gender that are not specifically tied to the presence or absence of a penis. Macduff's fleeting conviction, for example, that men "must" feel pain at the loss of loved ones, as well as rage, at least suggests that men are capable of feeling "feminine" emotions. We see, too, from the example of Lady Macbeth that women experience such "masculine" emotions as ambition. Through her madness and death, we see that conscience is far from easy to kill. But in the cases of multiple characters, desire to eradicate those humane, "feminine" presences that contribute to our humanity leads to catastrophic results.

In concluding our discussion of the play, it's worth thinking about how *Macbeth*'s focus on gender and sex maps onto the play's more explicit debates about fate and free will, action and passiveness. The spirits who hover above the foul air of this bleak world, and hold such power over it, are hermaphroditic ones, both male and female. It seems no mistake that these hermaphroditic spirits set into motion a series of events that hinge on the individual's ability to answer the following fundamental question: "How am I to become what I am determined to be?"[2] The complexity of the question as I've translated it resides in the double meaning of the word "determined," which can refer to the will of the individual ("I am determined to be the Queen") and the inevitable destiny of the individual ("It has been determined that I shall be the Queen"). The questions the play raises about gender determinism parallel quite neatly the ones it raises about determinism more generally. To what degree are my actions determined by my being a man or a woman? How much freedom do I have to alter the course of "nature," and what will be the consequences of my attempts to exercise this limited freedom?

And so we arrive back at the beginning, at the intersection between Shakespeare's and our own historically specific understandings of sex and gender. Though various models for thinking about sex and gender certainly were available to Shakespeare, his poetry and plays typically reveal a view promoted by the one-sex theory of human anatomy: that gender is not prescribed upon individuals, regardless of whether they are men or women. Rigid cultural constructions of gender, however, are repeatedly shown to exert considerable pressure on individuals. Shakespeare often dramatizes these conflicts between nature and culture in his characters, and in *Macbeth*, he goes so far as to explore the tragic consequences of them for an entire society. Though we moderns have dispensed with models of anatomy even remotely similar to the one-sex model popular before the eighteenth century, we have also moved beyond eighteenth- and nineteenth-century beliefs that gender is intrinsically tied to sexual-biological characteristics. Because culture's profound role in individual identity formation, and across the range of human interactions, is so well understood today, Shakespeare's numerous, complicated treatments of gender and sex can still seem remarkably relevant in the twenty-first century.

Notes

1. Strict laws governed homosexual and lesbian sex in the period. This paper is not focused on the subject, but interested readers should begin by consulting Goldberg, Smith, and Traub.
2. What Macbeth literally asks is whether he should "yield to that suggestion [murdering Duncan]" (1.3.134) or wait for destiny to play itself out naturally: "If chance will have me King, why, chance may crown me, / Without my stir" (1.3.142–43). Before Lady Macbeth changes his mind, in other words, he decides not to act.

Works Cited

Adelman, Janet. "'Born of Woman': Fantasies of Maternal Power in *Macbeth.*" *Cannibals,*

Witches, and Divorce: Estranging the Renaissance. Ed. Marjorie Garber. Baltimore & London: Johns Hopkins UP, 1987.

Asp, Carolyn. "'Be bloody, bold and resolute': Tragic Action and Sexual Stereotyping in *Macbeth.*" *Studies in Philology* 78 (1981): 153–169.

Garber, Marjorie. *Shakespeare After All.* New York: Anchor, 2004.

Goldberg, Jonathan, ed. *Queering the Renaissance.* Durham and London: Duke UP, 1994.

Laqueur, Thomas. *Making Sex: Body and Gender from the Greeks to Freud.* Cambridge, MA: Harvard UP, 1990.

Shakespeare, William. *Macbeth.* 1605. New York: Signet Classics, 1986.

Smith, Bruce R. *Homosexual Desire in Shakespeare's England: A Cultural Poetics.* Chicago: U Chicago P, 1991.

Traub, Valerie. *The Renaissance of Lesbianism in Early Modern England.* Cambridge: Cambridge UP, 2002.

"their sex not equal seemed": Gender, Sex, and Sexuality in Milton's *Paradise Lost*

David Gay

For an epic poet, the choice of subject is decisive because the poet's reputation will rest mainly on the success of a single work. The timing of its writing is also critical because it requires much intellectual and literary preparation. As an epic poet, Milton follows in the classical tradition of Homer and Virgil. Above all, however, he based *Paradise Lost* on the Bible. The Bible is a rich literary resource filled with stories, characters, and symbols. It is also a sacred text with a unique authority for early modern readers. *Paradise Lost* is an epic of the Protestant Reformation. Reformation for Milton was not simply a phase of political or religious history; it was a dynamic, revolutionary process energized by reading and debate. When Milton challenged monarchy, a sacred institution to many people, he drew from the Bible. When he argued for more liberal divorce laws, or against state censorship, or for church reform, he used the Bible to support his views. As we explore gender, sex, and sexuality in *Paradise Lost*, we will find the Bible underlying Milton's views. We can expect some authoritative statements in an epic poem, but also many interesting tensions that generate questions and debate. Milton announces his subject in the opening lines of *Paradise Lost*:

> Of man's first disobedience, and the fruit
> Of that forbidden tree, whose mortal taste
> Brought death into the world, and all our woe,
> With loss of Eden, till one greater man
> Restore us (1:1–5).

The first four lines refer to original sin or the "Fall" as told in the first three chapters of Genesis. It is a story of origins and loss. One "greater Man" later turns the story from loss to restoration. The first man is Adam; the second man is Jesus. This comparison of two biblical figures is called "typology," a method of reading set out by Paul in Romans 5:19: "For as by one man's disobedience many were made sinners, so by the obedience of one shall many be made righteous" (KJV). What about women? The answer is implied in both Milton and Paul: women bear children, producing "many" people over many generations. God commanded humans to be fruitful and multiply in paradise; when sin enters the world, it is propagated through generations living in a "fallen" world.

The typology of the invocation is dominantly male at the outset, but the feminine appears at the end: the Spirit of God is like a mother dove. It sat "brooding on the vast abyss / And mad'st it pregnant" when God made the universe. Milton identifies this Spirit with his feminine muse Urania, which he identifies in the invocation to Book 7. Milton's sources are biblical: Woman Wisdom in Proverbs 8:26–31 combines with the descending dove of Mark 1:10. As a model for *Paradise Lost,* the Bible is a source of poetic imagery linking different biblical texts.

Following Genesis 1–3, Milton emphasizes gender as an original, divinely ordained hierarchy, sex as part of the original goodness of creation, and sexuality as an original heterosexual marriage. All of these originals are affected by original sin. The original marriage is a hierarchy, with the man on top. This is a problem for many modern readers. Critics read Milton on gender, sex, and sexuality differently, but always with attention to hierarchy. As Roy Flannagan remarks, students "who believe that all humans are equal may have problems with the hierarchy of nature from the inanimate up to God, a hierarchy implied in all of Milton's works" (323). C. S. Lewis, for example, argues that "everything except God has some natural superior; everything except unformed matter has some natural inferior. The goodness, happiness, and dignity of every living being consists in obeying its natural superior and ruling its natural inferior" (73). Disregard for hierarchy can take the form of a "rebellious angel" (Satan) or an "uxorious husband" (Adam) (74). The word "natural" may concern contemporary readers; Lewis uses the word as Milton would: it signifies a hierarchy of virtue and wisdom in the original design of nature. Lewis writes to acclimatize readers to early modern hierarchy.

Feminist critics expose the history and consequences of hierarchy. Sandra Gilbert and Susan Gubar, for example, call *Paradise Lost* a "patriarchal etiology that defines a solitary Father God as the only creator of all things," and a "myth of origins, summarizing a long misogynistic tradition" (188). Let's examine the phrase "patriarchal etiology." An etiological story explains why things are the way they are (as in, how did the leopard get its spots?). Genesis 1, 2, and 3 are all etiological stories. Creation stories explain why there is a universe and where human beings are placed in that universe. Genesis 1 presents a simultaneous creation of man and woman:

> So God created man in his own image, in the image of God created he him; male and female created he them. And God blessed them, and God said unto them, Be fruitful, and multiply, and replenish the earth, and subdue it: and have dominion over the fish of the sea, and over the fowl of the air, and over every living thing that moveth upon the earth (Gen. 1:26–28).

After the six day's work of creation, "God blessed the seventh day, and sanctified it: because that in it he had rested from all his work which God created and made" (Gen. 2:3). As an etiological story, Genesis 1:1–2:3 explains why there is a sabbath, a special or "sacred" day.

In Genesis 2, God is like a craftsman fashioning a man out of the earth. He creates Adam first and Eve second from Adam's rib second. This story explains why there is marriage:

> And the rib, which the Lord God had taken from man, made he a woman, and brought her unto the man. And Adam said, This is now bone of my bones, and flesh of my flesh: she shall be called Woman, because she was taken out of Man. Therefore shall a man leave his father and his mother, and shall cleave unto his wife: and they shall be one flesh. And they were both naked, the man and his wife, and were not ashamed (Gen. 2:22–25).

Naming is a powerful theme throughout the Bible. "Adam" is Hebrew for "red earth." The new creature "shall be called Woman." She is renamed Eve or "mother of all living" after the Fall, while Adam's name suddenly signifies his mortality: "dust thou art, and unto dust shalt thou return" (Gen. 3:19–20). In the scene of judgment, patriarchal authority intensifies, as the Lord tells the woman: "I will greatly multiply thy sorrow and thy conception; in sorrow thou shalt bring forth children; and thy desire shall be to thy husband, and he shall rule over thee" (Gen. 3:16). As Desma Polydorou observes, "Prior to the Fall, there is no mention in the Bible of woman's subordination to man; female subordination is a postlapsarian condition imposed on woman by God in Genesis 3:16 for her role in the Fall" (23). As an etiological story, Genesis 3 may explain a hardening of patriarchy and the consequence of mortality of future generations.

Does Milton intensify the patriarchal elements of Genesis 1–3? For Gilbert and Gubar, who assess Milton's possible influence on later women writers, the answer is simply 'yes.' How does Milton look compared to women writers in his own time? Stimulated by feminist criticism, scholars have explored this question in detail (Wittreich 1–15). As Karen Edwards suggests, it is rewarding to see Milton's "representation of Adam and Eve in light of a very complex seventeenth-century historical and cultural context" (145). Catherine Gimelli Martin cites work on "the social/particular conditions of marriage, divorce, and patriarchal domination in western culture," noting that seventeenth-century women "participated in the most radical phase of Reformation and early revolutionary culture" and helped to "initiate the wholesale rethinking of marriage and the family in which Milton actively participated" (4). Notable seventeenth-century writers include Aemilia Lanyer, Rachel Speght, and Margaret Fell. Lanyer and Speght accepted gender hierarchy, while Fell, a Quaker, did not. Speght and Lanyer both empower women and conserve hierarchy because of a paradox in Christian theology: if Christ became weak to subvert worldly power, then women, the supposed "weaker vessel," enjoy a unique relationship to Christianity's central figure. Lanyer defends Eve within gender hierarchy:

> But surely *Adam* can not be excused,
> Her fault, though great, yet he was most too blame;
> What Weaknesse offerd, Strength might have refused,
> Being Lord of all, the greater was his shame (ll. 777–80).

Lanyer apportions blame between Adam and Eve. She sees abusive male authority as a misreading of Genesis 3 that exploits hierarchy and denies equality. For Lanyer, Speght, and Fell, misogyny is, by definition, anti-Christian.

There is tension between hierarchy and equality in Genesis 1 and 2. Rachel Speght, writing confidently at nineteen in response to an appalling misogynistic tract by Joseph Swetnam, "defends woman's spirituality by arguing for mutual equality between the sexes in marriage—man may be woman's head and guide, but for Speght this implies neither subjection nor inferiority" (Polydorou 24). Speght presents Eve's creation as immediate, in order to capture the simultaneous creation of Genesis 1 rather than the sequential creation of Genesis 2. Eve is God's gift: the "resplendent love of God toward man appeared, in taking care to provide him a helper before he saw his own want" (Nyquist 114). Mary Nyquist suggests that Milton would have resisted Speght's view. Where Speght emphasizes swift grace in the provision of a wife, "Milton foregrounds an Adam whose innocent or legitimate desires pre-exist the creation of the object that will satisfy them" (114). Unlike "Speght's transcendent lord of love, Milton's veiled but systematic insistence on the contractual form of the first institution is produced by a Protestantism pressed into the service of a historically specific form of individualism, an individualism paradigmatically masculine, autonomous, articulate, and preternaturally awake to the implications of entering into relations with others" (114–15). Milton slows things down to ensure Adam's autonomy and agency. In Book 8, Adam recalls a long period of autonomy and direct conversation with God prior to the creation of Eve. Eve, in contrast, enjoys only a short moment of autonomy before meeting Adam. In *Paradise Lost,* Milton imagines a marriage that is subject to growth and change. Growth depends on the choices people make. Choice depends on one prohibition—do not eat the forbidden fruit. Choice for Milton is a positive spiritual exercise, not an unhealthy repression. The prohibition disciplines the freedom and curiosity Adam and Eve enjoy; nevertheless, Adam's sense that he needs a mate comes from his sovereign reason, while Eve's recognition of Adam as her husband represents her deference as a rational choice.

Eden is the central setting for gender, sex, and sexuality, but other settings include these themes. The poem moves among Hell, Heaven, and Earth. Let's consider gender, sex, and sexuality in Hell and Heaven before returning to the Garden of Eden. The first two books of *Paradise Lost* are set in Hell. Milton names some of the defeated rebel angels in a procession of false gods and idols found in biblical narrative. At one point, Milton remarks on gender:

> With these came they who, from the bord'ring flood
> Of old Euphrates to the Brook that parts
> Egypt from Syrian ground, had general Names
> Of Baalim and Ashtaroth, those male,
> These feminine. For Spirits, when they please,
> Can either sex assume, or both; so soft
> And uncompounded is their essence pure,
> Not tied or manacled with joint or limb,
> Nor founded on the brittle strength of bones,
> Like cumbrous flesh; but, in what shape they choose,
> Dilated or condensed, bright or obscure,
> Can execute their aery purposes,
> And works of love or enmity fulfil (1:419–431).

This passage ascribes gender and sexuality to angels. Fallen angels assume "either Sex" in the form of "pagan" gods that mislead Israelites; yet they also take pleasure in sex. Their "works of love" are unconstrained by the material body. In Book 8, Adam asks the angel Raphael if good angels have sex. Raphael blushes, and assures Adam that what he "in the body enjoy'st" angels enjoy in "Eminence" (8:621–23). Angelic sexuality is consistent with Milton's general celebration of human sexuality, which we first encounter in Book 4.

The demonic procession also exposes "fallen" human sexuality. Milton refers to a violent event in Judges, a biblical text that connects gender and violence:

> And when night
> Darkens the streets, then wander forth the sons
> Of Belial, flown with insolence and wine.
> Witness the Streets of Sodom, and that night
> In Gibeah, when the hospitable door
> Exposed a matron to avoid worse rape (1:500–05).

Belial is a demon noted for sensuality. In Judges, "sons of Belial" attack a man's house. To appease them, the man thrusts a nameless concubine into the street, where the rioters "knew her, and abused her all the night until the morning" (Judges 19:25). Worse rape could imply a comparison of heterosexual and homosexual rape; however, Judges allows for a more ironic reading. A sanctimonious man who exposes an innocent victim to a horrific murder is no better than the drunken rioters at his door. A woman suffers for his principles, making his principles worthless. This reading comes from debating and questioning the text: biblical writers do not editorialize: the story itself condemns sexual violence when "*every man* did that which was right in his own eyes" (Judges 21:25).

At the end of Book 2, as he journeys to Earth, Satan encounters his family: Sin, who is both his wife and daughter, and Death, their son. Sin is the only other woman figure in the poem besides Eve. She "seemed woman to the waist, and fair, / But ended foul in many a scaly fold / Voluminous and vast, A serpent armed / With mortal sting" (2:650–53). She is conceived in the mind of Satan when he conceives pride within himself; she springs, in a parody of the birth of wisdom from the head of Zeus, from the left side of Satan's brow. She becomes his paramour in conspiracy against God, and conceives Death, their son, when Satan wages war in Heaven. Her dual form represents the initial attraction and ultimate repulsion of sin. Her grotesque lower body conflates the serpent that will later tempt Eve with the reproduction of original sin. Sin reveals Satan's narcissism: "Thy self in me thy perfect image viewing" (2:764). Satan, Sin and

Death are a demonic parody of a Holy Trinity. The Son of God is the express image of God the Father in Book 3. Thus, before we encounter Adam and Eve in the poem, we have already seen "fallen" sexuality as rape, narcissism, incest and mortality. Milton's harder challenge will be to represent innocent sexuality.

Adam and Eve first appear in Book 4:

> Two of far nobler shape, erect and tall,
> Godlike erect, with native honour clad
> In naked majesty seemed lords of all:
> And worthy seemed; for in their looks divine
> The image of their glorious Maker shone,
> Truth, wisdom, sanctitude severe and pure,
> Severe, but in true filial freedom placed,
> Whence true authority in men; though both
> Not equal, as their sex not equal seemed;
> For contemplation he and valor formed;
> For softness she and sweet attractive grace;
> He for God only, she for God in him:
> His fair large front and eye sublime declared
> Absolute rule; and hyacinthine locks
> Round from his parted forelock manly hung
> Clust'ring, but not beneath his shoulders broad:
> She as a veil, down to the slender waist
> Her unadorned golden tresses wore
> Dishevelled, but in wanton ringlets waved
> As the vine curls her tendrils, which implied
> Subjection, but required with gentle sway,
> And by her yielded, by him best received,
> Yielded with coy submission, modest pride,
> And sweet reluctant amorous delay (4: 288–311).

Adam and Eve are both created in the image of God in Genesis 1 and in the first five lines of this passage. Then, a division occurs. Adam and Eve are "Not equal, as their sex not equal seemed." As Karen Edwards observes, not equal could mean different rather than inferior (149). Milton emphasizes different body parts. Adam is "eye sublime" and "shoulders broad"; Eve is hair "down to the slender waist." Adam, like God, is identified with the sky; Eve, with her hair like a "vine," is identified with the garden. Words like "Dishevelled," "wanton," "coy" and "amorous" create a playful erotic tension. It is as if the unpredictable qualities of human nature affirmed in the Genesis 2 are gendered female, and require male "Absolute rule" comparable to God's in Genesis 1. "He for God only, she for God in him" asserts a hierarchy containing difference. Its source is Paul: "the head of every man is Christ; and the head of the woman is the man; and the head of Christ is God" (1 Cor. 11:3).

Three stages of marriage ensue: betrothal, wedding and consummation. Eve remembers awakening beside a pool and her betrothal to Adam:

> There I had fixed
> Mine eyes till now, and pined with vain desire,
> Had not a voice thus warned me, What thou seest,
> What there thou seest fair creature is thyself;
> With thee it came and goes: but follow me,
> And I will bring thee where no shadow stays
> Thy coming, and thy soft embrace, he
> Whose image thou art; him thou shalt enjoy
> Inseparably thine, to him shalt bear
> Multitudes like thyself, and thence be called
> Mother of human race (4:465–75).

The episode suggests Narcissus, but Eve experiences innocent wonder, not vanity. As Diane Kelsey McColley remarks, Eve "recognizes the risks of narcissism as she recounts her calling" (81). The tension here is between her initial solitude and her summons to a heterosexual marriage by a warning voice and by Adam. Autonomy as further solitude is a "vain desire." She makes a choice based on her perception of sexual difference: feminine "beauty is excelled by manly grace."

Eve creates an epithalamion or wedding poem. She first defers to hierarchy: "God is thy Law, thou mine." She then speaks a beautiful lyric poem celebrating mutuality:

With thee conversing I forget all time;
All seasons and their change, all please alike.
Sweet is the breath of morn, her rising sweet,
With charm of earliest birds (4: 639–42).

A biblical source is the Song of Solomon, an erotic love poem, which later Christian interpreters made into an allegory of Christ's marriage to his Church. Conversing could connote sex in Milton's time. Most importantly, Milton gives Eve a powerful poetic sensibility. As James Grantham Turner remarks, her relation to the garden is "entirely subsumed into her love for Adam" (237). Sexuality in Eden is "not a subcategory of experience," but a "transformation of the whole way of perceiving and being" (Turner 237). As in the Song of Solomon, sexual love is a paradigm of the harmony and energy of paradise. Consummation follows:

Into their inmost bower
Handed they went; and eased the putting off
These troublesome disguises which we wear,
Straight side by side were laid, nor turned, I ween,
Adam from his fair Spouse, nor Eve the Rites
Mysterious of connubial love refused:
Whatever hypocrites austerely talk
Of purity, and place, and innocence,
Defaming as impure what God declares
Pure, and commands to some, leaves free to all (4:738–757).

"Handed" betokens mutuality in sex. While Adam and Eve make love, the epic narrator denounces hypocrites who ascribe shame and guilt to sex. The passage interprets Hebrews 13:4: "Marriage is honourable in all, and the bed undefiled: but whoremongers and adulterers God will judge." As Turner suggests, Milton places sex at the center of Edenic life, guarding its sanctity against "Hypocrites on one side and Courtly Amorists on the other" (237). He impeaches both severe religious attitudes and the libertinism of the Restoration court, expressed in "Casual fruition" or in "Mixed dance, or wanton masque, or midnight ball" (4:767–68). The juxtaposition of innocent sex with court games is jarring. Milton's narrator makes readers process sharp contrasts between a lost paradise and their present reality.

During these episodes, Satan spies on Adam and Eve to plan their downfall. He is an envious voyeur. He inflicts a nightmare on Eve as she sleeps. Eve awakens in distress and relates the dream to Adam. The dream, a product of Satan's "devilish art," combines Genesis 1 and 2 to confuse Eve. She mistakes Satan's voice for Adam's. The voice leads her to the Tree of Knowledge, and then appears to her "shaped and winged, like one of those from Heav'n / By us oft seen" (5:55–56). She seems to eat the forbidden fruit at the angel's behest, and "Forthwith up to the clouds / With him I flew" (5:86–87). The experience is both sexual and transgressive, as she traverses the normal borders of day and night, earth and heaven. Milton alludes to Genesis 6:4: "the sons of God came in unto the daughters of men, and they bare children to them." This transgression provokes God to flood a wicked world. Satan's initial assault on Eve takes the form of a sexual fantasy that subverts the hierarchy of Genesis 1 and the etiology of Genesis 2.

Milton adds much to the short episodes in Genesis 2. His additions make sure that we do not equate original sin with sex, or assume that Eve is already partly guilty. The dream leads her to depend on Adam, but also develops her awareness of individual experience. As such, the dream completes the arc of episodes that began with her attraction to her own image by the pool. One illusion is productive; the other is destructive. Since Adam and Eve do not know about Satan, God sends the angel Raphael, a "sociable spirit," to offer instruction and friendship. Raphael's greeting to Eve is prophetic: "Hail Mother of Mankind, whose fruitful womb / Shall fill the world more numerous with thy sons / Than with these various fruits the trees of God / Have heaped this table" (5:388–91). His greeting alludes to the angel Gabriel's annunciation to Mary in Luke 1:28: by constructing the typology of the second Adam (Jesus) and the second Eve (Mary), Milton points ironically to the inevitability of the Fall. Raphael also names Eve according to her functions of maternal procreation and domestic labor. Procreation means "sons."

A naked Eve, who refills "their flowing cups" with unfermented "liquors," provokes an idealized "Love unlibidinous" in innocent "sons of God" (5:447–49). Eve then withdraws voluntarily in another gendered division of labor: intellectual discourse versus domestic service. We later learn that she prefers to learn from Adam, who would "solve high dispute / With conjugal caresses" (8:55–56).

In Books 5 to 8, Adam and Raphael share a long vegetarian lunch. The discussion ranges through cosmic history, astronomy, theology, and marriage. Their dialog presents another gendered relationship: male friendship. The juxtaposition of original marriage and male friendship reminds us that all social and sexual relationships have histories. As Thomas Luxon has shown, *Paradise Lost* is part of a long cultural negotiation between classical friendship and humanist marriage doctrines. For Milton, however, the tension between hierarchy and equality is unresolved: "Milton's marriage theories finally fail to do the work he imagines for them because Milton withholds from his marriage theories the linchpin of classical and humanist friendship doctrine—equality" (2). A male friendship seeks equality and a union of minds and souls; marriage, even in paradise, involves the production of a "helpmeet fit," and two becoming "one flesh. Adam and Raphael are not, however, entirely equal, since angels are higher in the hierarchy. Raphael sets aside his glory (just as Christ does in emptying himself of divinity to become incarnate man) and descends to converse with Adam "as friend with friend" (5:229). He tells Adam that humans will become angels if they are "found obedient." In Milton, hierarchy is fluid because matter and spirit are continuous. The angelic apex may, we might imagine, be as masculine as the names of the angels.

Adam's reason succumbs to passion and lust after his fall. Like reason and passion, spirit and matter, the senses exist in a hierarchy descending from the less corporeal (sight and sound) to the more corporeal (touch and taste). Adam collapses this hierarchy when he "sees" that Eve is "exact of taste." They take "their fill of Love and Love's disport / Took largely, of their mutual guilt the seal, / The solace of their sin" (9:1042–44). Lust and guilt are ironically equal in this passage.

In Book 10, Adam blames Eve: "Out of my sight, thou serpent, that name best / Befits thee with him leagued, thy self as false / And hateful" (10:867–69). This connection of Eve and the serpent, vigorously refuted by Margaret Fell, produced much misogynistic discourse. Milton, however, is not merely disparaging Eve; instead, he returns to the biblical theme of naming, particularly the power God gave Adam to name the animals in Genesis 2:19–20. Adam's rant reveals the instability of language after the Fall. Eve endures patiently and makes a practical suggestion: they could deprive Sin and Death of human offspring by committing suicide or practicing sexual abstinence. Adam is moved by her gesture, which helps to turn the action towards repentance and grace. Eve's suggestions show that advice is not exclusively male.

Books 11 and 12 present a vision of future history based on the Bible. Again, we find Adam in conversation with a male angel named Michael (Revelation 12:7). The narrative develops the commandment to be fruitful and multiply in the fallen world through successive generations that give structure to biblical history: Adam to Noah, Noah to Moses, Moses to David, David to the Babylonian captivity, Babylon to the birth of Christ, and Christ to the end of time. The narrative highlights male heroic figures, who are just men of faith. The wicked generations before the Flood illustrate "Man's effeminate slackness," according to Michael (11:634). Effeminacy is a sharp-edged word for Milton. He uses it to correct inversions of gender hierarchy. It situates "man" in what Luxon sees as an imperfect isolation in Milton's idea of masculinity. Adam is between a solitary, perfect God above and women below, setting conditions on the autonomous deliberation that Nyquist describes in her comparison of Milton and Speght. This isolation continues in the motif of the just men who typify Miltonic heroism in the fallen world.

Significantly, Eve has the last word in the poem. While Adam views history, Eve dreams of a second Adam. When she awakens, she and Adam reaffirm their marriage, look forward to sharing their separate revelations, and leave paradise holding hands in a final emblem of mutuality. The model for Eve's closing is the Book of Ruth:

> but now lead on;
> In me is no delay; with thee to go,
> Is to stay here; without thee here to stay,
> Is to go hence unwilling; thou to me
> Art all things under Heav'n, all places thou (12: 614–618).

> And Ruth said, Intreat me not to leave thee, or to return from following after thee: for whither thou goest, I will go; and where thou lodgest, I will lodge: thy people shall be my people, and thy God my God: Where thou diest, will I die, and there will I be buried: the Lord do so to me, and more also, if ought but death part thee and me (Ruth 1:16–17).

Ruth's name appears in Matthew's genealogy of Christ, as she became the ancestor of King David. Is Milton, as he did with the feminine Spirit that started the poem, adding a feminine dimension to the "generations" of fallen history Adam sees? Or is he subordinating Ruth's speech to a masculine genealogy consistent with her procreative purpose? Is it significant that Ruth makes her powerful declaration to another woman named Naomi at a point in their lives where they are alone, vulnerable, and destitute? Or is Ruth's marital and maternal destiny Milton's main focus? Milton's use of the biblical subtext may comment on the relationships among hierarchy, equality, and mutuality that he grappled with in the poem. Milton emulates the spirit of Hebrew scripture by raising questions about experience, and by alerting his readers to the ironies and tensions these questions reveal. It is never wise to boil a great poem down to a sound bite. While we may not accept all of Milton's premises, we can take up his questions and value his poem for making us more informed and historically aware critical readers. *Paradise Lost* remains a vital and rewarding text to explore the history and poetry of gender, sex, and sexuality.

Works Cited

Blessing, Carole. "Gilbert and Gubar's Daughters: *The Madwoman in the Attic's Spectre* in Milton Studies." *Gilbert and Gubar's The*

Madwoman in the Attic After Thirty Years. Ed. Annette R. Frederico. Columbia: U of Missouri P, 2009. 60–75.

Edwards, Karen L. "Gender, Sex and Marriage in Paradise." *A Concise Companion to Milton.* Ed. Angelica Duran. London: Blackwell, 2007. 144–160.

Fell, Margaret. *Women's Speaking Justified.* London, 1667.

Flannagan, Roy, ed. *The Riverside Milton.* New York: Houghton-Mifflin, 1998.

Gilbert, Sandra, & Susan Gubar. *The Madwoman in the Attic: The Woman Writer and the Nineteenth-Century Literary Imagination.* New Haven: Yale UP, 1979.

Lanyer, Aemilia. *Salve Deus Rex Judaeorum.* Ed. Susanne Woods. Oxford: Oxford UP, 1993.

Lewis, C. S. *A Preface to Paradise Lost.* New York: Oxford UP, 1961.

Luxon, Thomas. *Single Imperfection: Milton, Marriage and Friendship.* Pittsburgh: Duquesne UP, 2005.

Martin, Catherine Gimelli, ed. *Milton and Gender.* Cambridge: Cambridge UP, 2004.

McColley, Diane Kelsey. *Milton's Eve.* Chicago: U of Illinois P, 1983.

Milton, John. *Paradise Lost.* Ed. John Leonard. London: Penguin, 2000.

Nyquist, Mary. "The Genesis of Gendered Subjectivity in the Divorce Tracts and in *Paradise Lost.*" *Re-membering Milton: Essays on the Texts and Traditions.* Eds. Mary Nyquist & Margaret W. Ferguson. New York and London: Methuen, 1987.

Polydorou, Desma. "Gender and Spiritual Equality in Marriage: A Dialogic Reading of Rachel Speght and John Milton." *Milton Quarterly* 35 (2001): 22–32.

Speght, Rachel. *A Mouzell for Melastomus.* London, 1617.

Swetnam, Joseph. *The araignment of lewd, idle, froward, and unconstant women.* London, 1615.

Turner, James Grantham. *One Flesh: Paradisal Marriage and Sexual Relations in the Age of Milton.* Oxford: Clarendon Press, 1987.

Wittreich, Joseph. *Feminist Milton.* Ithaca: Cornell UP, 1987.

Sexuality and Gender in Victorian Sensation and Other Fiction

Thomas Recchio

"In the Victorian home swarming with children," writes Walter Houghton in *The Victorian Frame of Mind, 1830–1870* (1963), "sex was a secret. It was the skeleton in the parental chamber" (353). While sex was certainly not a complete secret in Victorian literature, the expression of sexual experience was constrained by "ideas of literary decorum" (Maynard 261). That sense of decorum has come down to us most memorably and comically in the observation of the character Podsnap from Charles Dickens' *Our Mutual Friend* (1865). Pompous and with faith unshakeable in the moral superiority of the "Englishman," Podsnap announces the following to a French dinner guest: ". . . there is in the Englishman a combination of qualities, a modesty, an independence, a responsibility, a repose, combined with an absence of everything calculated to call a blush into the cheek of a young person, which one would seek in vain among the Nations of the Earth" (180). Although Podsnap is a caricature of English middle-class self-confidence and complacence, for which Dickens felt nothing but contempt, Dickens' novels themselves were judged (sometimes as praise, sometimes as condemnation) as conforming to Podsnap's standards. Anyone, young person or old, male or female, could read him without blushing.

Today, of course, sexual references permeate nearly every aspect of culture, from advertising to self-help books and across all forms of mass media. As a result, when we read Victorian fiction, we are able to hear a multitude of sexual skeletons rattling around the closets of even the most conventional of Victorian stories. Consider Dickens' *Great Expectations*, for instance, a novel frequently included in anthologies of English literature produced for American high school students. Pip's first-person autobiography is presented in many classrooms as the coming-of-age story of a young boy who learns not to desire wealth and social position, but to be content with his moderate level of success and to accept his chastened spirit as a mark of maturity at the end of the novel; his "great expectations" are shown to be more a curse than a motive for growth. His love interest, though beautiful, is dis-embodied, abstract. Her name, Estella, is emblematic of a distant star, shimmering at an unattainable distance and redolent with the symbolism of wealth and status. Pip does not desire her body; he desires the social/material world she represents. While such a reading is certainly defensible, it ignores how the novel emphasizes aberrant physical experience—from the murder of Pip's sister and near murder of Pip by Pip's shadow and adversary Orlick (who also brawls with Jo, Pip's father-figure), to Estella's attraction to physical violence.

Estella's responsiveness to violence, in fact, suggests an element of sexual masochism emerging as her body matures, a physical effect of the psychological abuse inflicted by Miss Havisham. That suggestion is anchored by two visceral, physical details. The first involves her response to Pip's beating of the "pale young gentleman" at Satis House, a beating Estella witnesses and reacts to as follows: "[T]here was a bright flush upon her face, as though something had happened to delight her. Instead of going straight to the gate, she . . . stepped back into the passage and beckoned to me. 'Come here! You may kiss me, if you like'" (75). Up until that point, Estella had treated Pip coolly and disrespectfully, calling him a "boy" and mocking his "thick boots" and working-class life. When she witnesses Pip's physical strength in the fight, her body reacts, her face shows a "flush" of "delight" that requires satisfaction by a kiss, which she both demands—"Come here!"—and submits to—"if you like." Early in the novel, that detail seems merely a part of Estella's torment of Pip, but the physicality of her response to violence coupled with her decision later in the novel to marry Bentley Drummle, who is characterized as a brute and whom we subsequently learn beats her after they marry, become two visible signs of her sexual responsiveness to a violence that masters her. Those two physical details function as a sexual skeleton, whose outlines are quite visible on the surface of narrative, and they set in motion, for attentive readers, a resonance that brings other aspects of the novel into the sexual pathology they imply: for instance Jaggers' taming of his housekeeper, a murderess who turns out to be Estella's mother. We might tentatively conclude that the sex in *Great Expectations* is both concealed and revealed through heightened details of narrative actions, which are filtered through, if not completely motivated by, a particular sexual pathology. That conclusion does not imply a sexually symbolic reading; rather, it is attentive to the surface of the text, to what the bodies of the characters make legible. (Estella's "flush [of] delight" does not symbolize sex; it is a physical reaction to the violence she witnessed.)

The example given above is just one instance of what John Maynard calls "the conflict between restraint and expression that marks the age" (257). Victorian novels may not be explicit about the particulars of sexual activity among their characters, but sexual desire can be perceived as motivating behavior in contexts that, at the same time, rigidly constrain the possibility of acting on that desire. Or sexual desire surfaces in same-sex social relationships that develop in extraordinary circumstances, only for that desire to be transformed (or sublimated) into heterosexual marriage. The former case tends to characterize the way sexual desire emerges in mainstream Victorian novels, such as those by Dickens and Anthony Trollope, and the latter case tends to characterize the sensation fiction of the 1860s and can be found in the short fiction of canonical writers, such as Elizabeth Gaskell. Although Victorian fiction has been read as fundamentally conservative in matters related to sexuality and gender, as reinforcing what was more or less the "official" ideology of separate and complementary social and sexual spheres for men and women, readers in the twentieth- and twenty-first centuries have recognized patterns and energies in the fiction that revise such a reading. The first wave of revisionary reading could be described as readings that are sensitive to the ways in which the collision between "restraint and expression" erupts within a text. The second revisionary wave has emerged most influentially through the work of Eve Sedgwick, whose concept of "male homosocial desire" has broadened our understanding of the complex ways that Victorian fiction explores how sexuality and gender are tightly woven within male-dominated social, political, and cultural life. The remainder of this chapter will show how sexual "restraint and expression" animate the social relations between the Reverend Slope and Madame Neroni in Anthony Trollope's *Barchester Towers* (1857). Then, using the notion of "male homosocial desire" as an analytical frame, the chapter will demonstrate how the homosocial relation between Robert Audley and George Tallboys provides the dynamic energies that drive the narrative in Mary Elizabeth Braddon's *Lady Audley's Secret* (1862). Finally, there will be an exploration of the female variation of homosocial desire in Elizabeth Gaskell's short story "The Grey Woman" (1865). The net result will be to show that, while sex in its most literal and prurient sense may have been a partial secret to readers of Victorian fiction, sexuality and gender played a significant role in the forms of Victorian fiction that both challenged social-sexual orthodoxies and opened out ways to imagine social formations that enable more gender equity.

Barchester Towers is set in a cathedral town; consequently, "the manhood of Barchester consisted mainly of parsons" (77). Even though the male characters are for the most part sincerely committed to their religious vocation and have legitimate ambitions for success in that context, they are nonetheless physical beings with the same capacity for desire as non-religious men. And that capacity, given religious strictures about carnal desire, creates conditions for moral temptation and subsequent hypocrisy. The ambitious Reverend Mr. Obadiah Slope represents the most morally conservative, evangelical faction in Barchester, and his convictions are tested by the arrival in the town of Madeline Neroni (formerly Madeline Stanhope), a married (though separated) daughter of the aristocratic, eccentric, and nearly impoverished Stanhope family. "Though heartless," Trollope observes, "the Stanhopes were not selfish" (66), especially in their capacity not to judge (and not to care) about others. Madame Neroni, was "never more beautiful than at the time" of the story (65), but she is the most heartless of the Stanhopes, her *raison d'etre* being "to wound the hearts of men" (69). Trollope brings Mr. Slope and Madame Neroni together at a reception hosted by the Bishop, Mr. Slope intent on wooing a wealthy widow and Madame Neroni intent on creating "a sensation, to have parsons at her feet" (76–77). Slope is the first one smitten, and despite his continued plans to marry the widow, he pursues Madame Neroni aggressively, fully knowing "that her husband was living, and therefore he could not woo her honestly" (241). Slope was, he acknowledged to himself, "acting against the recognized principles of his life, [but] . . . passion was too strong for him" (242). And what of Madame Neroni? She "spitted him, as a boy does a cockchafer [beetle] on a cork, that she might enjoy the energetic agony of his gyrations. And she knew very well what she was doing" (242). Trollope sets up a situation rife with sexual energy in a language that renders that energy through a vividly comic image: the simile of the pierced insect gyrating on a cork communicates the quality of Slope's passion and its inevitable frustration. (The gyrations are the insect's death throes).

The coolness of Neroni's manipulation of Slope imposes an absolute boundary around the possibilities of Slope's achieving any gratification for that desire. Despite his loss of self-control, the scene is dominated by restraint, a restraint that results as much from Slope's financial ambitions as it does from Trollope's "literary decorum." That is, in the clash between Slope's clearly defined lust for money and position and his unfocused, but powerful, physical attraction to Neroni, money wins. If Slope were to succeed in seducing the still married Neroni, he would be disgraced, and he knows it. As a result, when Neroni calls his bluff—"Will you take me to your home to be your wife? Will you call me Mrs. Slope before bishop, dean, and prebendaries?"—Slope backs off. For by marrying Madame Neroni, he would, perforce, make her a bigamist. Thus the time, place, and legal circumstance impose an absolute restraint on the expression and field of action for Slope's sexual passion. He would have to exchange his worldly ambition for the life of a social outcast in order for his sexual desires to have any meaningful potential to be realized. The dialogue ends with Slope's declarations of love falling empty in the air. However, when he departs from Madame Neroni, his sexual impulses have not fully dissipated for he "promised that he would call again on the following day" (252). Caught between the expression of sexual desire and the necessity of restraint, he cannot control his passion fully; he may be figuratively released from his gyrations in the termination of the dialogue, but once released, he pins himself back on the cork. This dialogue in Trollope's narrative unambiguously registers sexual energies. The sexual motivation of Slope's interaction with Madame Neroni may reveal his hypocrisy, the sex may be more implied than explicit, but it is very much there, functioning as a muted challenge to those institutions that would restrain it.

The potential sexual subversion of two formative social institutions—the church and marriage—is raised as a possibility in Slope's and Neroni's flirtatious dialogue; if Slope succeeded in possessing Neroni sexually, whether in or out of marriage, he would violate marriage laws and his vows as a priest, in effect saying that both institutions unnaturally repress sexual expression. Of course, giving everything up for love is an old literary trope, and in this case, Trollope exploits that trope to comic effect. The implicit challenge to social institutions is deflected to the exposure of character, and the institutions themselves remain unchallenged. In *Lady Audley's Secret* and "The Grey Woman," however, the literary challenge to Victorian marriage laws is rendered more forcefully by not being restricted to sexuality as such. That is, the social relations between men that drive Braddon's sensation novel begin to blur the sharp gender distinctions that structure social and marital relations. Conversely, in Gaskell's sensation story, the cross-dressed social bonds formed between women in response to male oppression provide a vision of same-sex marriage that models gender equity in a way that transforms heterosexual marriage at the end of the tale. The possibility for social critique shifts in *Lady Audley's Secret* and "The Grey Woman" from sexuality to gender, from sex as a physical, genital activity to gender as the foundational construct upon which social institutions are built. By softening the rigidity of orthodox gender boundaries in those two stories, Braddon and Gaskell give narrative expression to a more fluid gender dynamic, which expands the possibilities of constructing human relationships more responsive to human need and the particularities of the individual lot.

Lady Audley's Secret traces the route by which Helen

Malden becomes Helen Talboys before becoming Lucy Graham and, finally, Lady Audley; the story then chronicles how Robert Audley traces Lady Audley's changes of identity in reverse order. The novel thus explores gender identity in terms of two characters: Lady Audley, who, chameleon-like, transforms her social position as she enhances the visible features of her feminine-gender identity in her search for status and security, and Robert Audley, who initially rejects the social expectations of his masculine-gender identity through what appears to be a cynical and perverse, though good-natured, passivity, only to embrace a conventional masculine-gendered identity in response to his attachment to his friend George Talboys. Rather than Robert's heterosexual desire being the catalyst that inspires ambition, action, and direction, it is his homosocial relationship with and subsequent loss of George—a plot element we would identify in film today as a "bromance"—that seems to produce his burst of masculine action. Before tracing out the trajectory and gendered nuances of Robert's actions, however, it is necessary to define the concept of the 'homosocial.'

In *Between Men: English Literature and Male Homosocial Desire,* Eve Sedgwick teases out the history of the word. "'Homosocial,'" she writes, "is a word occasionally used in history and the social sciences, where it describes social bonds between persons of the same sex . . . [and it is] meant to be distinguished from 'homosexual'" (1). Rejecting the implicit opposition between the homosocial and the homosexual that such a distinction implies, Sedgwick works "[t]o draw the 'homosocial' back into the orbit of 'desire,' of the potentially erotic," and she argues for "the potential unbrokenness of a continuum between homosocial and homosexual" (1). Her point is not to suggest that all homosocial relationships imply the possibility of homosexual desire—"I do not mean to discuss genital homosexual desire as 'at the root of' other forms of male homosociality" (2), she writes. She is, instead, interested in the "*structure* of men's relations with other men," a structure that includes some form of desire in many fine, subtle, and various gradations. Linking the homosocial with desire, we have an interpretive lens through which we can begin to understand features of gender instability, both male and female, in Victorian fiction. So with a definition of the homosocial that links the older notion of "social bonds between persons of the same sex" with Sedgwick's notion that such bonds include some form of desire, what we might call the erotics of sociality, we return to Robert Audley.

Robert is the nephew of Sir Michael Audley, a fifty-six-year-old widower, father of Alicia Audley, and the owner of the family estate, Audley Court. With Alicia in love with him and Robert affectionate though sexually indifferent towards her, and with Sir Michael's support for their marriage, Robert's prospects for inheriting the estate are secure. But Robert is strangely passive. He does nothing to indicate any real interest in marrying Alicia, and even though he earns the qualifications to become a lawyer, he never takes any cases and spends most of his time in his London rooms smoking a pipe, drinking good wine, and reading French novels. When Sir Michael meets Lucy Graham, a twenty-year-old governess whose blond curls were "the most wonderful curls in the world—soft and feathery, always floating away from her face, and making a pale halo round her head when the sunlight shone through them" (49), and he strikes "a bargain" to marry her (53) and thus potentially to produce a male heir, Robert responds by hoping sincerely for his uncle's happiness.

A short time after the marriage, Robert runs into an old friend from his school days at Eton, George Talboys. George had just returned from three-and-a-half years in Australia where he had made a minor fortune in gold; he was coming back to his wife, with whom he had not communicated during all those years and who, he finds out soon after his return, has just died (or so he is led to believe). On a visit to Audley Court to meet his uncle's new wife, Robert brings George, who soon thereafter disappears without a word or a trace. Robert's immediate and intense sense of loss is striking. As the narrator explains:

> If any one had ventured to tell Robert Audley that he could possibly feel a strong attachment to any creature breathing, that cynical gentleman would have elevated his eyebrows in supreme contempt at the preposterous notion. Yet here he was, flurried and anxious,

bewildering his brain by all manner of conjectures about his missing friend, and false to every attribute of his nature, walking fast (117).

Robert is stimulated to a degree beyond what he had ever experienced—except, he indirectly reveals, when he was a schoolboy with George at Eton: "I haven't walked fast since I was at Eton" (117), Robert whispered to himself. The memory of the boyhood bond coupled by the shock and uncertainty associated with the loss of his friend compel Robert to put his lawyer's training into action; he becomes, in effect, a detective, searching for his missing friend with an intensity that he expresses in a language of desire: "'To think,' he said meditatively, 'that it is possible to care so much for a fellow! But come what may . . . sooner than be balked in finding him, I'll go to the very end of the world'" (123). He goes even further in his expression of desire for his friend when he reflects, with some surprise, how he could "feel so lonely without him." Then, imagining the possibility of his marriage with Alicia—"I know of a certain little girl, who, as I think, would do her best to make me happy"—he declares in an inner monolog "that I would freely give up all and stand penniless in the world tomorrow . . . if George Talboys could stand by my side" (187).

Robert's search for his friend leads him to believe that George has been murdered. Early in his investigation, he suspects Lady Audley toward whom he "could not overcome a vague feeling of uneasiness" (121). As he traces her history backwards from her marriage to Sir Michael to her position as a governess back to her life with her father and her husband, he concludes that his uncle's young, beautiful, vivacious wife is also George's dead wife. The revelation that her identity was false, that as an already married woman she had married again after falsifying her own death, would be devastating to his uncle, blighting the twilight years of his life, so Robert hesitates to complete his investigation. If George is dead, what difference after all would it make, he reasons? It is better to leave his uncle in ignorance and in peace. He longs to be free from, as he puts it, "the office of a spy, the collector of damning facts that led on to horrible deductions" (218). At this point in the novel, however, the transference of his desire for George to his desire for George's sister changes his plans as his homosocial desire mutates into heterosexual desire.

When Robert first sees Clara Talboys, he is struck by her resemblance to George; when he "saw her face clearly for the first time . . . he saw that she was very handsome. She had brown eyes like George's" (219). "She was different," he muses, "to all other women he had ever seen" (222). And that difference seems to be related both to her resemblance to her brother and to the masculine strength of her intellect and character, to which he surrenders: "'I accept the dominion of that pale girl, with the statuesque features and calm brown eyes,' he thought. 'I recognize the power of a mind superior to my own, and I yield to it'" (227–28). There is a quality in the narrator's language in the sentences that follow that suggests a degree of discomfort with the same-sex motive that actualized Robert from a passive observer of the world to an active agent in the world. "I have been acting for myself," Robert observes, "and thinking for myself, for the last few months, and I'm tired of the unnatural business" (218). The judgment of the bond with his male friend as something selfish and unnatural reduces his motive to solve the mystery of his friend's disappearance/murder to a version of narcissism, as if he and George formed a single mutually self-regarding unit. The transference of desire from George to Clara, in this line of thought, serves as a corrective; it provides a culturally enabling social space that sanctions heterosexual desire and provides a field of action for the satisfaction of that desire. Rather than erasing the homosocial desire that functioned as the foundation of Robert's emotional development and subsequent activity in the world, however, homosocial desire remains a part of Robert's affective life. And that mutual desire on George's part may be said to have kept him alive.

As it turns out, Lady Audley did not succeed in killing her husband George when he confronted her at Audley Court on the day he disappeared. Although she pushed him down a well, he managed to claw his way up, despite a broken arm, and he left England for America, intending never to return and to leave her in peace. (Robert, of course, learns what Lady Audley did, but not that George had survived. Lady Audley then is forced to spend her last days in a lunatic asylum in Belgium where she dies young. Read the novel for the exciting details.) In America, where he "might have made plenty of friends," George longs for the sympathy of his friend, Robert. "I yearned," George said to Robert after his return from America and Robert's marriage to Clara, "for the strong grasp of your hand, Bob; the friendly touch of the hand which had guided me through the darkest passage of my life" (444). Note the physical quality of George's desire for the "grasp," the "friendly touch" of Robert's hand. Given the length of their friendship from schoolboys to marriage, to radical disappointment, suffering, and renewed stability, the physical quality of George's yearning grounds his long relationship with Robert on bodily affinity, a thread of desire winding its way through their homosocial bond and extending into what becomes a family relation: through Robert's marriage with Clara he and George become brothers. George Talboys, we are told on the last page of the novel, "is very happy with his sister and his old friend" (446). On that note, the novel delicately renders the paradox I have tried to articulate in my interpretation of how homosocial desire animates the bonds between Robert and George, and how that desire functions to destabilize gender relations in the novel, while at the same time providing an affective thread that connects Robert and George and extends out to their connection to others. Even though the novel notes that "it is not quite impossible" that George may one day "find someone who will be able to console him for the past," the hesitation in the phrasing ("not quite impossible") and the affirmation of the current *ménage a trois* among George, Robert, and Clara suggests that desire can thrive in any number of human arrangements. The insight that human desire need not be bound by the social constructs of gender relations glimmers throughout *Lady Audley's Secret*. In "The Grey Woman," that possibility is shown to be necessary for survival.

Critics have read "The Grey Woman" as a critique of the oppressive function of marriage for women, a critique, I think, that is part of the story's deeper exploration of the gender definitions upon which an understanding of marriage was based. In this sensation story, with its overlay of Gothic elements, Anna, who later becomes known as "the grey woman," is shown to be victimized by a gendered social system that circumscribes her every action, even, in fact, her very being. We first see Anna, some years after her death, in a painted portrait, which the narrator describes as follows: "It [the portrait] was that of a young girl of extreme beauty; evidently of middle rank. There was a sensitive refinement in her face, as if she almost shrank from the gaze which, of necessity, the painter must have fixed on her" (289). That brief passage presents Anna as a representative woman: her femininity is equated with beauty, she is middle-class, and she is subject "of necessity" to the gaze of men. The fact that the viewers (both women) of her portrait perceive her discomfort under the male gaze (assuming the artist was a man) suggests their sensitivity to the position of all women; they are, because of the gender inflected arrangements of their social system, always explicitly or implicitly subject to observation by men. The hint of subjugation perceived in the portrait is developed in some detail, first in Anna's fear of "admiration and notice" (292) in the days before her marriage; then in the preparation for the marriage itself when she feels "bewitched,—in a dream,—a kind of despair" as she prepares to marry a man with whom she "never felt quite at [her] ease" (296); then later in the descriptions of her new home, an isolated country estate in France, where she became "tame to [her] apparent imprisonment" (304) where she "always had the feeling that all the domestics . . . were spies upon [her], and that [she] was trammeled in a web of observation and unspoken limitation extending over all [her] actions" (309).

Anna's experience of the inherent oppressiveness of the gender roles required by her marriage is challenged when her husband hires a new maid, "[a] Norman woman, Amante by name" (302), who begins figuratively to challenge and re-write the gendered social scripts of marriage, by inspiring jealousy in Anna's legal husband, and by treating Anna in "quite tender ways" (303) in contrast to the coldness of her husband's behavior. A bond, sparked by desire for the warmth of a human connection that marriage seems to have subverted, begins to form between Anna and Amante. The necessity of that bond is then dramatized by the brutal behavior of the husband, who, it turns out, heads a gang of thieves and murderers. One night when Anna, with Amante's assistance, steals into her husband's room to retrieve a letter sent by her family, her husband, with a small group of men, climbs through the window, dragging a large bag, which he drops on the floor near where Anna is hiding. Her husband kicks the bag as Anna reaches out to feel what might be in it, when her "groping palm" fell "upon the clenched and chilly hand of a corpse" (311). After such a discovery (Anna eludes detection), it becomes clear that marriage for Anna means certain death. So she and Amante flee for their lives.

In order to elude capture, Amante put on "an old suit of man's clothes," "cut her hair to the shortness of a man's," and "by cutting up old corks into pieces such as would go into her cheeks, she altered both the shape of her face and her voice" (323). Transformed into a man, Amante then colored Anna's hair and blackened Anna's teeth, turning her into Amante's working-class wife. Anna herself "voluntarily broke a front tooth the better to effect [her] disguise" (323). Thus posing as husband and wife, Amante and Anna escape from two levels of oppression: from Anna's marriage, which had been rendered so vividly as a prison—even, perhaps, an execution chamber—and from the male gaze. Both levels of escape are enacted when Anna's husband walks into a blacksmith's home, where she and Amante had found work and refuge. With Amante looking like a man and Anna no longer a "beauty" from the middle-class, they become invisible as Anna's legal husband "looked all over the room, taking us in with about the same degree of interest as the inanimate furniture" (326). Freed from the gender constructions of the feminine, Anna is free to live.

After that close call, Amante and Anna take refuge in Germany. "We will still be husband and wife," Amante assures Anna; "we will take a small lodging, and you shall housekeep and live in-doors. I, as the rougher and more alert, will continue my father's trade, and seek work at the tailors' shops" (335). Some months later, Anna gives birth to a baby girl, for which she rejoices since, as she says, "a girl seemed all my own. And yet not all my own, for the faithful Amante's delight and glory in the babe almost exceeded mine" (335). Thus Amante and Anna live as a family, their roles determined by ability, mutual care, and love. By the end of the tale, however, Amante is killed (Anna's husband tracks her down and cuts her throat), Anna's husband is arrested and executed, and Anna herself is remarried to a doctor who takes on the responsibility as a father for her daughter. Still, the physical bond between Anna and Amante, born of need, necessity, and mutual care, functions as a corrective to the oppressions of gender. In place of a system that defines human potential in restrictive ways, "The Grey Woman" enacts a model human relationship, in which the expression of homosocial, homosexual, and heterosexual desire can bind people together in configurations determined by human need and the unpredictable particulars of the individual life.

Works Cited

Braddon, Mary Elizabeth. *Lady Audley's Secret*. Ed. Natalie M. Houston. Peterborough, Ontario: Broadview Press, Ltd., 2003.

Dickens, Charles. *Great Expectations*. Ed. Edgar Rosenberg. New York: W. W. Norton, 1999.

_____. *Our Mutual Friend*. Ed. Stephen Gill. Harmondsworth: Penguin, 1984.

Gaskell, Elizabeth. "The Grey Woman." *Gothic Tales*. Ed. Laura Kranzler. London: Penguin, 2000.

Houghton, Walter. *The Victorian Frame of Mind, 1830–1870*. New Haven: Yale UP, 1963.

Maynard, John. "The Worlds of Victorian Sexuality: Work in Progress." *Sexuality and Victorian Literature*. Ed. Don Richard Cox. Knoxville: U of Tennessee P, 1984. 251–265.

Sedgwick, Eve Kosofsky. *Between Men: English Literature and Male Homosocial Desire*. New York: Columbia UP, 1985.

Trollope, Anthony. *Barchester Towers*. London: Penguin, 2003.

Making Herself "for a Person": Gender and Jewishness in Anzia Yezierska's *Bread Givers*

Lisa Marcus

1. Becoming "Americanerin"

"I had just begun to peel the potatoes for dinner"—these are the opening lines of Anzia Yezierska's 1925 American novel, *Bread Givers*. Counter to Nick Carraway's catalog of privilege that opens *The Great Gatsby*, published in the same year as Yezierska's novel, the opening montage figures protagonist Sara Smolinski's assertion of her personhood while peeling potatoes and lamenting the dirt, hunger, and poverty that begrime her childhood. Yezierska's novel seems to rise from the famous ash heaps of Fitzgerald's quintessentially American tale. Unlike Fitzgerald's Carraway, with his pedigree and Wall Street job, Yezierska's protagonist Sara Smolinski works to "make [her]self for a person" in an America that cannot comfortably assimilate this immigrant daughter and in a Jewish community that cannot seem to abide female ambition and defiance against patriarchal tradition.

Young Sara, "thin and small like a dried-out herring," takes the burden of the household upon herself in the first chapter as she asserts herself to be a little "Rockefeller" (22) by turning a profit on the fishmonger's leftover squished herring. She exclaims:

> Nothing was before me but the hunger in our house, and no bread for the next meal if I didn't sell the herring. No longer like a fire engine, but like a houseful of hungry mouths my heart cried, "Herring – herring! Two cents apiece!" (22).

Sara's spirited endeavors to help her hungry family are referred to as "making [her]self for a person," and personhood is clearly aligned here with the ability to leave the domestic space of the family in order to make a profit in the new world. The *Gatsby* reference is instructive here, for just as that text is read as indicative of the possibilities and failures of the American Dream in its tale of the spectacular rise and fall of a "nobody," the (possibly ethnic) outsider James Gatz (who remakes himself as Jay Gatsby), *Bread Givers* also charts the allure and impossibility of the American Dream for this "sweatshop Cinderella." (This is the title of Suzanne Wasserman's short documentary about Yezierska; it comes from a moniker given to Yezierska by Hollywood publicists.) Like Gatz-turned-Gatsby, Sara discovers that assimilation has its costs, as she pursues the American Dream within the complex matrices of gender, ethnicity, class, and religion.

Sara's three sisters work in sweatshops to support the family—all while her Old World father sequesters himself with his Torah and holy books to be "alone with God." When not in such communion, Reb Smolinski assaults his wife and daughters with scripture insisting that:

> the prayers of his daughters didn't count because God didn't listen to women. Heaven and the next world were only for men. Women could get into Heaven because they were wives and daughters of men. . . . Only if they cooked for the men, and washed for the men, and didn't nag or curse the men out of their homes; only if they let the men study the Torah in peace, then, maybe, they could push themselves into Heaven with the men, to wait on them there" (10).

Reb's misogynistic rants are tolerated by his wife and the larger community, who suffer his abuses for other moments of seductive, beneficent religiosity. Sara, we soon see, will have none of that. She comes to see her father as a "tyrant more terrible than the Tsar from Russia" and reflects, "I'd wake up in the middle of the night when all were asleep and cry into the deaf, dumb darkness, 'I hate my father. And I hate God most of all for bringing me into such a terrible house'" (65–6). Yezierska explicitly aligns her critique of the patriarchal father, a man of God, with a critique of God proper. Sara's rebellion against father and family is also a break with religion, particularly the god of her father.

In the opening section of *Bread Givers*, this critique of patriarchal religious tradition is mapped onto a bildungsroman frame,[1] whose heteronormative marriage plot is also a target of Yezierska's analysis, leading readers of a feminist bent to cheer for Sara's escape from her suffocating home and father and explaining why this book was readily reclaimed by second-wave feminist scholars in the 1970s. (Alice Kessler Harris' 1975 introduction to *Bread Givers* charts this feminist reclamation.) Sara, youngest of the four Smolinski daughters and nicknamed "Blood and Iron" by her father for her passion and defiance, charts her difference from her three sisters by rejecting their submissive femininity as she sets out to claim Americanness and personhood as separate from her immigrant family. The tragedy of the three sisters, who are married off one by one to suitors of their father's choosing (though they all have chosen other lovers), forms the backdrop of Sara's initial quest for personhood. As each sister's spirit is broken in a patriarchal double-whammy (first father, then husband turn the sisters into spiritless drudges), Sara resolves to align herself with an imagined America, free of tyrannical fathers and religious prescriptions for dutiful daughterhood. The end of the first book of the novel has Sarah confronting her father:

> For seventeen years I had stood his preaching and his bullying. But now the hammering hell that I had to listen to since I was born cracked my brain. His heartlessness to Mother, his pitiless driving away Bessie's only chance at love, bargaining away Fania to a gambler and Masha to a diamond-faker—when they each had the luck to win lovers of their own—all these tyrannies crashed over me. Should I let him crush me as he crushed them? No. This is America where children are people (135).

It is important to note here the equation Sarah sets up between America and gender liberation, the new nation and the new woman. When her father responds that, "No girl can live without a father or a husband to look out for her. It says in the Torah, only through a man can a woman enter heaven" (136–7), Sarah repeatedly links herself with an America that promises freedom from patriarchal and

Old World religious tenets (this is, of course, just five years after women's suffrage was codified in the Nineteenth Amendment). When Sarah claims first that "In America, women don't need men to boss them" (137) and then, "I'm American" (138), she weds herself to what she imagines to be a New World anti-patriarchal ideology that promises freedom from the constricted lives her mother and sisters have been coerced into living because of religion, tradition, and the Old World—all lined up neatly as anti-modern and anti-woman. And the reaction of many twenty-first-century readers—students, teachers, and critics alike—is to cheer. Sarah, the protagonist of an ethnic-American woman's bildungsroman, confronts the restrictive traditional world and repressive family structure; she becomes a heroine journeying toward development of a new self and a new way to engage with the world. What's not to like?

We must be careful, however, about cheering too hard for both Sara's escape from and rebellion against the tyranny of Jewish patriarchy that makes an easy target for contemporary feminist readers. Reb Smolinski, who is described as looking like "he just stepped out of the Bible" (16), and spouting vile verses that (like the one cited above) testify to women's worthlessness, refuses to be a "bread giver"—which seems so improperly masculine to contemporary secular readers. My students are quick to hate him and his cartoon Judaism. But Yezierska's novel, in fact, demands a more complex reaction, positioning Sara's initial rupture from her family as that of a typical adolescent—an adolescent in a bildungsroman—whose departure from a provincial household is necessary to spur the journey toward a more mature selfhood. It is worth noting, moreover, that while there are many good reasons to find Reb Smolinski intolerable, hating Reb makes us love a falsely idealized America, love assimilation, and negate the immigrant's Otherness. Hating Reb makes readers also hate the Jew. And that's a bit of a problem for Yezierska. This essay's final section will return to this problem.

2. A Room of Her Own

[G]enius like Shakespeare's is not born among labouring, uneducated, servile people. It was not born in England among the Saxons and the Britons. It is not born today among the working classes. How, then, could it have been born among women whose work began, [. . .] almost before they were out of the nursery, who were forced to it by their parents and held to it by all the power of the law and custom? Yet genius of a sort must have existed among the working classes.

(Virginia Woolf, *A Room of One's Own*, 1929)

Virginia Woolf's feminist manifesto calling for space, place, and financial security for women was published four years after Yezierska's *Bread Givers*. While Woolf's pronouncements have become so enmeshed in the popular consciousness as to appear emblazoned on coffee mugs and T-shirts (a line of skin care products is sold at the domain name aroomofherown.com), few literary critics have noted that in *Bread Givers*, Anzia Yezierska—across the Atlantic and out of view of her upper class British contemporary—had already tested those ideas. Book Two of *Bread Givers* begins with an entire chapter devoted to Sara finding a "room of her own." Indeed, several times during the chapter titled "I Shut the Door," the language comes very close to Woolf's. Sara, having fled her father's house and been turned away from the shabby homes of her downtrodden sisters, declares, "I want a room all to myself" (158), knowing "what a luxury it was for a poor girl to want to be alone in a room" (158). When Sara finds the hoped-for room, she must battle a landlady suspicious of a single woman on her own. She thinks:

> Like a drowned person clinging to a rope, my tired body edged up to that door and clung to it. My hands clutched at the knob. The door was life. It was air. The bottom starting-point of becoming a person. I simply must have this room with the shut door" (159).

Woolf hypothesizes in the story of Shakespeare's Sister that a girl who "cried out that marriage was hateful to her," was "severely beaten by her father," and fled to a life of creativity in the city was doomed due to the treachery of her body and of men; Woolf imagines a suicidal end as the only available outcome to the undutiful artistic daughter. Yezierska has something else in mind, however. While the only window in her tiny room opens to an airshaft that serves as a garbage dump for her upstairs neighbors, and Sara struggles in "heart-choking dinginess" (162) "crucified in a torture pit of noise" (164), she nevertheless revels in her solitude and presses forward in her dreams to become a schoolteacher.

Much as Woolf argues in *A Room* that "one cannot think well, love well, sleep well, if one has not dined well" (18) in her brilliant juxtaposition of the wealthy male college's luscious luncheon with the spare and stringy meal at the poorer women's college, so Yezierska explores the sexual politics of food once Sara has secured her lodging. In "A Piece of Meat," hunger works on several levels. Sara is both physically and mentally hungry, and unlike her mother, who had saved the richest meat and fattiest broth for Sara's father, Sara cannot abide by such sexist prescriptions relegating the biggest and best portions to men. In a Hester Street cafeteria, Sara is "like a mad thing straining toward the pots of food" (167); she thinks of the server as "hold[ing] in her hands my life, my strength, new blood for my veins, new clearness in my brain to go on with the fight. Oh! If she would only give me enough to fill myself, this one time!" (167–8). When she is served only stringy bits of meat and potatoes, while the fat man behind her receives a plate heaped with chunks of beef, Sara ponders, "why did she give more to the man just because he was a man? I'm hungry" (169), and another woman answers, "Don't you know they always give men more?" (169). The sexist economics of food distribution (reproduced by other women) prove miserably unpalatable to Sara, who is fueled by a desire for a more just world. Only once she is educated at college and back in New York in a bright new room is her hunger quelled by "chops and spinach and salad" showing that education and upward mobility make the needs of the flesh less urgent—and more feminine. While Woolf asks, "what food do we feed women artists upon?" and answers with "prunes and custard" (53), as an explanation for why women's artistic production was so anemic (in quantity and style), Yezierska was illustrating this theory in her protagonist's struggles for "a piece of meat."

In Woolf's parable, Judith Shakespeare finds herself "with child" by a predatory theater manager—her artistic and sexual passion leading to her demise—as Woolf didactically cautions the college girls in her audience to keep their knickers on. Yezierska, again, has anticipated the passion-reason problem and worked it out in her fiction. In the chapter "A Man Wanted Me," Sara temporarily rebels against her claustrophobic room and unwavering, blinkered ambition. Courted by the pushcart peddler-turned-wealthy-capitalist Max Goldstein, Sara momentarily chooses passion over reason. Upon meeting him Sara thinks, "that man could wake the dead from their graves" (188). Max's "joyous youth," "slender body," and "full red lips" coupled with dancing at Harlem jazz clubs release and electrify Sara, while readers learn that she "had tasted pleasure" (194). Unlike Woolf, who impregnates her Judith, Yezierska does not pen such a fate for her heroine; she wants more from her. Max is revealed to be a "talking roll of dollar bills," and Sara rightly figures that, "A wife to him would only be another piece of property" (199). Sara has already rejected the idea proffered by her father and repeated by her badly married sisters of marriage as an inevitable or desirable outcome—she sees it plainly as a transaction of capital. The scene ends with Sara rejecting Max's marriage proposal and the pleasures of the body for those of the mind. She reclaims her books as her cherished companions:

> Nothing was so beautiful as to learn, to know, to master by the sheer force of my will even the dead squares and triangles of geometry. I seized my books and hugged them to my breast as though they were living things (201).

Yezierska herself rejected marriage (she was married twice, very briefly), and gave up custody of her only daughter to be a writer, a choice that is more vexed for readers than it apparently was for her (see Komy).

While Yezierska is not often regarded in the company of her modernist contemporaries, putting *Bread Givers* into conversation with Woolf's *A Room of One's Own* links Yezierska to a feminist project about art and economics, sex and space. Much ink has been spilled in calling out Woolf's uncharitable elitism, her proclamation (cited above) that genius is not "born among labouring, uneducated, servile people" (48); instead, I'd like to linger over Woolf's qualifying "yet." She finishes her thought, "Yet genius of a sort must have existed among women as it must have existed among the working classes" (48–9). Like Alice Walker, who also lingers on Woolf's "yet" in her attempt to reclaim the African American poet Phyllis Wheatley, and who reminds us that we have often "looked high when [we] should have looked high and low" (239), I think Woolf's "yet" leaves us an opening, an opening for Anzia Yezierska, whose "low" art and vernacular fiction may have predicted the feminist philosophies manifested four years later by Woolf.

3. "The Problem of Father"
"She's not a woman. She has a dybuk, a devil, a book for a heart."
     (Yezierska's father, quoted in her autobiography, *Red Ribbon on a White Horse*)

". . . my own daughter who is not a Jewess and not a gentile."
                              (Reb Smolinski, in *Bread Givers*)

Every time I teach *Bread Givers*, I assign my students a close-reading paper focused on the ending paragraphs of the novel. I never fail to be astonished at how many of them want to read Sara's conclusion as triumphant, how many cast her in some kind of feminist fairytale, wherein she becomes a teacher, wins the love of an intellectual equal and ethnic compatriot, and achieves reconciliation with her father and community—never mind the gymnastics they have to perform to ignore the ending's tone, tension, and incompleteness. Such a happy ending, though promised by the bildungsroman format and the American Dream mythology that the novel calls forth, is haunted by the shadow and chant that hover over the final scene. It must be read with a lens that attends to Sara as both a woman and a Jew, as a liminal figure, who straddles Old and New Worlds—of gender and ethnicity. Despite the anti-patriarchal rebellion and liberation spelled out by the novel's trajectory in its opening sections, the conclusion of *Bread Givers* shows that neither Sara nor Yezierska has solved the knotty "problem of father."

Sara is twice cursed by her father. These dramatic confrontations establish what seems to be an irreconcilable divide between father and daughter, Old World patriarchy and Americanized New Woman. In the first conflagration, when she leaves home, Sara deploys a New World rhetoric, declaring that "In America, women don't need men to boss them" (137); her father strikes her, calls her a "blasphemer," and spits out that "in the olden times the whole city would have stoned you!" (137). Sara declares her independence as she departs: "the Old World had struck its last on me" (138). But this isn't father's last strike. He reappears when she is settled in her New York room, after she has given up her lover Max Goldstein for the companionship of her books. She imagines her learned father, devoted to his precious books, would understand: "How rich with the sap of centuries were his words of wisdom! I never knew the meaning of his sayings when I had listened to him at home. But now it came over me like half-remembered, far-off songs, like music and poetry" (203). This desire to see him is actualized as he appears, "standing there like a picture out of the Bible" (203), but he has come not as a kindred spirit.

He is there to preach:

Pfui on your education! What's going to be your end? A dried-up old maid? You think millions of educated old maids like you could change the world one inch? Woe to America where women are let free like men" (205).

While Sara (and readers) appreciate this "America where women are let free like men," Reb singles Sara out as unnatural, "worse than an animal," "not a person at all" for defying what he views as the biblical command to marry and procreate. He rages:

"I give you up! [. . .] You're without character, without morals, without religion. What use are you to yourself or the world? [. . .] I disown you. I curse you. May your name and your memory be blotted out of this earth" (207–208).

This curse erases Sara's existence as a daughter and a Jew, leaving her alone with "No Father. No lover. No family. No friend" (208). In her father's cosmology, Sara's choice of education over marriage places her outside of the human and natural order. Sara and her father have fundamentally different versions of personhood; for him, a person exists in a fixed, hierarchical relationship to family and God; for her, personhood is separate from familial Old World tribalism, and is instead forged through education in an America that seems to promise liberation and self-realization.

As vicious and awful as the father comes across in these scenes, there is a sense in which both Sara and the novel internalize his logic—his accusation that, in striving for an educated self and a "room of her own," Sara cuts herself off from the Jewish sources of her humanity. Readers, still cringing from Reb's curses and physical blows, may well wish her good riddance of the old man and be happy to embrace an ethnically cleansed New Woman and reject Jewishness as oppressive and anti-modern. However, Yezierska does not allow for such a neat conclusion. The Jewish father and all he represents cannot be so easily disposed of. After aggressively pursuing her college degree, solidifying her vocation as a teacher, and securing a dirt-free and uncluttered "room of her own," Sara finds that indeed, as her father had warned, she is cut off from humankind. Walking among the grubby pushcarts of Hester Street, she laments, "my joy hurt like guilt" (281); she wishes to "divide [her] joy with the shivering pushcart peddlers" (281). The repressed father returns, as she stumbles upon Reb, reduced to shabbiness and selling chewing gum in the street. When he refers to himself as a Jewish "King Lear—broken—forgotten" (284), she plays Cordelia to rescue him, despite his earlier rejection of her. Sara soliloquizes:

> How could I have hated him and tried to blot him out of my life? Can I hate my arm, my hand that is part of me? Can a tree hate the roots

from which it sprang? [. . .] who gave me the fire, the passion, to push myself up from the dirt? If I grow, if I rise, if I ever amount to something, is it not his spirit burning in me? (286)

While her father's curse had earlier suggested that she wished to function outside of nature's law, here, Sara casts herself as a tree of life and accepts that she is at root conjoined with her father: she is attempting to read herself back into her father's cosmology.

But this is no father-daughter love fest. Sara has tried to forge a Jewish-American identity on her own terms: she has found a lover and future mate in school principal Hugo Seelig, whose gentle Jewishness and common ancestry open "all the secret places of [her] heart" (278). They discover that they are "Landesleute—countrymen," and repeatedly exclaim that they are "of one blood" (278, 280), both straddling Old and New Worlds as they teach the immigrant children correct English pronunciation in their Lower East Side school. The two of them represent a Jewishness that is both grounded in the Hester Street community and invested in an assimilationist project that seeks to allow the next generation to remain who they are as Jews, while being able to navigate the linguistic codes of the dominant culture (see Konzett).

All this must be kept in mind when assessing the final paragraphs of the novel. Cordelia-like, Sara offers her home to her father, even though she knows that "with him there it would not be a home for me" (295). She reflects "just as I was beginning to feel safe and free [. . .] the old burden dragged me back by the hair" (295). Upon meeting the old man, Hugo immediately ingratiates himself with Reb by requesting that he teach him Hebrew, which seems to indicate that Sara and Hugo will integrate her father into a new future, that Jewish identity, language, and tradition will be passed on to subsequent generations. While Reb happily accepts Hugo's invitation, he stubbornly continues to see Sara as transgressive and questions whether Sara can indeed be a Jew on his terms—that is, keep a kosher household and follow Jewish law. He twice notes her liminal religious status, referring to Sara as "my daughter who is not a Jewess and not a gentile" (293) and, responding to Sara's invitation, counters "Can a Jew and a Christian live under one roof?" (295).

Once again cursed or branded by her father as deficient, *traif*, outside the law, Sara does not, as previously, reject her father and flee; instead, as she thinks to herself, "I *almost* hated him again as I felt his tyranny" (emphasis added), she is overcome by a piercing "pathos" that recognizes him as an antiquated relic:

> In a world where all is changed, he alone remained unchanged – as tragically isolate as the rocks. All he had left of life was his fanatical adherence to his traditions. It was within my power to keep lighted the flickering candle of his life for him. Could I deny him this poor service? (296)

However, even in his impotence, Sara's father casts a pall over her future. The novel closes with a problem, "the problem before us—the problem of father—still unsolved" (296). This scene is set to the soundtrack of the sorrowful cadence of her father's chant from Job "*Man born of Woman is of few days and full of trouble*" (296). While the subsequent lines from Job, not quoted in the novel, "like a fleeting shadow, he does not endure," suggest that the father will soon expire, the shadow he casts will continue to haunt Sara's future: "It wasn't just my father, but the generations who made my father whose weight was still upon me" (297), for the "problem of father" is the problem of patriarchy.

If father remains an unsolved problem, so too does Hugo, who, some readers suspect, may be too easily schooled in Reb's theology along with his Hebrew lessons. For this reason, Hugo's grip, "tightened" on Sara's arm in the novel's final paragraph, seems a portent of danger: is her betrothed destined to become a copy of her father? An earlier scene at the school, when Hugo corrects Sara's pronunciation in front of her students by placing his hands on her throat, raises flags about Hugo's physicality, which is, at best, paternalistic and, at worst, potentially violent. Though there is much reason to believe that Sara and Hugo will soon marry, they aren't married within the pages of the text. If Yezierska's own marriage history is at all instructive—she was married to her first husband for all of twenty-four hours, and her second marriage disintegrated after the birth of their child—the romance plot is tenuous and insecure.

It is hard to see how this conclusion could lead readers to regard the novel as having a "fairytale ending," one that successfully marries New and Old Worlds, head and heart, Sara's desire to "make [her]self for a person," and the demands on a dutiful daughter. *Bread Givers* is a poignant example of how women's attempts to write themselves into libratory spaces of gender-equity and sexual freedom are inevitably complicated by issues of ethnicity, religion, and class.

Readers who are understandably drawn to the feminist project of this book must confront the fact that Yezierska is unwilling to sacrifice Sara's father and Judaism in order to envision Sara in a "room of her own." Sara doesn't ultimately get this room because she is (however uncomfortably) yoked to her father. While Woolf calls for the young women in her audience to "think back through [their] mothers"—through the books penned by their literary foremothers—Yezierska, addressing the "problem of father," cautions us that the Jewish proto-feminist must find a way to accommodate her father and his symbolic books. If the feminist and ethnic projects of this book exist in an unresolved tension, Yezierska also insists that they are inseparable. If we look to Yezierska as a literary mother to "think back through"—as much as I suspect she might hate such an honorific—we are challenged to resist reductive versions of feminist personhood.

Note

1. For a good distillation of literary definitions of the bildungsroman, see <http://www.victorianweb.org/genre/hader1.html>. Also see "The Bildungsroman Project," a digital project produced by Katherine Carlson at University of North Carolina, Chapel Hill, <http://bildungsromanproject.com/define/>.

Works Cited

Adelman Komy, Hannah. "Lies Her Mother Told Us: Louise Levitas Henriksen's Critique of Anzia Yezierska's Autobiography." *Shofar:*

An Interdisciplinary Journal of Jewish Studies 26.3 (Spring 2008): 33–47.

Fitzgerald, F. Scott. *The Great Gatsby*. New York: Scribner, 1925.

Kessler Harris, Alice. "Introduction." *Bread Givers*. 1925. By Anzia Yezierska. New York: Persea Books, 1975.

Konzett, Delia Caparoso. "Administered Identities and Linguistic Assimilation: The Politics of Immigrant English in Anzia Yezierska's *Hungry Hearts*." *American Literature* 69.3 (September 1997): 595–619.

Sweatshop Cinderella: A Portrait of Anzia Yezierska. Dir. Suzanne Wasserman. *Women Make Movies*, 2010. Film.

Walker, Alice. *In Search of Our Mothers' Gardens: Womanist Prose*. San Diego: Harcourt Brace Jovanovich, 1983. 231–43.

Wilentz, Gay. "Cultural Mediation and the Immigrant's Daughter: Anzia Yezierka's *Bread Givers*." *MELUS* 17.3 (Fall 1991): 33–42.

Woolf, Virginia. *A Room of One's Own*. 1929. Orlando, FL: Harcourt, 1989.

Yezierska, Anzia. *Bread Givers*. 1925. New York: Persea Books, 1970.

Claustrophobia: Containment and Queer Spaces in *Tea and Sympathy* and *Cat on a Hot Tin Roof*

Brenda Murphy

A woman in her mid-twenties enters the bedroom of a seventeen-year-old boy, shuts and bolts the door, and stands looking at the boy lying on the bed. With a *"slight and delicate movement,"* she unbuttons the top button of her blouse and moves toward the boy. Reaching the bed, she reaches out her hand, which he brings to his lips, and she says, "years from now . . . when you talk about this . . . and you will . . . be kind" (Anderson 312). The much-parodied ending of Robert Anderson's play *Tea and Sympathy* is one of the iconic images of 1950s American theater. After being repeated on Broadway 712 times between September 1953 and February 1955, it was enacted on film by Deborah Kerr and John Kerr (no relation), the same actors who had portrayed Laura Reynolds and Tom Lee in the play. Set in a boys' boarding school, the play and the film adaptation touch on anxiety-provoking subjects for the homophobic 1950s. Tom, who is in love with his young housemother, Laura, is suspected of being gay after he is seen swimming nude with Mr. Harris, one of the school's male teachers, who loses his job as a result of the rumor. Driven to prove his "manliness" by the taunting and ostracism of the other boys and the insensitivity of the housemaster, Laura's husband Bill, and his own father Herb, Tom tries to have sex with the notoriously promiscuous Ellie Martin, but is unable to perform, he later tells Laura, because he feels nothing for her. He then tries, unsuccessfully, to kill himself. The ending occurs after Laura has told Bill she is leaving him, and it is clear that Tom will be expelled from school.

By 1955, when Tennessee Williams was writing what many critics believe to be his best play, *Cat on a Hot Tin Roof*, *Tea and Sympathy*, and especially its ending, were so well known that Williams worried about the perceived similarities between it and his own play. He complained in a letter to his agent that Elia Kazan, who directed both plays, was pushing him away from his original idea for the ending and toward echoing *Tea and Sympathy*'s: "Here is another case of a woman giving a man back his manhood, while in the original conception it was about a vital, strong woman dominating a weak man and achieving her will" (554). In *Cat*, Brick Pollitt has stopped sleeping with his wife Maggie and stayed perpetually drunk after the death of his best friend Skipper. In the course of the play, it emerges that Brick hung up on Skipper when Skipper tried to tell Brick about the love he felt for him, and Brick feels guilt for Skipper's "cracking up" afterwards. Brick's own sexuality remains a mystery, but the play ends with Maggie finally succeeding at getting him into bed, hoping to make the lie she's told to his family about being pregnant into truth. In what Williams called the "Broadway Version" of the ending, written for the Kazan production, Maggie says: "Oh, you weak, beautiful people who give up with such grace. What you need is someone to take hold of you—gently, with love, and hand your life back to you, like something gold you let go of—and I can! I'm determined to do it—and nothing's more determined than a cat on a tin roof—is there? Is there, baby? [*She touches his cheek gently.*]" (215).

In both plays, the women offer the promise of normality to the men by means of affirming their "manliness" through heterosexual sex. In doing so, they return stability to an unstable sexual dynamic by reaffirming the heteronormative values of the plays' social institutions, the school and the family. The affirmation of heteronormative values was certainly a major element in mainstream American cultural consciousness in the 1950s. An important trope through which the heteronormative was emphasized was the metaphor of the closet, both in the particular sense of closeted homosexuality and as an example of what Bruce McConachie suggests in *American Theater in the Culture of the Cold War* was the dominant post-war cognitive metaphor for Americans, the figure of containment. Cognitive philosopher Mark Johnson writes in *The Body and the Mind* that the experience of containment involves both protection from or resistance to forces that are external to the container and the restriction of forces within the container (22). For gay men in the fifties, the metaphor of the closet was a powerful expression both of hiding from the societal and legal forces that threatened them and of the restrictions and limitations that action placed on their lives. It is no surprise that a closeted gay playwright, like Williams, would be adept at using restricted, airless, claustrophobic spaces in the staging of plays about gay characters, but it is intriguing to find an avowedly heterosexual playwright, like Robert Anderson, using this spatial metaphor to great effect as well.

Anderson always insisted in interviews that his subject in *Tea and Sympathy* was not homosexuality, but gender identity, or as he put it, "manliness." He said, in one interview, that "it's not a play about homosexuality. It's about manliness. . . . It was an attack on the macho image, the Hemingway man" (Bryer 20). Within the claustrophobic set of *Tea and Sympathy*, Anderson created what critics call a queer space, in which both gender identity and sexuality are far more fluid than the heteronormative conception prevalent in the fifties allowed for, and the setting and transgression of boundaries takes place constantly.

Besides Tom's transgressive relationship with Laura and his relationship with Harris, which initially took place in the open air, but was later closeted in his room because of the school rumors, the dormitory is the space for a continuum of queer or transgressive behavior, some of which is open and sanctioned by the heteronormative culture of the school, and some of which is tightly contained within the metaphoric closet. For example, the boys openly engage in the voyeuristic behavior of spying on the woman next door as she nurses her baby and make fun of Tom when he tries to stop them. Lilly, another faculty wife, who tells Laura that the boys think of nothing but sex, shows signs of exhibitionism, dressing as provocatively as the culture of the school will allow and saying, "I love watching them look and suffer" (233). An innocently fluid image of gender identity is established visually as Laura helps Tom with his costume for playing Lady Teazle in *The School for Scandal*. When Laura starts to dance with Tom, he says, "we'd look kind of silly, both of us in skirts" (242), and when Laura tells him,

"You're going to make a very lovely girl," he "*kids a curtsy*" (242). This is all behavior that is grudgingly accepted within the culture of the school, although not really approved of. Tom says, "My Dad's going to hit the roof when he hears I'm playing another girl" (239).

The rumors about a homosexual relationship between Harris and Tom are not permissible, however, and their innocent relationship is transformed into a punishable transgression of the sexual norm by the rumors themselves. Harris tells Tom that "the Dean's had me on the carpet all afternoon. I probably won't be reappointed next year . . . and all because I took you swimming down off the dunes on Saturday" (244). When Tom asks him what he did wrong, Harris answers, "Nothing! Nothing, unless you made it seem like something wrong" (245). When Tom tells him he hasn't even seen the Dean, Harris blames the "bunch of gossiping old busybodies" (245) on the faculty. This scene is immediately followed by a scene in which the other boys gossip about Harris and Tom being seen swimming "bare-assed" (245) off the dunes. When Laura's husband Bill tells her about the rumor, she says there wouldn't have been the same rise to judgment if it had been a big athlete out with Harris, and Bill admits, "It would have been different," but "Tom's always been an off-horse. And now it's quite obvious why" (251). Bill evokes stereotypical markers of homosexuality in the fifties to categorize the uneasiness he feels about Tom as he says, "Look at the way he walks, the way he sometimes stands . . . a man knows a queer when he sees one" (251). The boys, who have been calling Tom "Grace" because of his infatuation with the movie star Grace Moore, begin to use it with malevolence, referring to him as "a queer" and leaving the shower room when he comes in because "they don't want some queer looking at them" (269).

The homophobia of the boys is endemic to the culture, but Bill has a deeper reason for fearing any association with homosexuality. At the beginning of the play, Anderson makes it clear that before he married Laura, Bill was a confirmed bachelor, who never looked at women, and after his marriage, he is always with the boys, taking them on outings as well as being a housemaster and even taking some of the boys on his vacations with Laura. She tries to talk to him about the lack of intimacy in their marriage, saying he holds himself aloof, and they rarely touch anymore, so that "a tension seems to grow between us . . . and then when we do . . . touch . . . it's a violent thing . . . almost a compulsive thing" (280). At the end of the play, as she is telling Bill that she is leaving him, she says that he has resented her since the day they were married: "You never wanted to marry really . . . Did they kid you into it? Does a would-be headmaster have to be married? . . . You would have been far happier going off on your jaunts with the boys, having them to your rooms for feeds and bull sessions" (308). She feels that he had reached out to her for "help" before their marriage and that "in some terrible way I've failed you" (308).

The idea of a man seeking a woman to "cure" him of his homoerotic desires was common in mid-twentieth-century American culture. In Williams' *A Streetcar Named Desire*, for example, Blanche DuBois suffers from tremendous guilt for not "saving" her young husband Allen Gray from his homosexuality. In this context, the homosexual panic that Bill evinces in the face of the rumors about one of the boys in his house is not surprising. Laura says, "I've never seen you like this before" when he is telling her about the rumors (251). At the end of the play, Laura asks Bill whether it has occurred to him that "you persecute in [Tom] the thing you fear in yourself?" (309). As he turns a look of hatred on her, she says, "This was the weakness you cried out for me to save you from, wasn't it . . . And I have tried" (309).

The play's set is a queer space that visually contains all of this fluid sexuality and gender identity, but also suggests images of containment within it. The set is a small, old Colonial house that serves as a dormitory in the New England prep school. At stage right is the headmaster's study, the domain of Bill and Laura, at stage left, a hall and stairway that leads to the boys' rooms. Tom's small bedroom is connected to a sitting room off the landing of the stairs, which he shares with his roommate Al. An essential element of the staging, and of the play, is the use of the doors to the rooms. A door at the rear of the study leads to the private living quarters of Bill and Laura, never seen. The door to the hall is used as a signal to the boys. When it is closed, the study is an off-limits, private space. When it is ajar, *"there is considerable leniency in letting the boys use the study"* (231). During the play, the opening and closing of the door signals the shifting character of the study between public and private space and serves as a barometer of the intimacy of the interactions between Laura and Bill and Laura and Tom. Similarly, the door to Tom's bedroom can be open to the sitting room, allowing for Al and the other boys to use it more or less as a public space, notably when the boys come in to spy on the woman next door, or it can signal Tom's willing or unwilling enclosure in a private space. For example, when Mr. Harris comes to his room to discuss the accusation with him, he closes the bedroom door, and Tom *"regards this action with some nervousness"* (244). At the end of Act One, after Laura reveals that she has tried to help Tom fight the rumor by inviting him and a girl to tea, Tom runs upstairs and shuts the door to his bedroom, leaning against the doorjamb as he seeks its privacy.

The use of the study door also builds toward the ending, beginning with the opening scene in the study when Tom, who is *"deeply in love"* with Laura, expresses his emotion as a sort of *"delayed puppy love"* (236). He tries to establish a private, intimate space by closing the door, but she tells him to leave it open in case some of the other boys want to drop in for tea, and is amused when he opens it "the merest crack" (237). A different form of containment is established when Laura closes the study door as Bill is telling her about the rumor of Harris and Tom swimming nude together, an attempt to contain the rumor. In Act Two, when Laura is trying to keep Tom in the study so he doesn't go to meet Ellie Martin, she opens the door wide when she sees him in the hall, and then shuts it gently after he comes in, saying "It'll be nice just to stay here by the fire" (189). Later in the scene, he opens the door and starts to leave after she offers to teach him to dance, and then closes it when she says, "Please, for me" (294). At the end of the scene, Tom kisses Laura, and then awkwardly rushes out when she dissuades him from kissing her again, and then Bill returns unexpectedly with a group of boys from the outing he has been leading, leaving the door to the study open. Laura "sadly goes to the door and slowly and gently closes it" (296), metaphorically reestablishing her private relationship with Bill and shutting Tom out. When Tom sees the door close, he stands looking at it for a moment, and then goes out to his disastrous date with Ellie. In the final scene, Laura first comes into Tom's bedroom and looks at him lying miserably on the bed, then she goes through the sitting room to the hall door and closes it, returns to the bedroom and closes the door to the sitting room, and then bolts it, suggesting both the containment of their relationship in a private space apart from the rest of the house and a sense of its closeted transgressive nature.

It is the intrusion of Laura, a sexualized mother figure, into the private space of Tom's bedroom that promises to effect his salvation from the devastating effects of his homosexual panic and his seeming failure at heterosexual sex. As Anderson said, "the beautiful irony in the play is that the boy would never have been in bed with the woman if he hadn't been accused of being a homosexual. They were forced into each others' arms by what the boys did to him and what her husband did to her" (Bryer 20). Laura's action essentially heterosexualizes the private space of Tom's bedroom, transforming the forbidden space of closeted homosexuality and bringing it into the realm of the "normal," that is, the heterosexual that is approved in this world. In this context, a woman in her twenties seducing a seventeen-year-old is represented as salvation rather than exploitation or abuse. There are transgressions that are tolerated, after all, and those that aren't. For example, Tom's father is tolerant and even boastful of his son's sexual transgression when he believes that Tom is being expelled for having sex with Ellie Martin, saying "the circumstances are so much more normal" (300) than the incident with Harris. But he is devastated when he hears that Tom wasn't able to perform: "I'm drawing no conclusions. This sort of thing can happen to a normal boy. But it's what the others will think . . . Added to the Harris business. And that's all that's important. What they'll think" (303).

The queer space that Tennessee Williams imagined in *Cat on a Hot Tin Roof* was there from the beginning, in the short story from which the play developed, "Three Players of a Summer

Game" (1952). In the story, Brick Pollitt is an alcoholic who lost control of his drinking two years after his marriage to Margaret, who has undergone a transformation during the marriage, from a pretty Southern Belle to a powerful woman to whom Williams gives many of the 1950s markers of lesbianism. She now has "a firm and rough-textured sort of handsomeness" (306), cuts her hair short, goes around with dirty fingernails, and develops "a booming laugh that she might have stolen from Brick while he was drunk" (109). At the end of the story, she drives Brick's car "with a wonderful male assurance, her bare arms brown and muscular as a Negro field hand's" (324). Williams describes the dynamic of the marriage with vampire imagery: "It was as though she had her lips fastened to some invisible wound in his body through which drained out of him and flowed into her the assurance and vitality that he had owned before marriage" (306). The effect of this is Brick's emasculation—he says that he could feel his "self respect" being "cut off [him]" (312)—which is the stimulus for his drinking and for his engaging in a love affair with Isabel Grey, the wife of the town's young doctor.

In the course of the story, it becomes clear that Brick and Isabel have administered a fatal dose of morphine to Isabel's husband, who was suffering from a brain tumor, and the Victorian house where she lives has become a metonymic representation of containment, a "walled palace," a "suffocating enclosure," in which the lovers spend their time living with their secrets as if "bound in a closet" (303). The house functions as a containment trope, both in protecting the lovers from the town and its knowledge of their transgressions and in restricting their freedom. At the end of the day, they come out of the house "with the buoyant air of persons just released from a suffocating enclosure" (303).

Margaret wins the contest between her and Brick in the story, which ends with her driving Brick through the town in his Pierce Arrow, waving, and shouting greetings to everyone in the town "as if she were running for office," while Brick nods and grins "with senseless amiability behind her" (325). The narrator comments that "it was exactly the way that some ancient conqueror, such as Caesar or Alexander the Great or Hannibal, might have led in chains through a capital city the prince of a state newly conquered" (325). When Williams returned to the material for the play, he removed the lesbian markers from Margaret, instead making her an aggressively heterosexual, but sexually frustrated, woman whose husband Brick refuses to sleep with her, ostensibly because she had sex with his best friend Skipper once before his death. In the play, Brick is not trying to control his drinking as he is in the story, but has "that cool air of detachment that people have who have given up the struggle" (19).

The setting of the play has shifted to the bedroom where Brick and Maggie are sleeping at the family plantation, and Williams planned the play, which never leaves this room, to have a claustrophobic sense of containment. As Maggie says, "I'm not living with you. We occupy the same cage" (35). In his "Notes for the Designer," Williams described the room as Victorian "with a touch of the Far East" (15) and linked it crucially with its original inhabitants, a gay couple named Jack Straw and Peter Ochello, who were the owners of the plantation before it passed to Brick's father, Big Daddy. The room "is gently and poetically haunted by a relationship that must have involved a tenderness which was uncommon." The set has "the grace and comfort of light, the reassurance it gives, on a late and fair afternoon in summer, the way that no matter what, even dread of death, is gently touched and soothed by it" (15). Thus, like the Victorian house in the short story, the room is a version of the closet, but rather than being shut in with the memory of a crime and death, Brick and Maggie are surrounded by the comforting atmosphere of a tender gay love relationship.

This very atmosphere provokes anxiety for Brick, who strikes out physically at Maggie when she tries to talk about his friend Skipper's love for him. When, during their long private conversation in Act Two, Big Daddy suggests that there was something "not exactly *normal* in your friendship" (114), Brick responds with fury that "you call me your son and a queer. Oh! Maybe that's why you put Maggie and me in this room that was Jack Straw's and Peter Ochello's, in which that pair of old sisters slept in a double bed where both of 'em died!" (115). In the course of this private conversation between them, "Brick is transformed, as if a quiet mountain blew suddenly up in volcanic flame" (117), his homosexual panic erupting in his outrage that his father thought he and Skipper "did, did, did!–*sodomy!*–together" (117), that they should be compared to "a pair of dirty old men . . . ducking sissies? Queers" (118). Being shut up in this room with its "big double bed" (16) is doubly torturous for Brick, who has broken his ankle trying to run the hurdles on the high school athletic track, as it is the site of both his daily battle against Maggie's desire to have sex and the reminder of tender homoerotic feelings that he is trying desperately to deny.

As Anderson did in *Tea and Sympathy*, Williams made full use of doors in the set to indicate containment, suggesting the desire for privacy associated with the closet and the inevitable intrusion of prying and often malevolent outsiders. The bedroom has a door to the hall and two sets of double doors to the gallery or balcony, through which numerous intrusions are attempted. In the long scene between Brick and Maggie in Act One, the desire for privacy is emphasized when Maggie slams and locks the door to the hall "to give us a little privacy for a while" (40). Her attempt to seduce Brick is immediately thwarted when Big Mama calls through the hall door and rattles the knob. After calling Maggie to open the door, she goes around and comes through the gallery door, saying "I hate locked doors in a house" (42) and demonstrating the futility of Maggie's effort. Preferring greater containment to exposure, Brick hides from Big Mama in the bathroom, coming out only when she's gone. At the end of the scene, when Maggie is making her final desperate plea for Brick to sleep with her, Dixie, one of the "no-neck monsters"—Maggie's name for the children of Brick's brother Gooper and his wife Mae—bursts into the room and fires a cap pistol at Maggie. The desperation of her desire for privacy comes out in the *"cool fury"* of her speech: "Little girl, your mother or someone should teach you—[gasping]—to knock at a door before you come into a room. Otherwise people might think that you—lack—good breeding" (60). This, of course, is futile, as Dixie demonstrates the bad breeding of the Pollitt family by shooting the cap pistol again and taunting Maggie: "You're just jealous because you can't have babies" (61), something she's heard her parents say.

This scene is immediately followed by the mass intrusion of the family members from the gallery into the room for Big Daddy's birthday celebration at the beginning of Act Two. Big Daddy succeeds in emptying the room when he decides to have his private conversation with Brick, but immediately catches Mae eavesdropping. His awareness of the constant intrusions on Brick and Maggie's privacy is evident in his telling Mae he's going to move her and Gooper away from this room. "You listen at night like a couple of rutten peephole spies and go and give a report on what you hear to Big Mama an' she comes to me and says they say such and such and so and so about what they heard goin' on between Brick an' Maggie, and Jesus, it makes me sick" (82). Although he, at first, says it's too hot to close the doors to the gallery, Big Daddy does this, "as if he were going to tell an important secret" (90), when he begins to tell Brick that he was afraid he had cancer. The scene between the two of them is constantly interrupted by intrusions, however, twice by Big Mama, whom he finally shouts at to "GIT!– outa here" (103), sending her out sobbing, once by Gooper, twice by children, and once by the Rev. Tooker, who is looking for the bathroom. These intrusions are as annoying for the audience as for the participants and a reminder that privacy is not something that is available in this family, even in one's own bedroom, even for Big Daddy.

In the version of Act Three that Williams said he "much preferred" (*Letters* II: 569), the room becomes a contested site as the family battles for power over Big Daddy and the plantation. This time, it is Mae closing the door, as she and Gooper try to orchestrate the revelation to Big Mama that Big Daddy has terminal cancer without letting Big Daddy hear. Big Mama insists on having the door open, declaring that "nothing's going to be said in Big Daddy's house that he can't hear if he wants to" (133). The family succeeds in "surroundin" Big Mama and making the revelation, with the proceedings spiraling into a fight for control of the estate. Seeking to avoid all of this, Brick keeps escaping to the gallery, but drifts back in toward the end of the scene, singing "Show Me the Way to Go Home." Maggie's announcement that she is pregnant and Big

Mama's departure to tell Big Daddy that his dream has come true ends the battle, with Mae slamming the door to the hall and leaving Brick and Maggie together. Finally, Maggie throws Brick's liquor bottles off the gallery and comes back, closing the door behind her.

The ending of the Broadway version is quoted in the second paragraph of this essay. In the earlier version that Williams preferred, Maggie says, "Brick, I used to think that you were stronger than me and I didn't want to be overpowered by you. But now, since you've taken to liquor—you know what?—I guess it's bad, but now I'm stronger than you and I can love you more truly" (163–64). Brick says finally that he has nothing to say, and Maggie says, "Oh, you weak people, you weak, beautiful people!—who give up.—What you want is someone to . . . take hold of you.—Gently, gently, with love!—And I *do* love you, Brick, I *do*!" (165–66). Echoing Big Daddy's earlier statement about Big Mama, Brick, "smiling with charming sadness," says "Wouldn't it be funny if that was true?" With Maggie's victory and Brick's amiable capitulation, this is a kinder, gentler version of the ending of "Three Players of a Summer Game" and an echo of *Tea and Sympathy,* which was strengthened in the Broadway version, at Elia Kazan's urging, with the line about Maggie handing Brick's life back to him. Like Laura's, Maggie's promise of heterosexual sex represents not only Brick's salvation from the debilitating confusion of the queer space in which he has been contained, but also his defeat and imprisonment within the claustrophobic space of the now "normalized" bedroom.

There is an important difference in the endings in that Anderson intended the viewer to understand that the sexual encounter was a single event, serving to put Tom on the straight road to heterosexuality, while Williams intended a permanent shift in the relationship between Brick and Maggie. Anderson said that he added Laura's famous line after his wife asked him whether they went on to have a love affair. When he wrote the screenplay for the film adaptation, he was even more overt about this, creating a frame that occurs ten years later in which Tom, now married, comes back to the school for a reunion and receives a letter from Laura that explains what has happened since their "afternoon together." In *Cat*, while Williams dropped the vampire imagery and the transformation of Maggie into a "butch" lesbian that is in the story, he still wanted to indicate that the ending implies Brick's surrender to Maggie and the shifting of power in their marriage. As he wrote to his agent, it was not meant to be about "a woman giving a man back his manhood," but about "a vital, strong woman dominating a weak man and achieving her will" (*Letters* II:554). Writing to Kazan during the rehearsal process, he said he had come to believe that "Brick *did* love Skipper" (555, emphasis in original) and that "in the deeper sense, not the literal sense, Brick is a homosexual with a heterosexual adjustment" (556). After his conversation with Big Daddy, "he's faced the truth . . . and maybe the block is broken. I just said maybe. I don't really think so. I think that Brick is doomed by the falsities and cruel prejudices of the world he comes out of, belongs to, the world of Big Daddy and Big Mama" (558). To Williams, the tragedy of *Cat on a Hot Tin Roof* was always the paralysis of Brick, the loss of will, and at the play's end, it is Maggie's will that has taken over. For Williams, Brick is a gay man trapped in a heterosexual marriage, not a straight man who is set free.

Works Cited

Anderson, Robert. *Tea and Sympathy*. 1953. *Famous American Plays of the 1950s*. New York: Dell, 1962. 229–312.

Bryer, Jackson. "Robert Anderson." *Speaking on Stage: Interviews with Contemporary American Playwrights.* Eds. Philip C. Kolin & Colby H. Kullman. Tuscaloosa: U of Alabama P, 1996.

Johnson, Mark. *The Body in the Mind: The Bodily Basis of Meaning, Imagination and Reason.* Chicago: U of Chicago P, 1990.

McConache, Bruce. *American Theater in the Culture of the Cold War: Producing and Contesting Containment, 1947–1962.* Iowa City: U of Iowa P, 2003.

Tea and Sympathy. Screenplay by Robert Anderson. Dir. Vincente Minnelli. Perf. Deborah Kerr, John Kerr, Leif Erickson, and Edward Andrews. MGM, 1956. Film.

Williams, Tennessee. *Cat on a Hot Tin Roof. The Theatre of Tennessee Williams,* Vol. 3. New York: New Directions, 1971. 1–216.

_____. *The Selected Letters of Tennessee Williams: Volume II 1945–1957*. Eds. Albert J. Devlin and Nancy M. Tischler. New York: New Directions, 2004.

_____. "Three Players of a Summer Game." *Tennessee Williams Collected Stories*. New York: New Directions, 1985. 303–25.

Killing the Queen: Yeats, McDonagh, and Punk

Mary M. Burke

> Maybe McDonagh really can do . . . what Johnny Rotten did . . .
> (Sean O'Hagan, "The Wild West")

Cathleen ni Houlihan, an influential one-act play by W.B. Yeats and Lady Gregory, was first staged in 1902 at the very height of the Irish Literary Revival, one of a number of cultural flowerings inspired by Irish nationalism. The title character of *Cathleen ni Houlihan* first appears as an old woman who becomes instantly recognizable as a personification of an Irish nation divested by colonization when she describes how she has been robbed of four "beautiful green fields" (the four Irish provinces). (This language was immediately resonant because it drew upon a rich and long native Irish tradition of personifying the oppressed nation as a wronged woman, often called Cathleen ni Houlihan or Dark Rosaleen.) Cathleen urges young men to sacrifice their lives on her behalf, and mission accomplished, the play closes with the old woman transforming into "a young girl" with "the walk of a queen." *Cathleen ni Houlihan* became the most famous play of the Irish Revival because its highly emotive dénouement held out the promise to the Abbey Theatre's nationalist audience of the revitalization that would occur with Irish independence from Britain. Cathleen was an Irish alternative to the only recently deceased Queen Victoria, and her assurance of Irish sovereignty in the near future (should enough Irish men be willing to sacrifice their lives) also implicitly promised that this reassembled Ireland would be one that would be self-sufficient enough to halt the long tradition of Irish emigration to Britain and elsewhere. In fact, after independence in 1922, when political self-determination did not align with the promised economic success, Irish emigration to England continued apace, peaking successively in the post-war (post-WWII) years, in the 1980s, and again in the first decade of the twenty-first century, in the wake of the collapse of the "Celtic Tiger" economy.

Cathleen ni Houlihan's resonant central image of the nation-as-woman/queen has become one that later generations of Irish dramatists respond to and critique. This exploration will suggest that this image inspired little respect in the drama produced by the conflicted post-war Irish in England in particular, who felt allegiance neither to the motherland they were obliged to leave nor to their adopted mother, Britannia. This outlook will be linked to the punk movement of 1970s Britain, which was arguably one in which the offspring of post-war Irish immigrants played a pivotal role and whose anarchist message was disseminated worldwide by a defaced image of Queen Elizabeth II. Such analysis will be used to contextualize the work of British-Irish playwright Martin McDonagh, who has been repeatedly labelled a "punk playwright," and to suggest that the reduced "queen" of his most iconoclastic play, *The Beauty Queen of Leenane* (1996), negates both the female sovereign of the land of his birth and Yeats and Gregory's seemingly failed Irish alternative. Strikingly, in a 2013 assessment of emigration from Ireland after the founding of the Irish State in 1922, cultural commentator Fintan O'Toole suggests that it is an illusion to believe that Ireland has been reigned over by a reinstated Cathleen ni Houlihan since independence. For this sometime critic of McDonagh, the "public story of liberation from the British empire" is a deceitful veneer that masks a repeated reality: repeated economic crises and the resultant emigration mean that a good many men and women born in Ireland since independence still die as subjects of Queen Elizabeth II:

> [In this] alternative Irish history . . . , there is no break with anything—there is a continuity of mass emigration over centuries. There is no liberation from the British empire. Where are our emigrants still going? To places whose stamps still have Queen Elizabeth's head on them. The biggest long-term impact of the British empire on Ireland was that it opened up places for Irish people to emigrate: North America, Australia, and, of course, Britain itself (O'Toole, "We're Brilliant at Plan B" 12).

In such a telling, the sovereignty of Cathleen ni Houlihan and the putative independence of those who stayed in Ireland was maintained only by sacrificing excess population to the former colonial power. Rather than being the nurturing mother/queen, Ireland is, in the evocative phrase of another famous Irish exile, James Joyce, "the old sow that eats her farrow." In rejecting *Cathleen ni Houlihan* in *The Beauty Queen of Leenane*, McDonagh simultaneously repudiates both the Irish state and the early twentieth-century drama that urged it into existence. In a typically punk maneuver, McDonagh casts himself as one who disrupts rather than maintains tradition, be those traditions respect for one's artistic antecedents or the reflexive patriotism to the motherland expected of the emigrant obliged to leave Ireland.

Exile or Escape? Post-War Irish Emigration to Britain

In 1955, when emigration to England out of the most deprived districts of the rural Irish West was at its height, the Irish government published a report by the Commission on Emigration and Other Population Problems. The commission sat from 1948 until 1954 and was comprised of high-grade and generally Dublin-based civil servants, members of the clergy, and economists. A senior government lawyer and member of the commission quite openly noted, in an addendum to the report, that emigration should be considered a useful tool in the maintenance of the *status quo*:

> I cannot accept . . . the view that a high rate of emigration is necessarily a sign of national decline or that policy should be over anxiously framed to reduce it. . . . In the order of ***values, it seems more*** important to preserve and improve the quality of Irish life . . . ***than it is to reduce*** the numbers of Irish emigrants. . . . High emigration, granted a population excess, ***releases social tensions*** which would otherwise explode and makes possible a stability of manners and customs which would otherwise be the subject of radical change (Fitzgerald 222).

The 1937 Bunreacht na hÉireann/Constitution of Ireland, the replacement for the 1922 Constitution of the Irish Free State, guaranteed that state policy would maintain "on the land in economic security as many families as in the circumstances shall be practicable" (Bunreacht na hÉireann, Article 45.2.v: 150). In hindsight, the final word of the pledge seems to allow for the purging of surplus citizens when required. This semi-official state policy was in stark contrast to the lip-service paid to the tragic nature of emigration in popular culture and by other sectors of the state, which often framed such population loss as unwilling "exile." In the dramas by McDonagh, Frank Carney, and Tom Murphy considered below, bitterness regarding the economic inequalities and policy insufficiencies of home that force the less well-educated and well-connected to emigrate to Britain mean that leaving could well be experienced as a liberating flight from the cruel mother(land) as much as a wrenching departure (Murray 6).

The most striking evidence that the Irish who emigrated to Britain were considered a small loss in Irish elite circles is that they had no commonly agreed-upon designation in Irish public discourse, a fact that speaks to the voicelessness of the constituency. The cover blurb of the 1998 Vintage edition of McDonagh's plays refers to this London-born son of Irish parents as "Anglo-Irish." This designation that will strike a false note with anyone familiar with Irish history, since the designation "Anglo-Irish" actually refers to English settlers in Ireland as well as their descendants. Unlike its American equivalent, members of this population do not present Ireland with a consoling image of what the emigrant from Ireland can achieve. In the popular imagination and in the work of dramatists considered below, this is a grouping associated with high levels of poverty, alcoholism, psychiatric illness, and social isolation. As such, Britain was understood to function as the dumping ground for those who could not fit in at home or who lacked the initiative or capital to make it across the Atlantic.

Irish Emigrants to Britain in Post-War Abbey Theatre Drama: Frank Carney

During the post-war period, when emigration to England was at its highest, some of the most popular productions presented by the state-funded National Theatre—the self-same Abbey—seemed to subtly endorse the view that emigration to England could function as a safety valve, through which to dispose of undesirables. *The Righteous Are Bold*, a 1946 drama set in the present tense by the Tuam-educated Frank Carney, played for one of the longest runs in the history of the Abbey. It centers on Nora Geraty, who has recently returned from England to her modest home in the Irish West in a disturbed condition. Nora is stridently critical of the Irish state, and the action seeks to ascertain whether she is speaking truth to power, merely mentally ill or, as certain locals believe, demonically possessed. The play initially challenges state policies that seem designed to expel the non-conformist and disadvantaged, but closes with a hasty re-affirmation of all that has been interrogated. Although Nora's father appears to be accepting of his lot, it is quickly discovered that his economically unviable holding is actually being maintained by the remittances of his other emigrant children. His farm can only support his unmarried son Patrick, a young man who openly denounces the passivity engendered by a rigid class system and the thriftiness urged upon the poor by the struggling new state. (In a radio address delivered on the religious holiday of St. Patrick's Day in 1943, President Éamon de Valera, a veteran of a 1916 Rising that had promised social as well as political transformation, famously spoke of his ideal Ireland as "the home of a people who valued material wealth only as a basis for right living, of a people . . . satisfied with frugal comfort. . . . " [Lee 334].) On his sister's return, Patrick's rage is directed towards what he perceives to be the Catholic Church's support of the inequitable and stagnant social order conserved by emigration. Although she shares her brother's views, Nora's smashing of a statue of the Virgin Mary is interpreted as an indisputable manifestation on Irish soil of her demonic possession. The Virgin often functioned as a Catholic iteration of Cathleen ni Houlihan in a mid-century Ireland, in which devoutness had become deeply entwined with nationalism, and the generally pious Abbey audience of the time reacted with great disturbance to this scene. Moreover, Nora's vulnerability to demonic possession as an emigrant to England would have made sense to a mid-century audience schooled by sermons that painted secular Britain as a godless space in which Irish emigrants often "lost their religion," which in the socio-political context of the period, amounted to an abjuration of the mother culture. The play closes with Nora's exorcism, and the previously atheistic Patrick appears to have a kind of conversion experience on witnessing the event, after which the siblings recant their quasi-socialist critiques of Church and state. Carney's drama began by addressing the most challenging issues confronting the new state: high rates of psychiatric illness among the emigrant cohort in England, institutional and popular sanction of emigration, reliance on delayed marriage and remittance as economic policy, prejudice against returned emigrants, and individual and collective acceptance of Church domination. Nevertheless, the drama ultimately concludes with an explanation of supernatural agency that reinstates a reactionary and fundamentalist Catholic worldview.

Irish Emigrants in Britain in Post-War London Drama: Tom Murphy

The protest of the post-war Irish emigrant to Britain ultimately stifled in Carney's play, for the National Theatre in Dublin later bellowed loudly on the London stage, however. Tom Murphy's *A Whistle in the Dark*, set in a violent Irish immigrant enclave in Coventry, England, was one the first Irish dramas to unconditionally critique the manner in which the former colonial power was used by the new Irish state as a dumping ground for its unwanted citizens. The Tuam, County Galway-born Murphy was nine years old when his father emigrated to England in 1944. Murphy himself also spent some time as an emigrant in England as a young man, as did a number of his nine siblings. It is notable, in light of the success and final message of *The Righteous Are Bold,* that Murphy had originally submitted *A Whistle in the Dark* to the National Theatre, but was rejected by its then Managing Director, Ernest Blythe. *A Whistle in the Dark* eventually premièred at the Theatre Royal, Stratford East in London in 1961, and Blythe was famously overheard disparaging the play as "rubbish" when it transferred to the Olympia Theatre in Dublin a year later, a production that many Irish commentators interpreted as a London-facilitated racial slur on Irish manhood rather than a critique of Ireland's use of nearby England as a dumping ground for undesirables.

A Whistle in the Dark centers on the West-of-Ireland Carney clan, consisting of Dada (that is, Daddy) and his five sons, and their troubled relations with both their urban English host community and other Irish immigrants in Coventry. The victims of class prejudice in their Irish hometown, the Carney men have begun to enact the barbarity they have been unjustly accused of all their lives. Theirs is a squalid and chaotic world in which the moderating presence of the mother or any other female is entirely rejected, symbolic of the manner in which these immigrants have been spurned by both host and birth nation. The Carneys have internalized the incivility projected onto them by more respectable elements in *both* their Irish hometown and adopted post-war English city; Ireland, as much as England, has coarsened these men. It was this clear-eyed assessment of how emigrants to England of that generation were neither mourned at home nor warmly welcomed by Mother England that made *A Whistle in the Dark* so controversial in an Ireland in which it was convenient for those who could afford to stay behind to speak of emigration in the sentimental language of exile and lamentation.

Murphy went on the write a number of plays centered on Irish emigrants throughout his career, and it is striking that in *A Whistle in the Dark* and his later "emigrant dramas," his inarticulate male characters are generally more liable to suddenly burst into a snatch of sentimental emigrant ballad than they are to speak coherently of their anger towards the rejecting mother/land. The ferociously abrupt song snatches of Murphy's emigrant characters and the fact that such singing is often accompanied by sudden violence point to the antipathy that lies beneath the consolatory balladry of exile, which was often the only expression of emigrant sentiments recognized by those "at home." On some level, these emigrants understand that they are disposable, a hard truth masked by the syrupy language of the emigrant ballad that can only be revealed by a spitting singing style. The guttural intonations of Murphy's emigrants are precursors to the sounds of punk that were to explode in London in the 1970s. Murphy depicts the inarticulate protests of the post-war generation of West-of-Ireland immigrants in England, who would birth some of the central figures of punk music and, in the case of Martin McDonagh, *the* "punk dramatist" himself.

Contemporary London-Irish Drama and Punk: Martin McDonagh

In terms of generation, background, favored themes, and a shared initial rejection by the Abbey Theatre, Martin McDonagh and his work might be said to be Tom Murphy's offspring. McDonagh was born in London in 1970 and raised in London-Irish, working-class enclaves by his West-of-Ireland parents. Their jobs were typical of the kind of work found by disadvantaged post-war Irish emigrants to London: his Galway father worked in construction; his Sligo mother was a part-time cleaner. McDonagh's postmodern dramas, which draw equally on the grotesques who people J. M. Synge's Revival drama and the stylized violence and referential nature of contemporary filmmakers, such as Quentin Tarantino, persistently examine the fractured and globalized nature of contemporary Irish identity, which is traced in his work as being in no small part due to the history and impact of emigration to Britain and America. Indeed, McDonagh himself embodies this fractured identity: though repeatedly critiqued and marketed as an "Irish playwright" and as someone who draws from time spent with his grandparents in the West of Ireland during childhood summers, he is of course, culturally British. As he notes in a 2001 interview, "I don't feel I have to defend myself for being English or for being Irish, because, in a way, I don't feel either. And, in another way, of course, I'm both" (O'Hagan 32). This lack of allegiance to either world finds its way into *Beauty Queen*, in a poignant scene in which Pato, an Irish emigrant vacationing in the Irish West, describes (in the heightened Hiberno-English dialect of Synge) the confusion "coming home" engenders: "***And when I'm over there in London and working in rain and it's more or less cattle I am*** . . . it's here I wish I was. . . . But when ***it's here*** I am . . . it isn't *there **I want to be**.* . . . But I know it isn't *here I want to be* either" (McDonagh scene 3, 31). In a similar refusal of attachment, McDonagh notes that he is not "into ... any kind of -ism, politically, socially, religiously. ..." (O'Toole, "Nowhere Man" 1).

Punk music emerged in London in the 1970s as self-consciously working-class anti-art. It was played in a loud, fast, and rasping style, and the shouted lyrics were deliberately offensive and provocatively anti-establishment. At its "purest," punk was ideologically opposed to skilful musicianship as bourgeois affectation. In short, any quick definition of the genre could easily be applied to McDonagh's positioning of himself within the broader Irish-British dramatic tradition; in interviews given just after he had exploded onto the scene with a series of well-crafted plays in the mid-1990s, McDonagh claimed to have hardly ever attended theatre, and when asked what he thought of canonical dramatist David Hare's *Skylight* on its opening night in 1996, McDonagh replied, "Well, I didn't write it so it's crap" (Eyre 364). Such iconoclasm ensured that the label "punk" quickly attached itself to the young playwright, and McDonagh has explicitly invoked the Sex Pistols in discussing the confrontational nature of his work (O'Hagan 32) and noted recently that theatre had seemed "upper-class" and "dull" when he was younger, which drove him to "come at it with a punk rock attitude" (Booth online).

However, McDonagh can be linked to punk in terms of his social and cultural roots as much as his dismissive attitude to canonical drama. The most influential punk band of all time, the short-lived Sex Pistols, was formed in London in 1975, and the articulate and politically radical lead singer's background was strikingly similar to that of McDonagh. Johnny Rotten was born John Joseph Lydon in an Irish community in London in 1956 to working-class Irish parents; if Murphy might have been McDonagh's father, then Lydon could have been his older brother. (Strikingly, the punk singer's father hailed from Murphy's hometown of Tuam.) Like McDonagh, Lydon spent every childhood summer in a modest farm house in rural Ireland, and as in the case of the playwright, this continual back-and-forth across the Irish Sea between underdeveloped and depopulated rural Ireland and the largest and most diverse city in England seems to have engendered a critical distance from both countries. Lydon's awareness of the prejudice against Irish immigrants in the period his parents settled in London is reflected in the subtitle of his autobiography, *Rotten: No Irish, No Blacks, No Dogs*; the title references the kinds of signs found in urban English boarding house windows in the 1950s and 1960s, when discrimination against Irish immigrants was rife.

The Sex Pistols' second single, "God Save the Queen," was released during Queen Elizabeth II's Silver Jubilee in 1977. The single's raucous soundscape and post-Empire lyrics ("God save the queen/She ain't no human being/There is no future/In England's dreaming") was condemned as an attack on the monarchy, while its then-shocking cover of a mutilated image of the Queen has functioned ever since as visual shorthand for the whole punk scene. What is often left unremarked is that anti-monarchism was extremely common among the London Irish in the 1970s, whose antipathy was often directed at *both* the former colonial power and an Irish state that had failed them. (An added complication was the IRA's bombing campaign in 1970s London—mocked in the 2001 McDonagh play, *The Lieutenant of Inishmore*—which contributed to anti-Irish immigrant sentiment.)

Religious as a child while enrolled at Catholic school, McDonagh traces the stirrings of his art and his loss of faith at the age of twelve to "listening to his brother's punk-rock records. . . ." In particular, McDonagh's exposure to London-Irish punk band Pogues, The, whose members married the violent energy of the Sex Pistols with traditional Irish music, showed him that he could "make use" of his heritage: "Just as the Pogues set harsh new lyrics to old Irish tunes, McDonagh's plays subject the pieties of Irish Catholicism and nationalism to impudent satire." (O'Toole, *A Mind in Connemara* 40).

McDonagh shares Lydon's disdain for the Irish priests they were both educated by in London Catholic schools, though McDonagh's tone is merely derisive in comparison to Lydon's deep bitterness. However, the very "punk" anti-monarchist streak in McDonagh's persona highlights the manner in which he rejects the sacred cows of British as well as Irish culture. In 1996, when he attended the prestigious *London Evening Standard* Theatre Awards ceremony to collect the Most Promising Playwright Prize, he refused to toast Queen Elizabeth II and, thereby, got into an altercation with actor Sean Connery that made the tabloids. Defending his response later, McDonagh asked, "Do these people take no account of how many people in there were actually British, let alone how many even supported [the Queen]?" (O'Hagan 32). Nevertheless, Irish shibboleths remain the usual target of McDonagh's dramas.

Killing the Irish and British Queens: McDonagh's *Beauty Queen of Leenane*

The action of *The Beauty Queen of Leenane* takes place in the 1990s, and it is one of a number of McDonagh plays set in Connemara, the rugged region on Ireland's west coast. In a ruthless reprimand to its bucolic image in tourism brochures and sentimentalizing Revival depictions, the McDonagh's Connemara could be mistaken for the punk scene of a 1970s London, rife with high unemployment and social unrest: it is an anarchic, unprincipled wasteland in which authority has collapsed and visceral violence is commonplace. *Beauty Queen* blends black comedy, tragedy, and a self-consciously melodramatic plot, full of deceptions, secrets, betrayals, and turnabouts that reference Shakespeare, *Psycho*, and cheesy daytime soap operas of the kind enjoyed by the play's characters. The action takes place in a shabby cottage kitchen, whose soundscape of Australian soaps and sentimental Irish ballads blaring from the TV and radio signifies the play's postmodern mash-up of a century of Irish drama with a contemporary globalized Ireland. The idealized coastal Irish cottage settings of Revival staples, such as *Cathleen ni Houlihan*, which served as backdrops with which to highlight the unadorned nobility of peasant culture, are undercut by the play's crowded kitchen setting, which amplifies mother and daughter Mag and Maureen's claustrophobic mutual hatred. Maureen takes care of the manipulative Mag because her other sisters refuse to deal with the difficult old woman. Mag is the Joycean sow, who eats her farrow, the devouring Mother Ireland who drives her children away or drives the only one who returns to hatred. Like Nora Geraty in *The Righteous Are Bold*, forty-year-old Maureen has been forced to return to the parental home as a result of psychiatric illness, and she is emotionally tormented about this and her other failings by her malicious mother. The disconnect between idealizing literary depictions in the service of cultural nationalism and the harsh reality of Connemara's poverty and high emigration rates underlines an exchange Maureen recalls from her immigrant days working as a cleaner in urban England, when she experienced the anti-Irish prejudice that likely contributed to her subsequent incarceration in an English psychiatric hospital:

> "Get back to that backward fecking pigsty of yours or whatever hole it was you drug yourself out of." Half of the swearing I didn't even understand I had to have a black woman [and fellow cleaner] explain it to me. . . . And a ***calendar with a picture of Connemara*** on I showed her one day, and "What the hell have you left there for?" she said (McDonagh, Scene 4: 44).

The mother-daughter antipathy comes to a histrionic head when the incensed daughter fatally injures her mother, and it is a mark of McDonagh's skill as a (melo)dramatist that audiences generally find Maureen sympathetic. The grotesquely unmaternal Mag undermines the ideal of the passive, suffering Catholic mother, who was a common personification of Ireland/ Cathleen in twentieth-century Irish culture. Mag practices poor hygiene, simulates invalidity in order to torment Maureen, and undermines her daughter's attempt at happiness by spitefully revealing Maureen's prior hospitalization to potential suitor Pato. Unfulfilled by his life as an immigrant construction worker in England, Pato seems to be urging Maureen to emigrate to America with him, which underlines the often hidden truth that emigration functioned as escape as often as it was experienced as "exile." As Pato notes in reference to the social control of Leenane, "In England they don't care if you live or die, and . . . that isn't altogether a bad thing" (McDonagh Scene 3, 32). In a moment of tenderness, Mag is referred to as a "beauty queen" by Pato, a title that may be somewhat pitying, given her age and doleful situation. This designation gains ironic resonance at the dénouement, with its explicit echo of the revelation of the queen that closes *Cathleen ni Houlihan.*

As well as undermining sanctified Mother Ireland in the play, McDonagh attacks hypocrisy regarding the mother tongue, which became intrinsic to the official ideology of the Irish state after independence. One of the more ambitious aims of the Revival was to spread Irish (Gaelic) as a means of general social intercourse. Irish was the native language that had been largely pushed to the most isolated regions of the western seaboard, such as Connemara, after the Famine. As a result, the Irish language and the use of Hiberno-English (the Irish dialect of English that utilized Gaelic syntax) were considered more "authentic" than Standard English by Revival dramatists, such as Yeats and Gregory. After independence, a state language policy that made Irish mandatory at all education levels and enabled fluency in the language as a shortcut to career advancement within the public sector, politicized and fetishized the language as a marker of cultural authenticity available only to the well-educated or those fortunate enough to hail from the deprived, Irish-speaking West (Burke 67). Part of the fallout of this vocabulary of cultural and linguistic purity was the inference that speaking "the conqueror's language" (English) or making one's home in Britain was unpatriotic. This insinuation became a source of conflict for the economically marginalized citizen who had no choice but to emigrate in order to make a living, particularly if that emigrant happened to be from one of the *Gaeltachtaí*, the Irish-speaking western districts that received state attention due to their status as repositories for the native tongue. It should be stressed that the Leenane of McDonagh's title is a small town in Connemara, the most fetishized *Gaeltacht* of the Irish mainland. In light of such facts, Mag and Maureen's extraordinary exchange regarding what would, in all likelihood, have been the first language of many residents of Leenane even into the 1990s, amounts to an extremely provocative attempt on McDonagh's behalf to mock the hypocrisy of post-independence policies regarding the mother tongue and emigration:

MAG: It's Irish you should be speaking in Ireland.

MAUREEN: . . . Except where would Irish get you going for a job in England? Nowhere.

. . .

MAG: If it wasn't for the English stealing our language, and our land, and our God-knows-what, wouldn't it be we wouldn't need to go over there begging for jobs and for handouts?

MAUREEN: *(Pause.)* Except America, too. . . . If it was to America you had to go begging for handouts, it isn't Irish would be any good to you (McDonagh, Scene I: 8–9).

McDonagh's reduced queen hails from a region in which inhabitants were privileged by the official state language policy, but implicitly considered disposable according to state policy on emigration. (I actually attended the original 1996 Druid Theatre/ Royal Court production in the West-of-Ireland capital city, Galway, which prides itself as being the most "Gaelic" city in contemporary Ireland in terms of the use and promotion of the Irish language. This exchange was met with stony silence by the Galway audience, a stark contrast to how the play's sharp humor was otherwise received.) The hypocritical nature of post-independent language and emigration policy reveal the mother (land) to be one who dissimulates. She must be violently murdered, even if, in McDonagh's nihilist and postmodern punk vision, no alternate future is proffered other than a repetition of events. In an image that simultaneously recalls the most resonant visual in Hitchcock's *Psycho* and the final scene of *Cathleen ni Houlihan*, the close of *Beauty Queen* sees Maureen transforming into what Pato's brother Ray calls the "'exact fecking image'" of the mother she has murdered: she sits in her mother's chair and orders Ray about in the manner of her dead parent, even as she forgets his name, precisely as Mag used to do (McDonagh, Scene 9: 83). Just as an oppressive state and Church apparatus stepped into the vacuum left after the withdrawal of the British in 1922, the successive governments of the seemingly failed independent Irish state are destined to merely replace one degenerate queen/bad mother with another, time after time. The mother gets murdered, only to return, more grotesque than ever. Various Cathleens replace Victoria, but social exclusion and emigration to Britain continues, regardless of which queen rules. The close of *Beauty Queen* explicitly reverses the movement towards a renewed future promised by Yeats and Gregory. The "beauty queen" becomes her aged mother rather than the more youthful self that was a fleeting possibility when Pato seemed to offer the hope of change, and in so doing, closes off any possibility of transformation or escape.

Works Cited

Booth, William. "Dripping Blood in the Snow." *Washington Post* 21 Jan. 2008. Web. 14 February 2014.

Bunreacht na hÉireann / Constitution of Ireland. 1937. Dublin: Stationery Office, 1964.

Burke, Mary. "Synge, Evolutionary Theory, and the Irish Language." *Synge and His Influences: Centenary Essays from the Synge Summer School*. Ed. Patrick Lonergan. Dublin: Carysfort P, 2011. 55–71.

Eyre, Richard. *National Service: Diary of a Decade at the National Theatre*. London: Bloomsbury, 2004.

Fitzgerald, Alexis. "***Reservation No. 2***." [Appendix to] *Report of the Commission on Emigration and Other Population Problems*. Dublin: The Stationery Office, 1955. 222.

Lee, Joseph. *Ireland 1912–1985: Politics and Society*. Cambridge: Cambridge UP, 1990.

Lydon, John (a.k.a. Johnny Rotten), Keith Zimmerman, & Kent Zimmerman. *Rotten: No Irish, No Blacks, No Dogs*. New York: St. Martin's P, 1994.

McDonagh, Martin. *The Beauty Queen of Leenane*. The Beauty Queen of Leenane *and Other Plays*. New York: Vintage, 1998. 1–84.

Murrary, Tony. *London Irish Fictions*. Liverpool: Liverpool UP, 2012.

O'Hagan, Sean. "The Wild West." *Guardian* 23 March 2001: 32.

O'Toole, Fintan. "Nowhere Man." *Irish Times. Weekend* supplement. 26 April, 1997, 1.

_____. "A Mind in Connemara." *New Yorker*. 6 March 2006. 82.3: 40.

_____. "We're Brilliant at Plan B." *Irish Times* 31 Dec. 2013:12.

A Road More Travelled: Gay and Lesbian Lives in Irish Fiction Since 1989

Rachael Sealy Lynch

Early Journeys

A reader browsing the fiction shelves in a bookstore in Ireland today is very likely to pick up a novel containing at least one prominent gay or lesbian character. Jennifer Johnston, Colm Tóibín, and Emma Donoghue, to name but three important and widely-read contemporary authors, portray gay and lesbian lives in much of their work. In this fiction, "out" characters are increasingly presented as men and women living their lives, interacting with their families, falling in love, making mistakes, and growing as individuals, exactly like their peers. They just happen not to be heterosexual. However, while Irish novels have featured homosexual characters since at least the early years of the twentieth century, the way in which these characters' stories are told has changed significantly.

In order to realize how substantially contemporary gay and lesbian Irish fiction has evolved, we need a little earlier context for comparison. In her seminal essay, "A Trackless Road: Irish Nationalism and Lesbian Writing," Ann Owens Weekes writes eloquently of these early days, arguing that not even the decriminalization of male homosexual acts in Ireland in 1993 initially made much of a difference, especially to lesbians, who were never "criminalized under the British legal codes that the Free State adopted" (123). Weekes argues that in fact, "Lack of criminalization was not a sign of acceptance, of course, but a negation of women's agency . . . the suppression of women in Irish law is mirrored by the almost complete absence of lesbian characters from Irish fiction in general" (123). She does, however, allow that "the slim thread of lesbian fiction courageously questions, leads, and participates in a dialog with Irish society, whose changing perceptions as regards sexuality precede the legal revolution and emerge in the fiction" (123). Weekes discusses several key early fictional lesbian figures, including Marda in Elizabeth Bowen's *The Last September* (1929), Jessica in Molly Keane's *Devoted Ladies* (1934), and Agatha in Kate O'Brien's *Mary Lavelle* (1937). It is notable, however, that Marda and Agatha live their lives outside Ireland, and Jessica self-destructs. The climate for these lesbian characters was equally unfriendly in the real world; a later Kate O'Brien novel, *Land of Spices* (1941), was banned by the Censorship Board in 1942. Weekes attributes the chilliness and suppression lasting through the 1950s to the effects of President Éamonn de Valera's 1937 Constitution, which "dismissed women's concerns with respect to sexuality and denied them agency" (130). The Constitution's focus on home and traditional family values, and on the centrality of Roman Catholicism, had a smothering effect on homosexual expression.

Attempts to legislate for compulsory heteronormativity are of course implausible and doomed to fail, as Irish writers have long been well aware. Jennifer Johnston recognizes the inherent impossibility in such a project, and *This Is Not a Novel* makes a powerful case for the dangers, indeed impossibility, of suppression, and the need to address openly what the narrator's closeted father refers to as the "longings down all the years that I have not dared to face, that even now I cannot write down" (166). While this novel was written in 2002, the narrator is looking back at events that culminated with her brother's disappearance in the pre-Dorcey climate of 1970. The narrative's interrogation of homosexuality makes two key points: that disgust, shame, and references to disease are not useful or appropriate responses and that suppression and attempts at eradication are doomed to fail. Johnston emphasizes these points via a multigenerational narrative, in the course of which she portrays three gay Irish men from the same family. The first, Harry, has been sent to Rugby, the elite British boarding school, from which he is expelled for "performing frequently gross, shameful homosexual acts" (174). Harry's case is apparently so woeful that only death at Suvla Bay in 1915 can finally eradicate the contagion rampant in his body. As the headmaster wrote, "Homosexuality is a sickness that must be stamped out" (174). Harry's father feels that participation in The Great War "will make a man of him," and if death is the price of manhood, so be it (176). Given the "possibility of future intolerable scandal brought on the whole family," the only way open to Harry to "purge his sin" is "by going to fight for his country" (64).

However, the family secret refuses to be buried, and we witness, following Freud, a return of the repressed a generation later, in the person of the narrator's father. He makes every possible attempt to stifle his self-knowledge: marrying, having children, and living a respectable upper-middle class existence as a doctor. Yet the "longings down all the years" cannot be extinguished, and although nothing is ever openly acknowledged, even by the narrator herself, Edward Bailey shares the end of his life with "a quiet middle-aged man called Gregory" (61). In a desperate attempt to expunge his nature, Edward cleans house, as it were, by attempting to force his son Johnny to be what he himself could not. Johnny, like his great uncle Harry, is a champion swimmer, and his father is determined that he will compete in the next Olympics. However, there exists a fatal hitch to Edward's plan: Johnny is also gay, and less adept than his father in the practice of closeted behavior. Distraught at the messy disintegration of his relationship with his lover Bruno, and left without direction or hope for the future, Johnny swims out to sea, never to return. The multigenerational familial gay connection running from Harry through Edward to Johnny suggests powerfully that the "sickness" of homosexuality cannot, in fact, be stamped out, and attempts to do so are worse than futile. It cannot be excluded from nor contained within an institution like Rugby, or, as Edward discovers, marriage. In a symbolic paying forward, inevitable eruptions continue to recur.

1989—A Changing Landscape

Mary Dorcey is a towering transitional figure in the Irish fictional landscape. Weekes stresses the novelty and power of Dorcey's 1989 collection of short stories, writing that "*A Noise from the Woodshed* burst triumphantly upon the scene, joyfully presenting the delight of lesbian love and heralding alternatives that the 1993 law would uphold" (146). Lesbian desire is uncloaked in these stories, and, as Weekes notes, Dorcey gives full weight both to its "addictive nature" and its "cost in terms of lack of comprehension, ridicule, and violence" (147). Weekes places Dorcey in the context of emerging Irish women's and gay rights movements from the 1960s through the 1980s, granting her pride of place: " . . . although the stage was prepared by 'shifts in perception,' Dorcey is braver than any of her predecessors in her refusal to go gently, to make her lesbianism or her radicalism palatable to heterosexuals" (147). Furthermore, as Weekes stresses, Dorcey integrates her lesbian characters "into a wide spectrum of Irish life . . . the whole panoply of Irish life in the 1970s and 1980s" (147). Looking back now, twenty-five years later, we can identify this key shift into the mainstream as the beginning of a new, inclusive portrayal of gay and lesbian lives in Irish fiction.

The eponymous noise from the woodshed is the sound of lesbians making love, initially alarming and unrecognizable even to other lesbians. It serves as a fitting metaphor for emergent self-awareness and for early eruptions of lesbian sexuality into the public sphere. One of the listening lesbian characters notes, "We should have known . . . I mean recognized it. . . . It wasn't, after all, for the want of hearing it" (16). Two stories from this collection, "The Husband" and "Introducing Nessa," serve as particularly useful illustrations of Dorcey's concerns, amplifying and elucidating these intoxicating, frightening sounds. The focalizing husband, in the story named for him, also hears the sounds and is appalled: "like cats in heat!" (73). He is caught in the crosshairs of his wife's discovery of her sexuality and does not fare well as they contemplate the virtually trackless road before them. Yet he is not portrayed as a villain. He is intelligent, educated, willing to try to understand, and deeply invested in a marriage that has brought him much happiness. "He would always be grateful for what he had discovered with her" (69). Both husband and wife are shown to be struggling with old habits after years of wedlock, finding it extremely difficult to slough off years of comfortable marital performance. Martina offers her body to her husband on the very day she leaves; she continues to brew coffee and bake bread right up until the end; and when she does leave, "her lips were white" (80) and her wedding ring still on her finger. However, for her, the way is clear; a new climate that has rendered such discovery imaginable has made her aware that she is attracted to women, and she has found a new partner.

Possibility for Martina cannot be other than abandonment and betrayal for her spouse. Seized in turn by disbelief, anger, clichéd thinking, hope, and denial, the husband finds that his own well-worn patriarchal prejudices impede any chance of epiphanic breakthrough. He is convinced that any right-thinking person, and Irish law, will be on his side and deny Martina custody of their daughter: "The instant they discovered the truth, who and what she had left him for, they would snatch Lisa from her as ruthlessly as they would from quicksand" (67). He relies upon a sense of certainty that he is "normal" (70), wronged, and in the right, and he clings with desperation to the notion that Martina is in the grip of a temporary bout of insanity and will return to him because she "was too fundamentally healthy, and too fond of the admiration of men" (70). His stance is understandable, given his lack of tools with which to address the situation, but it is not productive.

We meet Anna in "Introducing Nessa" after she has left her marriage, which she does before she experiences the consciousness-raising that leads, in turn, to her discovery of her lesbian identity. When Anna returns to Ireland with her daughter at the end of a five-year marriage in Canada, she is shocked at how "women were treated here: the patronage and contempt that were a part of daily life" (135). Her sense of injustice leads her to a women's group, where, she says, "in the company of women who were self-sufficient, self-directed, who . . . bestowed on each other an authority nowhere else given to women, I felt an amazed elation, a sense of coming home, though it was a home I could not have imagined" (136). She meets and falls in love with Nessa and, intoxicated with previously unimaginable bliss, ignores Nessa's warnings of the rocky road ahead: "It's going to be hard for you when they start demanding lies" (133). Anna learns a new language of lesbian love and desire. "I would stare back into the glass and slowly shape the words: love, lover, in love, rehearsing them as though they were not the most commonplace in the language, but rather phrases of initiation to some secret rite" (140). As her story progresses, Nessa's predictions come true and

Anna increasingly chooses secrecy, to the point where her way forward is entirely blocked. She is out only to Nessa and the group, and the ugly climax to the story comes when she betrays and denies her lover to visiting friends from Canada.

However, despite all of Anna's fear and missteps, the ending of this story leaves us in the realm of hope, even joy. Anna is shown to be wrong in her continued adherence to patriarchal beliefs mirroring those of Martina's husband. One of her greatest fears is that discovery of her affair with Nessa will cause her to lose her daughter (who, as the action unfolds, is spending the vacation in Canada with her father). In fact, what her friends Ben and Karen come to tell her is that her ex-husband Harry has come out as gay. Faced with Anna's self-protective wall, Karen—who, despite Anna's best efforts, completely understands the situation—tells Nessa instead.

The story ends with Anna's experiencing an epiphany, realizing with a jolt that "she had sold herself" to earn the approbation of "solid citizens" she did not even know. She asks herself, "Was she prepared to trade everything she had discovered, to keep a little corner in their world private, safe, accepted?" (155). Her answer to this potentially life-altering question is implicit in her courageous telephone call to Nessa and the potent connection between the two after Nessa tells Anna Harry's news. "And so, there they were . . . holding tight to their receivers and carried over the distance; bouncing, gushing like water, unstoppable, laughter ran along the wires that joined them" (159).

With her 1989 collection of short stories, Dorcey opened the floodgates, enabling successors like Emma Donoghue and Colm Tóibín to gush, unstoppable, behind her. Both these writers inherit from Dorcey a sense of legitimacy and an inclusiveness of approach. Their gay and lesbian characters seek and find visibility and sure footing in a world in which their sexual expression is still not the norm. However, the Ireland in which these characters live is shown to be increasingly accepting of their choices. Donoghue gratefully identifies Dorcey as her guide and enabler, noting that "Since Dorcey's ground-breaking collection, fictional Irishwomen have been kissing other women all over the place" ("Noises" 167).

Dorcey's writing profoundly impacted and encouraged Donoghue, helping her to answer the question "How is a woman who loves women to live as an Irishwoman?" (Quinn 147). Donoghue found in Dorcey somebody to show her the way: "*A Noise from the Woodshed* ... fell into my hands like a gift the year I was coming out in College and needed to know that 'lesbian writer' was not a limiting label" ("Noises" 166). While this essay focuses on Donoghue's 2007 novel *Landing*, her earlier novels *Stir-Fry* and *Hood* also represent stages in the Irish writerly journey towards the eradication of such limiting labels. In *Stir-Fry*, the focus is on lesbian self-discovery, while *Hood*, narrated by the lesbian character Penelope, or Pen, charts her coming to terms with her grief at the loss of her partner Cara in an environment where her bereavement does not count as significant in the way it would be had she and Cara been a heterosexual married couple. While Pen is still in the closet at work (like Anna, she teaches in a convent school), she gradually comes out to a fellow teacher and also realizes, belatedly, that Mr. Wall, her partner's father, has known all along. Pen is seeking a way to live as a lesbian in Ireland on her own terms, not an easy task as she does not feel that she shares much in common with high-visibility communities of women, like the Amazon Attic, of which Cara was a core member. We leave Pen as she is about to come out to her mother, thinking to herself as she prepares to open up, "This birth is long overdue, mother. It'll be a tight squeeze. You'd better open your arms to this screaming red bundle, because it's the only one I'll ever bring you" (309).

Take-off and *Landing*

Very recent and contemporary Irish fiction continues, unsurprisingly, to place an increasing focus on a range of sexualities. Gay, lesbian, and bisexual characters are no longer shocking or unexpected to us or to those with whom they share the pages of the narratives that tell their stories. Colm Tóibín's *The Blackwater Lightship* (1999) is a fine example of a novel in which gay characters move towards inclusion in an Ireland that is still struggling to weave alternate sexualities into its societal fabric. However, here Tóibín is more concerned with the universal than he is with the particular, interrogating love, abandonment, grief, and loss. His characters, whatever their sexual orientation, grapple with very similar issues, and help one another to understand and come to terms with their situations. An extended family and an assortment of friends come together to allow Declan, a young man dying of AIDS, a final visit to his grandmother's house, where he spent a key portion of his childhood. Two gay characters, Declan and François, struggle with loss and a sense of abandonment after the death of one or both parents, but so does Declan's sister Helen, through whom the story is focalized. After their father's death from cancer when they were both still children, and without the chance for goodbyes, Declan seeks refuge in commitment-free promiscuity, while Helen spends years mired in bitterness and anger towards her mother and grandmother and afraid to love her husband without reservation. She tells Paul, Declan's friend and François' partner, "I associated love with loss, that's what I did. And the only way that I could live with Hugh and bring up my children was to keep my mother and my grandmother away from me" (188). She explains the psychic damage she has incurred: "I had put away parts of myself that were damaged and left them rotting" (187). It is only when Helen confronts this damage that she can begin to free herself from years of unhappiness. After Helen's mother Lily shares with her daughter her inability to cope with her husband's illness and death, and the reasons why she had sent Helen and Declan to live with their grandparents, Helen finally comes to the understanding of the situation she had so badly needed. "There's something I never realized before, that's just struck me now," Helen tells her mother, "I've always believed that you took him away and you never brought him back. I know it's irrational, but that's what it was, that's what I felt" (245).

    The gay experience in this novel is of real intrinsic importance to the narrative. Most notably, perhaps, Tóibín portrays the continuing difficulties experienced by gay Irish men as they come out, right into the 1990s. Declan does not come out to his mother or grandmother until close to death, and Lily's initial response to the news makes it clear that his reservations were justified. Paul describes the homophobic prejudice to which he is subjected at school, and

Declan's friend Larry narrates, with poignant hilarity, his outing on national television. He recounts his inclusion in President Mary Robinson's landmark invitation of "gay men and lesbians to Áras an Uachtaráin," the presidential residence (144). This actual December 1992 event is credited by Weekes with "setting the mood for the nation" as the gay movement in Ireland gained ground (144). In Larry's telling, faced with an appearance on the six o'clock news in front of his parents, in a family where his siblings, "even the married ones—still haven't told my parents that they are heterosexual," he rushed home and "stood like an eejit in front of the television," trying to prevent their seeing the news (145–46). His final wry comment on the situation is that had he been discovered to be in the Irish Republican Army the news would have been "more normal" (146).

Yet at the heart of this narrative, binding all the characters together, is what Helen identifies as "this web of unresolved connections" (232). Gay or straight, we are bound by our humanity, and Declan's grandmother responds to his dying loneliness as one human being to another. Upon learning that he has no partner, Dora responds, "sadly," that Declan has "nobody of his own, and that's why he came down here. I didn't understand that before, Helen, we'll have to do everything we can for him" (130). Such human warmth grants this often tortured narrative a note of optimism.

Emma Donoghue's *Landing* (2007), which is set in the final years of the economic boom in Celtic Tiger Ireland), grants its gay and lesbian characters the freedom to live their lives as people who happen to be homosexual. Nobody comes out in the course of this narrative, and Dublin is portrayed as a city where a lesbian can—for the most part—live, work, and recreate in a supportive, accommodating atmosphere. Síle Sunita Siobhán O'Shaughnessey is not only lesbian but also biracial; her mother, "Sunita Pillay, glamorous Air India stew" (311), died when Síle was three. Síle does not completely escape homophobia or xenophobic racism, but the manifestations are relatively infrequent and not at the forefront of the narrative. For example, when Síle kisses her visiting Canadian lover, Jude Turner, as they wait in the rain for a cab, "drunken lads started making mwah-mwah sounds" (186). However, the lovers outface the threat: "Síle went on kissing her. Now one of the guys was pretending to puke. Síle tucked her arm tightly through Jude's and stared ahead at the taxis" (186). The most confrontational moment in Dublin occurs between lesbians at a gay club when Síle's ex, Kathleen, turns her fury on Jude, and the worst instance of gay-bashing occurs, ironically, outside a Detroit bar after Jude and Síle break up. Jude has been drowning her sorrows with her ex (but still legal husband) Rizla, and she is mistaken for a man. "I guess getting gay-bashed has novelty value," the strictly heterosexual Rizla comments later in the hospital. 'Next time we go out I'm making you wear a skirt and heels. I can't believe we got taken for a couple of fags!' (273).

Rizla is not initially comfortable when his bisexual wife leaves him, putting a fist through a wall when he first hears that his "wife [is] a dyke" (272). Other instances of biphobia occur in the novel, too, most notably when Síle expresses extreme discomfort with Jude's past: "I thought you were a dyke. So you're still bi, is that what you are telling me?" (137). Síle is clearly still limited by binary thinking, despite having come so far herself.

Yet, at its core, this novel interrogates the importance of place and the nature of love far more than it does sexual orientation and gender identity and expression. Síle and particularly Jude are comfortable with their sexuality, although they display marked differences in its expression, in part because Síle is fourteen years older. As she comments to Jude, "It's two generations, musically and demographically: I'm a tail-end Boomer and you're Gen Y" (122). Also the rural Canadian Quaker community, in which Jude came of age, is markedly more tolerant than was Síle's Ireland. Síle provides Jude with an account of her lesbian journey, stretching back to an initial conscious-raising experience that she describes as "a dramatic and somewhat traumatic result of joining a feminist group at College" (72). She notes that "we aged crones of thirty-nine definitely used to pronounce" Coming Out "in capital letters" (72). Síle's age in the 2004 of the novel means that her coming out experience would have been akin to Mary Dorcey's, or Dorcey's character Nessa's. However, she is unusually lucky in her well-off Southside Dublin father, "a die-hard liberal" (72), and finds acceptance within her family. As a flight attendant, Síle (unlike the teachers Nessa and Pen) also works in a gay-friendly work environment and recognizes her good fortune, noting that "nobody gives me a hard time for being queer, not since that one pilot who moved to Quantas" (86). While her friend Marcus shoots back with "That's the law, not a basis for gratitude" (86), Síle still knows that in other Irish workplaces an open lesbian might not fare so well, even in 2004.

Jude's bisexual coming of age and her gradual realization that, actually, she prefers women, is described as a gentler process, unconstrained by what Síle calls "the old labels" and boundaries that she still finds troubling at times. By Síle's standards, Jude's early adventures veered into promiscuity and lacked the expected differentiation between lesbian and heterosexual experiences. In response to Síle's question, "Did it feel any different with the girls?" Jude answers, "Sex is always different, depending on who you're with" (154). Another key difference between the two women's experiences is that Jude never felt a need to come out. She says, "I'm not sure I was ever in. I wasn't too concerned about being 'normal,' maybe because Quakers aren't keen on dogma or fitting in. I brought home some boys and some girls, and Mom never expressed a view (though I'm sure she had her preferences)" (71).

While of course it is of importance in the narrative that Síle and Jude are lesbians, what is far more central is that they are people, with as many differences as similarities. Their love story addresses these differences, such as Jude's stay-at-home nature; frugality and simple tastes; and dislike of credit cards, email, and mobile phones, as opposed to Síle's glitzy consumerism and fondness for travel. They are not concerned with coming out or with being lesbians, but with how to stay together, how to make their relationship work. They are divided not only by age and temperament but by the Atlantic Ocean, and the key to success in their relationship is mastery of "the trick of being happy together" (293).

Every couple portrayed in the narrative, whether gay, lesbian, or heterosexual, struggles with the same questions: what makes us happy, and how do we create this happiness in the relationship? What can and does go wrong? Síle's parents, Shay and Sunita, both clearly thought that they had found "The One," against all odds and despite formidable obstacles between them and marital bliss. Their initial meeting as Sunita offered Shay more champagne on "The Flying Ranee Service, on a Super Constellation, London-Cairo-Bombay" (81) led to a marriage in which it was required of Sunita to make the leap of faith and all the compromises. As Síle writes in an email to Jude, "My Amma was Hindu, but the Church insisted she convert to marry Da (already pretty much lapsed, ironically), and he claims it was 'simpler for her to change everything' (country, job, primary language, religion, marital status) all at once" (68). As the narrative unfolds, Síle is forced to confront the nature of her mother's early death, a probable suicide brought about by unhappiness and caused by deliberate mismanagement of her diabetes.

Síle and her long-time partner Kathleen break up not because Síle has met Jude (although Jude is the catalyst of change), but because the passion and sexual expression in the relationship have long since dried up. The couple remain stuck in a comfort zone, stagnant but afraid of movement, until the spark of their meeting (also on an airplane) ignites the process of change. As she walks up the stairs to Kathleen's flat to initiate the break-up process, "It wasn't indecision that was wracking Síle, not at all. It was the torque of a decision that she realized she'd made some time ago" (100). Similarly, Jude has remained open to sex with Rizla, thinking "It was so hard to climb out of ruts. Old habits, old jokes, old arguments, tease, nag, tease, nag, push, pull" (94). However, after her mother's death (the onset of her mother's final illness during a visit to her sister in England was the reason for Jude's encounter with Síle on the airplane) and the instant electric connection she feels with Síle, Jude abandons her rut in favor of long-distance monogamy.

Síle's closest friend, Jael, and her husband, Anton, also navigate turbulent marital waters. Jael is bisexual and, like Jude, uncomfortable with binaries, "the whole straight-slash-queer thing" (229). She and Síle came of age in Dublin together, in the heady atmosphere of consciousness-raising groups, and "Jael had been a lesbian then, all battered leather and ties from Oxfam" (42). When Jael opts for an apparently fulfilling marriage with the stolid Anton, Síle idealizes what she sees as a happy monogamous union, telling Jael that "you're an inspiration to me" (297). Jael has previously hinted that maybe her bisexual days are not fully behind her, also noting the irony of her having become "a has-bian in the early nineties, just when the lot of Irish queers was about to improve" (197). However, her response to Síle's admiration is an emotional confession that she has a female lover. "One person isn't enough," Jael explains, "for a lifetime" (298). Jael's need for "a little bit extra" (298) comes, of course, at the expense of honesty in the marriage and leaves Síle extremely uncomfortable.

Lastly, Síle must work through the disintegration of the initially idyllic union between her friend Marcus and his partner Pedro. She, Jude, and Jael's family attend Marcus and Pedro's extravagant pagan commitment ceremony. However, the relationship is soon shattered, and Síle is shaken by Pedro's inability to commit to one partner: "'Pedro's never been faithful to one man in his life,' said Marcus, gravel-voiced, 'but I suppose I'd deluded myself that I'd converted him'" (307).

In her own quest for happiness ever after with "The One," Síle must sort through the vast pile of baggage heaped about her by her family and friends. She and Jude meet at a time when they are both aware of the need for a fresh start. However, they must also acknowledge and work through the reasons why they might have chosen to pin their hopes on so distant a prospective partner, with neither of them wishing to relocate, and decide what sort of relationship they do actually want. Both women genuinely believe that they have finally met the exclusive life partner of their dreams. However, to earn this dream union, they must be fueled not only by the power of love, but also by two key ingredients so lacking in the narrative's other relationships: compromise and a willingness to change. Donoghue grants her lovers the beginning of a fairy-tale ending, but not until Síle makes an emigrant's leap of faith, just as her mother did, and is met half-way by Jude, whose unwillingness to move beyond her little town of Ireland, Ontario, is overcome by a crashing epiphany: "A place was nothing on its own; it hit her now; it was only people who carved it into meaning" (318). Jude's new perspective leads to the compromise and the offer she was until now unable to make:

> "So what do you think—is there any chance that would make the leap possible for you, if we split the difference? Between Dublin and here, she explained when Síle didn't answer.
> "Could you imagine living in Toronto?"
> "Yes, but—are you serious?"
> "Why not? I guess I could get used to a city if you can get used to a new country" (320).

What Jude does not, at this point, realize is that Síle has already made the leap and is talking on her mobile just a few yards away. Jude's honest and sincere offer brings a healthy equality to the new, no-longer-long-distance relationship. No emotional debts will now need to be paid. Jude and Síle, "coming up the drive, out of the dark . . . her suitcase cutting a trail, her cat in a small cage, snowflakes snagged in her hair," are granted a real chance at happiness. In this lovely ending, the couple's sexual preference takes a back seat to their solution to "the trick of being happy together" (293). In this contemporary work of Irish fiction, gay and lesbian lives are ordinary ones; like everybody else, the characters work through life's challenges. The road is now well trodden and also increasingly well lit.

Works Cited

Donoghue, Emma. *Hood*. Los Angeles: Alyson, 1998.

_____. *Landing*. Orlando: Harcourt, 2007.

_____. "Noises from Woodsheds: Tales of Irish Lesbians, 1886–1989." *Lesbian and Gay Visions of Ireland*. Eds. Ide O'Carroll and Eoin Collins. London: Cassell, 1995. 158–70.

Dorcey, Mary. *A Noise from the Woodshed*. London: Onlywomen, 1989.

Johnston, Jennifer. *This is Not a Novel*. London: Review, 2002.

Quinn, Antoinette. "New Noises from the Woodshed: the Novels of Emma Donoghue." *Contemporary Irish Fiction: Themes, Tropes, Theories.* Eds. Liam Harte & Michael Parker. New York: St. Martin's, 2000. 145–64.

Tóibín, Colm. *The Blackwater Lightship.* New York: Scribner, 1999.

Weekes, Ann Owens. "A Trackless Road: Irish Nationalisms and Lesbian Writing." *Border Crossings: Irish Women Writers and National Identities.* Ed. Kathryn Kirkpatrick. Tuscaloosa: U of Alabama P, 2000. 123–56.

Trans/Forming Girlhood: Transgenderism, the Tomboy Formula, and Gender Identity Disorder in Sharon Dennis Wyeth's *Tomboy Trouble*

Michelle Ann Abate

Angela M. Gooden and Mark A. Gooden, in a 2001 article discussing picture books, noted: "Although female representation has greatly improved since the 1970s, gender stereotypes are still prevalent" (89). A survey conducted by Sue Jackson and Susan Gee affirmed this observation. After examining books for pre-adolescent readers that were published during the past five decades, they discovered: "Notably, positions as 'tomboys,' girls who look and act similar to boys, were not available in the texts. . . . [M]ore broadly, positions that resist or challenge traditional notions of femininity were absent" (126). As a result, pre-adolescent children "grow up learning about the 'correct,' dominant worldview about the ways of being masculine and feminine" (Jackson and Gee 117). This phenomenon has prompted David A. Anderson and Mykol Hamilton to lament the widespread "reinforcement of gender stereotypes by picture books read during the formative years" (par 1).

This essay will confront this literary and cultural tendency by examining an illustrated book for young readers that defied this trend: Sharon Dennis Wyeth's *Tomboy Trouble* (1998). Rather than avoiding nontraditional gender identities, the text—along with the pictures by Lynne Woodcock Cravath that accompany it—addresses the issue directly. As its title suggests, *Tomboy Trouble* chronicles a young girl's construction of a tomboyish gender role and the various forms of peer and parental "trouble" that result. Showing the eight-year-old main character engaging in an array of activities that fall outside the realm of conventional femininity—from playing baseball and cutting her hair to wearing boy's clothes and partaking in rough-and-tumble games at recess—the book does more than deliver the pat feminist message that girls can do anything that boys can do. *Tomboy Trouble* engages in the more ambitious, and decidedly more subversive, task of calling into question the socially constructed nature of gender roles. Rather than presenting masculine and feminine traits as rigidly tied to biological sex, it presents these elements as fluid and malleable. In this way, *Tomboy Trouble* advocates a gender identity that transcends the categories of maleness and femaleness, or one that could be cast, in the lexicon of contemporary LGBTQ studies, as transgender.

By condoning cross-gender identification and even inviting young readers to question assumptions about the naturalness of masculinity and femininity, Wyeth's book takes the exploration of gender roles in general and the construction of girlhood in particular to places that previous narratives for pre-adolescent readers never went. To borrow the language of UK sociologist Emma Renold, *Tomboy Trouble* positions its central female character "not as a passive recipient that is imprinted upon or 'socialised' by 'society,' but as a subject imbued with agency and self-knowledge" (372). In stark contrast to the portrayal of pre-adolescent children in previous illustrated books, Wyeth presents Georgia as actively constructing her own social world. This different approach to presenting how the eight-year-old girl "does gender" shifts the concepts of femininity and masculinity "from 'roles' that males and females 'learn' to an understanding of the forming of gender identities as relational, multiple and diverse" (Renold 372). In short, it opens up the space for the creation of feminin*ities* and masculin*ities*.

The resistance that Georgia encounters to this project is as illuminating as her successes, for the "tomboy trouble" that Wyeth depicts in her text resonates with the "gender trouble" which Judith Butler famously identified as a defining characteristic of contemporary writing for adults. Calling similar attention to the way in which gender is artificial and often even performative, the text breaks the longstanding silence surrounding iconoclastic constructions of girlhood in books for young readers. Especially when placed against the backdrop of the current cultural interest in and accompanying growing social anxiety about 'tweens, Wyeth's narrative becomes even more socially relevant and critically important. In books like Claudia Mitchell and Jacqueline Reid-

Walsh's *Seven Going on Seventeen* (2005), cultural historians, developmental psychologists, and literary and film critics have explored the ways in which pre-adolescent girls negotiate societal pressures to conform to traditional expectations about femininity. *Tomboy Trouble* joins as well as disjoins this discussion, illustrating the pressure that 'tween girls face to adhere to conventional forms of female gender performance but also offering modes of productive and, at times, even radical resistance. In this way, Wyeth's book defies the longstanding project in picture books of reinforcing what Renold and other sociologists refer to as "hegemonic femininity" (17) and instead introduces forms that are iconoclastic, Other, and even queer.

When these elements are taken as a collective, *Tomboy Trouble* poses a challenge to the American Psychiatric Association's assertion that young girls who are tomboyish, transgressive and even transgender suffer from a psychological condition, commonly known as "Gender Identity Disorder." Making its debut in 1980 in the third edition of the *Diagnostic and Statistical Manual of Mental Disorders*, GID received increased media attention as well as growing societal importance in the years following its initial appearance. As Eve Kosofsky Sedgwick, Judith Halberstam, and William Spurlin have written, during the early 1990s, anxiety about Gender Identity Disorder of childhood ceased to be merely a concern of the medico-scientific community and began to impact national childrearing strategies and societal attitudes about gender nonconformist girls. First published in 1998, *Tomboy Trouble* can be read as a response to this phenomenon. Wyeth's eight-year-old main character forms a rare instance in which an unconventional, iconoclastic and even queer female gender identity is not simply depicted in writing for and about pre-adolescent readers, but proudly defended.

"T" is for "Transgender," "Q" is for "Queer Theory"
Although the term "transgender" has received so much attention in recent years that it seems to have always been part of American cultural and linguistic life, it is actually a relatively new concept. The *Oxford English Dictionary* records the first use of the term only

a little over twenty years ago, in 1984. Meanwhile, the word itself made its debut in the *OED* even more recently, as a draft entry for the March 2004 revision: "Of, relating to, or designating a person whose identity does not conform unambiguously to conventional notions of male or female, but combines or moves between these."

Tomboy Trouble embeds this extant definition of transgenderism in both the written portrayal of its tomboyish main character and the pictures that accompany it. The narrative chronicles a young girl's construction of a tomboyish identity that transcends stereotypical gender roles and addresses the various forms of peer and parental "trouble" that arise from it. Moving to a new school in the opening pages of the text, eight-year-old Georgia also gets a chance to move into an entirely new gender identity that falls outside the boundaries of conventional notions of maleness and femaleness. An avid baseball player whose long hair causes her to overheat on the field, Georgia happily gets her locks cut short in the opening pages of the book.

Georgia's new haircut serves as the springboard for Wyeth's investigation of gender roles in general and the introduction of cross-gender transgression in particular. Recalling the common definition of transgenderism, the book's young female character refrains from saying that she wants her hair to look like a boy's. Eight-year-old Georgia repudiates the common societal association of short locks with masculinity and instead says more neutrally that she wants "a haircut" (5). In addition, the youth does not refer to the man cutting her hair as a masculine "barber" or more feminine "hairdresser." Instead, she simply refers to him by the non-gender specific term "the hair cutter." Finally, the young girl's desire for shorter locks is precipitated by her enthusiasm for playing the traditionally masculine sport of baseball, not the more feminine one of softball. As these details indicate, even in its opening pages, *Tomboy Trouble* reveals its intention of troubling notions of masculinity and femininity and even maleness and femaleness.

Although Georgia is thrilled with her short hair, this new tomboyish gender identity almost immediately causes various forms of "trouble." First, the young girl's mother dislikes her new coif.

When Georgia instructs the man cutting her hair to make it "'very short "' (8), her distressed mother attempts to dissuade her:

> "This short?" asked the hair cutter.
> "Shorter," I said.
> "Maybe not *that* short," said Mommy.
> "I want to see my ears," I said.
> "Your ears?" said Mommy. "Really?" (7, italics in original)

Lest the parental concern is not apparent from this conversation, the illustration that accompanies it presents Georgia's mother sitting with her hand near her mouth and a worried look on her face.

When the hairdresser is finished trimming Georgia's locks, such concern only increases. Although the eight-year-old girl delightfully exclaims upon seeing her new haircut, "'Wow!,'" and declares, "'I like it'" (7), her mother has a drastically different reaction. Seeing her daughter's new coif, she says disapprovingly, "'That's *short*, Georgia,'" and then, as the hairdresser sweeps up her daughter's shorn hair, the youth observes, "Mommy looked sad" (7, italics in original). When these tactics fail, the mother takes comfort in a fact that has consoled the parents of countless tomboys: the barber reminds her that Georgia's hair will grow back, insinuating that her daughter's "natural" femininity will be eventually, even inevitably, restored.

When Georgia begins attending her new school, concerns about her tomboyish identity deepen. As Emma Renold has aptly observed, primary school is powerful site of "the intersection of gender essentialism (femininity as female), gender polarity (masculinity and femininity as binary opposites) and compulsory and gendered heterosexuality (heterofeminity and heteromasculinity)" (27). Given the way in which traditional gender roles are policed, maintained, and perpetuated within this environment, it comes as no surprise that from the first time Georgia's classmates meet their new peer, they are frustrated by their inability to determine whether she is a boy or a girl. Echoing Barbara Chatton's observation that "Young children typically assign gender by appearance and behavior traits" (57), the schoolmates use external visual cues about gender like clothing style and hair length as reliable physical manifestations of her biological sex. As a result, they repeatedly mistake Georgia for a boy. When the tomboyish main character stands in the girl's line at recess, for instance, several boys try to correct this "mistake" and wave her over to their side. "'Hey you! You're in the wrong line. Come over here,'" one of them shouts, and a good old-fashioned battle of "No, I'm not" / "Yes, you are" ensues (10–13).

The illustrations that accompany the incident further reinforce this message, inviting pre-adolescent readers to question the likely numerous messages that they have received about traditional gender roles and the "appropriate" behavior for boys and girls. In the pictures by Cravath, all but one of the students in the girls' line has long hair and is wearing a dress or skirt; the one exception has on a pair of lavender-colored shorts and a pink shirt. Meanwhile, all of the boys in the boys' line—again, save one—have short hair, jeans, and a T-shirt. The one exception is donning black shorts and a solid-colored t-shirt. Even more significantly, the boy who tries to usher Georgia over the boys' line could be her doppelganger. Like the tomboyish title character, the young man is wearing jeans, a solid t-shirt and a baseball cap. Even his reddish brown hair color matches hers exactly. Thus, the boy's motivation for both making this initial remark and repeating it—as Georgia notes, "Every day I stood in the girls' line. Every day the boy called me stupid" (19)—may arise not only from the tomboyish girl's defiance of traditional gender categories but also from his own "gender panic." If a fellow student could look like him and act like him but be a girl, then the accuracy and stability of his gender identity is called into question. By juxtaposing images of more stereotypical-looking boys and girls with the nontraditional Georgia, Cravath's illustration underscores the message in Wyeth's text. The pictures allow pre-adolescent readers to see a gender identity that exists between the polarities of masculine and feminine, thereby suggesting that two seemingly opposing elements may not be so mutually exclusive after all.

The boy who teases Georgia in the school line is not the only one who expresses frustration about the tomboy's unconventional gender identity. When the class frolics on the playground, one youngster repeatedly insists that the new student, in spite of her instance to the contrary, must be a boy. After pointing to her jeans, baseball cap and haircut as evidence, he concludes, "'You're a boy but you say you're a girl. That's stupid'" (17). A few moments later, another male classmate takes this line of reasoning even further. After surveying Georgia's appearance and behavior, he declares: "'Your real name is George. . . . You're a boy. A boy who's so stupid that he really thinks he's a girl'" (20). Before long, various avowals and disavowals about the young girl's gender identity grow so heated that a teacher intervenes. Once again, the illustration that accompanies this episode accentuates its message. The picture, which occupies a full page, shows the black boy and white girl as having different races but analogous gender identities: Georgia's t-shirt is solid green with a ribbed collar and his is exactly the same style only red. Likewise, Georgia is wearing jeans and he is wearing jean shorts. Finally, both children have nearly identical pairs of white tennis sneakers; the only difference is that Georgia's shoes have a blue stripe along the side.

These incidents prompt Georgia to engage in the subversive task of calling into question the socially-constructed nature of gender roles and their independence from biological sex. In yet another example of Wyeth's presentation of Georgia as an active agent who negotiates her social world rather than a passive subject who merely absorbs and acquiesces to it, the eight year old realizes that being female doesn't obligate her to look and act feminine. When Georgia is teased for wearing "boy's sneakers" and "a boy's cap," for instance, she responds with a clever comeback that undercuts the purported naturalness of maleness and femaleness: "'These are my sneakers and my cap'" (14). Similarly, when she is mocked for having a boy's haircut, she asserts: "'This is not a boy's haircut. This is *my* haircut'" (14, italics in original). Finally, when a new classmate asks her "'Are you a tomboy?'" later in the narrative, she responds in a way that dislodges this concept from its grounding in essentialist notions of gender: "'I'm no kind of boy. I'm just my own kind of girl'" (47–8).

The presence of juvenile gender iconoclasm and the various forms of trouble that arise from it, however, are not limited to the tomboyish main character in Wyeth's book. This phenomenon extends to another iconoclastic figure named Robin, who is the mirror image of Georgia in many ways. With his long hair, gender-ambiguous name and love for singing, Robin defies the conventions of masculinity in the same way that Georgia defies the ones of femininity. When the protagonist first meets Robin, in fact, she mistakes his gender identity. Recalling the way in which Georgia's classmates assume that she is male, she initially assumes that Robin is female. Once again, visual markers of identity such as hair length and clothing style play a key role in the young girl's formulation of this conclusion. A conversation that takes placed between the pair offers one of the most direct and illuminating interrogations of gender in Wyeth's book:

> "Are you a boy or a girl?" asked Robin.
> "A girl."
> "You can't be," said Robin.
> "Why not?"
> "Because I'm a boy. And you're my new friend."
> "You're a boy?" I said.
> "Of course I am," said Robin.
> "You have long hair," I said.
> "And your hair is short," Robin pointed out.
> I laughed. "I thought you were a girl."
> Robin laughed. "I thought *you* were a boy" (36, italics in original).

When Georgia discovers her mistake, however, she does not cling to the divisions between maleness and femaleness as her classmates had done a few pages earlier. Instead, she uses the experience to deepen her knowledge about the malleability of gender. Upon discovering that Robin is a boy, Georgia responds with the wise and knowing, "'Just goes to show'" (36). Whereas the young girl's tomboyishness had previously made her aware of the socially-constructed nature of femininity, her friendship with Robin now makes her aware of the similarly artificial nature of masculinity. Going beyond simply asserting that girls can have short hair and boys can have long locks, Georgia argues that individuals should adopt the external gender identity that most accurately reflects their internal personality or self-image, even if this role does not conform to societal notions about masculinity and femininity. As Georgia matter-of-factly tells her mother: "'I like short hair. Especially on me. But not on Robin. Because Robin likes his hair long. So I hope he never gets a haircut'" (46).

In these and other passages, Wyeth's book and her gender-bending tomboy engage with contemporary discourses about queerness. Karen Coats has provided an excellent overview of this pervasive but sometimes nebulous concept in contemporary LGBTQ studies: "Queer theorists . . . resist both heteronormative and homonormative classifications; they resist norms of all kinds, including the modernist mandate that a person be one thing or another, sexually speaking" (110). *Tomboy Trouble* applies this ethos about adult human sexuality to childhood gender identity. Georgia does not advocate for traditional notions of masculinity and femininity, but rather for ones that exist outside of these categories. In the words of Coats once again, "The queer subject exists in a fluid space, resisting the specificity that comes with sexed identification, and hence, resisting in some ways modernist identity itself" (110). By frustrating the formerly rigid distinctions between male and female, masculine and feminine, boy and girl, Georgia and her tomboyish gender identity are iconoclastic, non-normative or, more simply, queer.

Tomboy Trouble's portrait of the artificial and even arbitrary nature of masculinity and femininity may be unique to books for pre-adolescent readers, but its underlying theoretical premise is not. Wyeth's text is in dialogue with one of the leading contemporary critiques of gender. The "tomboy trouble" that eight-year-old Georgia encounters echoes the "gender trouble" which Judith Butler has famously identified as a defining trope in contemporary writing for adults. In what has become an oft-quoted passage from the final chapter of Butler's book, she argues: ". . . external acts, gestures, and enactments of gender are *performative* in the sense that the essence or identity that they otherwise purport to express are *fabrications* manufactured and sustained through corporeal signs" (136). Rather than reading outward visual cues as accurate indicators of an individual's internal identity, they are, to quote another one of Butler's oft-referenced passages, "mere copies of a copy" (31). Far from being stable signs, such elements are unstable significations. As Butler asserts, "the performance of the gendered body in such daily activities as dress, mannerisms and behavior has no ontological relationship with what may constitute its inner reality" (136). Given the way in which gender is a false index of identity, it is, as the title of Butler's book suggests, always the site of trouble. Notions of masculinity and femininity are semiotic (mine) fields of perplexity, puzzlement and even misdirection. In the words of Butler once again: "The construction of coherence conceals the gender discontinuities that run rampant within heterosexual, bisexual, and gay and lesbian contexts in which gender does not necessarily follow from sex" (135).

The construction of Georgia's tomboyish gender identity reflects this idea. In keeping with the central tenet of *Gender Trouble*, *Tomboy Trouble* calls repeated attention to the artificial and even performative nature of gender. The eight-year-old main character frequently asserts that the outward, public manifestations of her identity—such as her short haircut, blue jeans and baseball cap—are not accurate predictors of her internal, biological sex; rather, they are unreliable indices. As such, they become, like the title of Wyeth's text indicates and the storyline repeatedly demonstrate, sites of trouble. By willfully violating and openly transgressing hegemonic forms of femininity, Georgia demonstrates that not simply female gender roles but, by extension, all gender performance is just that, a performance. The discontinuities, gaps and fissures that she exposes in this supposed fixed system reveal the artificial nature of masculinity and femininity and creates the possibility for alternatives; in short, for masculinit*ies* and feminin*ities*. These elements radically upend the message in countless previous illustrated books for young readers that gender is fixed, stable and immutable. Eight-year-old Georgia reveals how gender is not something that "is," but rather something that is continually becoming by being produced and reproduced. Because gender is socially constructed, it can be reconstructed.

"Poor Mommy"

In an even more daring implication, the way in which *Tomboy Trouble* embeds elements of *Gender Trouble* also offers a literary challenge to the growing pathologization of gender-bending young girls. Beginning in 1980 with the advent of "Gender Identity Disorder" in the American Psychiatric Association's *Diagnostic and Statistical Manual of Mental Disorders (DSM-III)*, female figures who defied traditional feminine gender roles generated increased scientific interest along with social anxiety. Although the APA asserted that this new type of childhood psychological condition was "not merely the rejection of stereotypical sex role behavior as, for example, in 'tomboyishness' in girls or 'sissyish' behavior in boys" (264), it nonetheless described this illness in language that was eerily reminiscent of tomboyism. According to the *DSM-III*, girls with Gender Identity Disorder "regularly have male peer groups, an avid interest in sports and rough-and-tumble play, and a lack of interest in playing with dolls or playing 'house' (unless playing the father or another male role)" (264). Only more rarely, the description went on to note, did a girl suffering from GID express more pronounced disavowals of her gender through "claims that she will grow up to become a man (not merely in role), that she is biologically unable to become pregnant, that she will not develop breasts, or that she has, or will grow, a penis" (*DSM-III* 264). Indeed, the *DSM-III* attested: "Some of these children, particularly girls, show no other signs of psychopathology" than the gender-bending traits listed previously (*DSM-III* 264–5).

The fourth edition of the *Diagnostic and Statistical Manual of Mental Disorders* (1994), published only four years before *Tomboy Trouble*, introduced additional modifications that revealed the heightened societal interest in Gender Identity Disorder in girls and also extended the condition's steadily growing similarity to tomboyism. Before readers even considered the changes to GID in the *DSM-IV*, they were likely to notice the increased attention devoted to it. Whereas discussion of this condition occupied around three pages of text in the *DSM-III* and *DSM-III-R*, it received more than six pages in this new edition.

Together with revealing the way in which the diagnosis of Gender Identity Disorder acquired added importance in the 1990s, several of the changes further eroded the already crumbling distinction between it and tomboyism. Indeed, the newly revised and expanded description of GID in girls could easily have been used to describe a tomboy:

> Girls with Gender Identity Disorder display intense negative reactions to parental expectations or attempts to have them wear dresses or other feminine attire. Some may refuse to attend school or social events where such clothes may be required. They prefer boy's clothing and short hair and are often misidentified as boys, and may ask to be called by a boy's name. Their fantasy heroes are most often powerful male figures, such as Batman or Superman. These girls prefer boys as playmates, with whom they share interests in contact sports, rough-and-tumble play, and traditional boyhood games. They show little interest in dolls or any form of feminine dress up or role-play activity (*DSM-IV* 533).

These similarities further undercut the APA's longstanding assertion that Gender Identity Disorder was "not meant to describe a child's gender nonconformity to stereotypic sex-role behavior as, for example, 'tomboyishness' in girls" (*DSM-IV* 536). While this qualifier was still included with the description in theory, it no longer applied in practice.

Given the suggestive echoes between tomboyism and Gender Identity Disorder indicate, more masculine forms of this code of conduct were not merely unpopular or discouraged; they were now pathologized. As Judith Halberstam, Eve Kosofsky Sedgwick and William Spurlin have discussed, together with encountering family disapproval and peer ridicule, these young women were now also subject to gender reorientation counseling, aversion therapy and even institutionalization. As Spurlin has documented, these aggressive, invasive and often harmful tactics are "self-righteously performed in the name of the 'best interest' of the gender-atypical child" even when the boys and girls being treated do not express discomfort with their iconoclastic gender identities (83). As a result, he rightly concludes that GID can more accurately be seen as treating the parental concerns and social anxieties surrounding gender nonconformity, rather than an illness that ostensibly ails children (81–4).

Written and released four years after the publication of the *DSM-IV*, the eight-year-old main character in *Tomboy Trouble* mirrors many of the traits for GID. While Georgia does not possess any of the more pathological symptoms of the disorder—like assertions that "she is biologically unable to become pregnant, that she will not develop breasts, or that she has, or will grow, a penis" (*DSM-III* 264)—she does embody an array of the tomboyish ones that the APA identifies as being constitutive of Gender Identity Disorder. For example, reflecting the extensive diagnostic criteria in the *DSM-IV*, the young girl prefers "boy's clothing and short hair" and is "often misidentified as a boy." In addition, she has "little interest in dolls or any form of feminine dress up or role-play activity." Throughout *Tomboy Trouble*, in fact, Georgia is never shown playing with, or even owning, any traditionally feminine toys. Finally, the eight year old displays "intense negative reactions to parental expectations or attempts to have them wear dresses or other feminine attire." When Georgia's mother suggests that she could wear a dress as a means to keep her new classmates from misidentifying her as a boy, she responds with the emphatic: "'No way!'" (31).

Such heightened concern about GID in girls during the late 1980s and throughout the decade of the 1990s was rooted in fears that childhood gender nonconformity would lead to adult sexual nonconformity. As Emma Renold has written, the display of "an 'abnormal' or questionable [gender] identity also throws into doubt . . . [a child's presumed future] hetero-sexuality, thereby creating potential for their behaviour/practices to be 'homosexualized'" (377).[1] For these reasons, tactics for treating gender nonconformity in feminine boys and masculine girls are generally characterized as being "in the best interests of the child," but, as William Spurlin has pointed out, they are more accurately seen as being "specifically tied to adult anxieties about the possibility that a child may become gay or lesbian" (83). Indeed, Shannon Minter has said about the clinical creation of Gender Identity Disorder: "Much of this research was touted as a means to identify 'prehomosexual' and 'pretranssexual' children and to prevent them from growing up to be gay or transsexual" (11–12). In light of these details, homosexuality may have been officially removed from the American Psychiatric Association's *Diagnostic and Statistical Manual* in 1973, but it resurfaced via Gender Identity Disorder of childhood in the very next edition. In the words of Sedgwick, "the *de*pathologization of an atypical [sexual] object-choice can be yoked to the *new* pathologization of an atypical gender identification" (21, italics in original). Likewise, in language that is even more direct, Matthew Rottnek has asserted: "Here, homosexuality-as-pathology is simply reconfigured as a childhood disorder" (1).

The scientific blurring between childhood tomboyism, Gender Identity Disorder, and adult homosexuality raised anxiety among many parents. A segment that appeared on the April 14th, 1995 broadcast of the popular television newsmagazine *Dateline NBC* and tellingly titled "Sugar and Spice" demonstrated the way in which changing scientific attitudes about female gender nonconformity were rapidly changing national attitudes about tomboyism. As anchor Jane Pauley asserts in the lead-in to the piece, a new research project being conducted by scientists at Northwestern University "is the first long-term study of its kind to determine if there's a link between tomboyish behavior and sexual preference." While viewers watch a group of young girls engage in various forms of rough-and-tumble play, the reporting journalist gives ominous statistics about the incidence of homosexuality among the general population and the projected rate among tomboys: "Right now, one percent of the general population is thought to be lesbian. The scientists at Northwestern think ten percent of the tomboy population will be gay." After hearing these statistics, the mother of one of the young girls participating in the study changes her attitude about tomboyism. Having been rather blasé about her daughter's gender-bending behavior before, she now says, "No, I didn't like it," and then later and even more anxiously, "Yes, I was alarmed."

Tomboy Trouble was written and released amidst this growing anxiety about gender-bending behavior among pre-adolescent girls. Together with troubling prevailing beliefs about the naturalness of masculinity and femininity, the text also troubles the social wisdom and even scientific accuracy of Gender Identity Disorder. Rather than offering medicalized or even pathologized reasons for Georgia's excitement about her new short haircut, *Tomboy Trouble* offers ones that embody a proud declaration of individuality and a clever critique of gender roles. When the eight-year-old girl's mother informs her, "'When I was a little girl . . . I wanted my hair long,'" Georgia puts on her baseball cap and responds with the matter-of-fact, "'Not me'" (8). This seemingly simplistic retort embeds a sophisticated awareness about the myriad forms of human nature. Georgia's remark recognizes that people are unique and thus express their personality and gender identity in different ways. What constitutes an appropriate outward image for one individual—such as her mother's feminine desire to have long hair—embodies an inaccurate and unacceptable one for another person, like the tomboyish young girl.

Confronted with this reaction, Georgia's mother tries to elaborate on her reason for wanting long hair and, by extension, why her daughter should want it too: "'I didn't want my ears to show,' said Mommy. 'Why not?' I asked. Mommy said she didn't like her ears" (8). Even more so than the mother's previous attempt, this strategy backfires. Rather than finding her mother's reason persuasive, Georgia is disturbed. In a remark that cleverly inverts the question of which one of these characters possess a dysfunctional and even dysphoric reason for wanting her hair a certain length, Georgia responds, "'Poor Mommy'" (8). With just these two words, the eight-year-old character transforms her mother's seemingly "normal" and "healthy" desire for long locks into one that is rooted in the "abnormal" and "unhealthy" basis of low self-esteem, poor self-image and a desire to hide or at least obfuscate a perceived physical flaw. While Wyeth's book never explicitly mentions GID or the growing pathologization of gender-bending young girls, it tacitly invites readers to question which character can more accurately be seen as suffering from an "identity disorder": the tomboyish and self-assured Georgia or her feminine but self-conscious mother. Later, when Georgia and a fellow female classmate named Rose, who—in a surprising revelation that is clearly meant to be seen as liberating—has also cut her hair short are teased because of their appearance, such sentiments recur. In a direct inversion of previous narrative instances when peers called Georgia and Robin "dumb" because of their perceived gender confusion, the pair asserts that individuals who cling to rigid notions about masculinity and femininity possess this quality. In a passage that makes the youths sound like world-weary queer theorists for whom gender roles are antiquated facets of a by-gone era, they engage in the following exchange about individuals who dwell on it: "'People are dumb,' said Robin. 'Don't they have anything better to do?' said Rose" (42).

In a daring message not only for picture books but especially for those released during the 1990s, Sharon Dennis Wyeth's *Tomboy Trouble* does not suggest that the gender-bending main character needs to abandon her iconoclastic identity. Instead, the narrative a compelling case for continuing such behavior and questions both its social stigmatization and scientific pathologization. In doing so, *Tomboy Trouble* may ostensibly invite its young audience readers to "step into reading," but it simultaneously allows them to step into tomboyish, transgender and even queer conceptions of girlhood.

Copyright © 2008 The Johns Hopkins University Press. A version of this article was first published in The Lion and the Unicorn *32.1 (January 2008), 40–60. Reprinted with permission by Johns Hopkins University Press.*

Note

1. This phenomenon of what gender theorists often refer to as the "heterosexualization of gender" has prompted Chrys Ingraham to coin the terms "heterogender" and more specifically "heterofemininity" and "heteromasculinity." As she explains in "The Heterosexual Imaginary: Feminist Sociology and Theories of Gender," these terms more accurately convey the firm alignment of conventional male and female gender roles with heteronormative sexuality.

Works Cited

American Psychiatric Association. *Diagnostic and Statistical Manual for Mental Disorders—III*. 3rd ed. Washington, DC: American Psychiatric Association America, 1980.

_____. *Diagnostic and Statistical Manual for Mental Disorders—IV*. 4th ed. Washington, DC: American Psychiatric Association, 1994.

Anderson, David A., and Mykol Hamilton. "Gender Role Stereotyping of Parents in Children's Picture Books: The Invisible Father." *Sex Roles: A Journal of Research*. 52. 3–4 (February 2005): 145–51.

Butler, Judith. *Gender Trouble: Feminism and the Subversion of Identity*. New York: Routledge, 1990.

Cart, Michael, & Christine Jenkins. *The Heart Has Its Reasons: Young Adult Literature with Gay/Lesbian/Queer Content, 1969–2004*. Metuchen, NJ: Scarecrow, 2006.

Chatton, Barbara. "Picture Books for Preschool Children: Exploring Gender Issues with Three- and Four-Year-Olds." *Beauty, Brains, and Brawn: The Construction of Gender in Children's Literature*. Ed. Susan S. Lehr. Portsmouth, NH: Heinemann, 2001. 57–66.

Coats, Karen. *Looking Glasses and Neverlands: Lacan, Desire, and Subjectivity in Children's Literature*. Iowa City: U of Iowa, 2004.

Gooden, Angela M., & Mark A. Gooden. "Gender Representation in Notable Children's Picture Books." *Sex Roles: A Journal of Research*. 89.1–2 (July 2001): 89–101.

Halberstam, Judith. "Oh Bondage Up Yours!: Female Masculinity and the Tomboy." *Sissies and Tomboys: Gender Nonconformity and Homosexual Childhood*. Ed. Matthew Rottnek. New York: NYU, 1999. 153–79.

Ingraham, Chrys. "The Heterosexual Imaginary: Feminist Sociology and Theories of Gender." *Sociological Theory* 12.4 (July 1994): 203–19.

Jackson, Sue, and Susan Gee. "'Look, Janet,' 'No you look, John': Constructions of Gender in Early School Reader Illustrations Across 50 Years." *Gender and Education*. 17.2 (May 2005): 115–28.

Minter, Shannon. "Diagnosis and Treatment of Gender Identity Disorder in Children." *Sissies and Tomboys: Gender Nonconformity and Homosexual Childhood*. Ed. Matthew Rottnek. New York: NYU, 1999. 9–33.

Mitchell, Claudia, & Jacqueline Reid-Walsh. *Seven Going on Seventeen: Tween Studies in the Culture of Girlhood*. New York: Lang, 2005.

Renold, Emma. *Girls, Boys and Junior Sexualities: Exploring Children's Gender and Sexual Relations in the Primary School*. London: RoutledgeFalmer, 2005.

Rottnek, Matthew. Introduction. *Sissies and Tomboys: Gender Nonconformity and Homosexual Childhood*. Ed. Matthew Rottnek. New York: NYU, 1999. 1–5.

Sedgwick, Eve Kosofsky. "How to Bring Your Kids Up Gay." *Social Text* 29 (1990): 18–27.

Spurlin, William. "Sissies and Sisters: Gender, Sexuality and the Possibilities of Coalition." *Coming Out of Feminism?* Eds. Many Merck, Naomi Segal, and Elizabeth Wright. Oxford: Blackwell, 1998. 74–101.

"Sugar and Spice." *Dateline NBC*. Narr. Victoria Corderi. NBC, New York, 14 Apr. 1995. Transcript.

"Transgender." Draft Entry. *Oxford English Dictionary*. March 2004. Web. 5 March 2006. < www.oed.com>.

Wyeth, Sharon Dennis. *Tomboy Trouble*. Illus. Lynne Woodcock Cravath. New York: Random House, 1998.

Border-Crossing and Evolution: From Violence to Love in Cristina García's *Monkey Hunting* and *The Lady Matador's Hotel*

Barbara Frey Waxman

Introduction: Gender, Cultures, and Borders

Cristina García, born in 1958, crossed a geographical and cultural border when she came to New York from Cuba as a child. She is now one of a cadre of US authors of Latino/a descent. The term *Latino/a* refers to Spanish-speaking people from the Americas and Caribbean. Debate persists about use of the terms *Latino/a* versus *Hispanic*; many use *Latino/a,* as I do here, because *Hispanic* is associated with the colonialism of Spain's *conquistadores*. Some scholars of US Latino/a studies use *Latino/a,* but prefer to identify authors' nations of origin more precisely, like, for example, designating García as Cuban American. Regardless of terminology, US Latino/a authors have garnered critical acclaim, like García; a large readership, like Sandra Cisneros and Julia Alvarez; won Pulitzer Prizes, like Oscar Hijuelos and Junot Díaz; and transformed American literary history.

García creates fictional characters who cross linguistic, cultural, religious, and gender borders, including African slaves, indentured servants from China, and others seeking economic betterment. These fictional immigrants' *destinos* suggest optimism about the long-term gains of border-crossing, arguably more for male characters than for female. Readers of US Latino/a literature may be reminded of the ground-breaking theoretical work of Chicana (Mexican American) lesbian feminist Gloria Anzaldúa in *Borderlands/La Frontera,* a text taught frequently in Chicano studies, Latino/a studies, and women's studies courses. A reading of García's fiction may be productively informed by Anzaldúa's work, especially when examining García's Asian characters, like Chen Pan in García's third novel, *Monkey Hunting (*2003*),* and Won Kim and Suki Palacios, in her fifth novel, *The Lady Matador's Hotel* (2010). These characters, especially the males, Chen Pan and Won Kim, cross cultural borders and create meaningful lives by moving into a space of atypical gender-performance. Specifically, they challenge the dictates of *machismo*, which, in its extreme, may be defined as a "syndrome of hyper-or traditional masculinity" typically associated with "a denigration of females" (Basham 126). Against this ideology, García's two male characters develop respect and love for their women and create new cultural and spiritual territory with gentle masculine behavior toward wives and offspring.

Suki's performance of *machismo/a* is more problematic. Her cultural border-crossings are evident in Suki's pursuit of bullfighting and aggressive seduction of men. Suki, born of a Mexican American father and a Japanese mother, crosses into a *macho/a*[1] territory of cold coupling and violence. However, the fate of *matadora* Suki seems more ambiguous than Won Kim's. It could be argued that Suki's brand of *machismo* is negatively portrayed in both bullring and bedroom, while her Asian heritage, represented in her recurring visions of her dead mother, portends Suki's release from *macho* behavior and embrace of a more humane life. In the novel's final bullfight, she vows to return to medical school, in order to learn to heal others.

Other female border-crossers in both novels stake out new spiritual and emotional turf, too. In *Monkey Hunting*, Lucrecia, a freed African slave, evolves as Chen Pan's African-Cuban-Chinese wife; however, dying young, she only dwells briefly in this borderland. Berta, Won Kim's teenage Latina lover, is a tender partner for her Korean companion. And prospects are good for her long life. She bears his son, which regenerates him. Love raises humanity to a higher level in both novels.

Love and Evolution: Gilligan, Anzaldúa, Darwin, and García's Feminism

Both novels espouse an ideology of love and an ethic of care reminiscent of feminist psychologist Carol Gilligan's work. Gilligan's research ascribed this ethic to women and an ethic of justice to men. In García's novels this ethic of care is performed by some female *and* male characters who have crossed cultural borders. These characters suggest García's hope for humankind and her feminism ("Buckner Lecture Series"). In 1982, Gilligan wrote, "To admit the truth of the women's perspective to the conception of moral development is to recognize for both sexes the importance throughout life of the connection between self and other, the universality of the need for compassion and care" (98). García imagines both male and female characters whose moral development is evident in their deepening compassion.

Anzaldúa's notion of border-crossing is instructive here: crossing borders is unsettling, but can dismantle the dualistic thinking and behavior that constrain identities, like Latino/a and Anglo, male and female, gay and straight. Anzaldúa notes that from a "racial, ideological, cultural, and biological cross-pollinization" comes a more flexible and inclusive way of thinking, a "new *mestiza* consciousness" (99, 101). García's novels celebrate individuals who dismantle dualities as they embrace multiple languages, cultures, and gendered subject-positions. While Anzaldúa focuses mainly on Latina women in her exploration of a new *mestiza* consciousness, this essay means to extend the notion to García's Asian and multiracial characters in Latino settings. Anzaldúa also includes Latino men in discussing *machismo*, suggesting that they are injured by adherence to *machismo* and by *machismo's* devolution into a "false *machismo*" (105); sprung from Anglo culture's marginalization of Latino men, this false *machismo* replaces men's role as women's protectors with violent denigration of women. García's gentle Asian males suggest agreement with Anzaldúa: men (Asian and Latino) must relinquish false *machismo*, learning, like Chen Pan and Won Kim, to care for others.

Also argued here is that Anzaldúa's thinking about human border-crossings are metaphorically linked to Darwin's ideas about migration of animals to places that force them to acquire survival traits and to cross-breed. Anzaldúa argues that borderland-living creates new ways of being human and fresh ways of thinking: "Living on borders and in margins, keeping intact one's shifting and multiple identity and integrity, is like trying to swim in a new element. . . . There is an exhilaration in being a participant in *the further evolution of humankind,* . . . [in which] dormant areas of consciousness are being activated, awakened" (xvii, italics added). Darwin similarly noted that significant migrations to new borderlands bring significant changes in the migrating animals. Hardy species that adapt reproduce new species: natural selection.

References to Darwin's work within Won Kim's storyline suggest this link to Anzaldúa's ideas on human evolution and borderland consciousness. Won Kim has translated Darwin's *Origin of Species* into Korean; moreover, his passion for butterflies links him to Darwin, who, like other nineteenth-century scientists, including his colleague Alfred Russel Wallace, did fieldwork on the evolution of species of migrating butterflies in the New World. As biographer Janet Browne observes of Wallace's work, "butterflies were destined to become evolution's most elegant practical support. . . . Wallace produced his own analysis of insect mimicry as a form of protective coloration, revealing his belief in the efficacy of natural selection . . ." (226). Like butterfly species' evolution, Won Kim's changes in the novel prefigure a further evolution of humankind.

García's ideas about cultural border-crossing and human evolution inform her portrayals of multicultural characters in *Monkey Hunting* and *The Lady Matador's Hotel*. These characters evolve to a higher human form through cross-cultural relationships—with love and an ethic of care as means to survival, adaptation, and procreation. Further, García's portrayals of multiracial characters and their relationships challenge others' silence about Cuba's multiracial identities and the broader Latino/a *mestizaje* (Caminero-Santangelo 100). In her craft, García is both historically accurate and forward-thinking.

Examining the Love of Chen Pan and Lucrecia in *Monkey Hunting*

Despite the grim historical setting of slavery, indentured servitude, and racism in nineteenth-century Havana, Chen Pan's "border-crossing" movements successfully blend Spanish, Cuban, Chinese, and African cultures in his relationship with Lucrecia. Caminero-Santangelo argues that, in García's novel, hybridity is associated with "the violence that produces it" (104): Lucrecia's birth is the product of her mother's rape by a Spaniard, and Lucrecia is herself raped and impregnated by her father. Yet Chen Pan and Lucrecia's love, crossing cultural, racial, and spiritual borders, produces beloved offspring; this familial love challenges hybridity's association with violence. Richard Rodriguez also offers an erotic definition of hybridity as transracial desire in *Brown: The Last Discovery of America.* Like him, critic Doris Sommer notes in her study of nineteenth-century Latin American novels: "Miscegenation was . . . the way of redemption in Latin America" (Caminero-Santangelo 103). Lovers of different nationalities become metaphors for the binding of national groups in Cuba's story of national origin. Authors like García forge narratives of "'national romance'" (Caminero-Santangelo 103) that contest representations of hybridity as colonialist violence. Such is the case with Chen Pan and Lucrecia.

Chen Pan's humane values develop from the mid-nineteenth century to the early twentieth century. Like Sean Moiles, who suggests utopian literature is an important generic model for *Monkey Hunting*, I see Chen Pan's heroic behavior—resisting Cuban racism and creating an egalitarian union with Lucrecia—as utopian. His background as the son of a Chinese poet, his moral courage, and his love counteract the violence of the Spanish presence in Cuba.

García explores the flowering of humanity in Chen Pan. On the ship traveling to Cuba, Chen Pan exhibits an ethic of care, inspired by his father's poetry, when he soothes the other passengers' suffering. Later, in the sugarcane fields, Chen Pan subverts slavery's inhumanities by interacting with the Africans, in particular Cabeza de Piña, in friendship; Cabeza protects Chen's health by feeding him yams, while Chen teaches Cabeza "Chinese exercises . . . to strengthen his body" (26). Cabeza's compliment that Chen Pan, "like him[self], was a son of the God of Fire," Changó in his Yoruban religion, suggests that Chen Pan is a border-crosser. Chen Pan's development of transcultural values and intolerance for evil prompt his murder of the overseer, El Bigote. He flees servitude and the plantation.

Chen eventually enters Havana. There, he again displays an ethic of care by intervening in a fight to save the life of a Spanish gentleman. He is rewarded for his courage financially, allowing him to establish a lucrative antiques store. He adapts well to this setting, demonstrating survival of the fittest. Love, however, is the real key to his survival.

Chen Pan's most courageous border-crossing occurs when he buys Lucrecia and her son, freeing them from slavery, and then loves them both. Lucrecia stays with him because of his humane view of women and because he adopts her son. In this conduct, he is ahead of his time, as historian Karen Y. Morrison's research on nineteenth-century Cuba suggests: "Although white and Asian men [in Cuba] frequently were sexual partners of women of color—including slaves—these relationships were rarely legitimated. In fact, interracial marriages were actively discouraged by both law and racist beliefs" (61). Although Chen Pan and Lucrecia do not have a marriage ceremony in the Catholic Church, theirs is a legitimate lifelong union. Chen Pan embodies a higher humanity in his devotion to Lucrecia and to their hybrid offspring.

In the development of his humane outlook, Chen Pan is aided by the transcultural self-fashioning of Lucrecia. Their shared religious practices reveal the couple's skilled border-crossing. They express reverence for Buddha (Lucrecia makes an offering to Buddha before crucial decisions) and for the African deity Yemaya (Lucrecia's mother was Yoruban); there are shrines to both in their home. And Lucrecia makes candles for Catholic holidays, including "gilded votives for La Virgen de la Caridad del Cobre, Cuba's patron saint" (135). As Caminero-Santangelo notes, Lucrecia's references to her saints also suggests "the already syncretic *santos*, or *orishas* of Cuban Santeria, in which deities of Yoruban origin are merged with Catholic saints" (106). As Buddhists, the couple visits the Chinese cemetery for the grave-sweeping holiday and make food offerings to their ancestors (164).

Through her Chinese cooking, readers recognize how far into Chinese space Lucrecia has crossed: "Chen Pan remembered how Lucrecia had learned to bake . . . mooncakes for him. She'd tried everything to please his Chinese side" (245). Lucrecia becomes "Chinese in her liver, Chinese in her heart" (138). This passage might, to some feminist readers, suggest a colonization of Lucrecia's body, but it is noteworthy that she *chooses* to become Chinese out of love and cross-cultural tolerance. Moreover, her cultural syncretism remains evident in her cooking: chicken with ginger and smoked duck (Chinese style); *ajiaco* stew (a signature Cuban dish whose ingredients emblematize the multiculturalism of Cuba (Caminero-Santangelo 106), and fried sweet potatoes (her African roots). She is an African-Spanish-Cuban-Chinese woman. The novel shows that her partnership with Chen Pan is secure and mutually nurturing.

In telling Lucrecia's story, García is reaffirming the border-crossing *mestizaje*, a consciousness that Anzaldúa defines: "[The new *mestiza*] is willing to share, to make herself vulnerable to foreign ways of seeing and thinking" (104). Lucrecia embodies the new *mestiza:* "She lit a candle here, made an offering there, said prayers to the gods of heaven and the ones here on earth. She didn't believe in just one thing" (129). Lucrecia's spiritual beliefs and cultural practices epitomize the "Cuban national narrative that has fully embraced . . . the notion of racial and cultural *mestizaje* for the Cuban people" (Caminero-Santangelo 107).

Chen Pan also exemplifies Cuba's cultural syncretism in his evolving ways of seeing and thinking. For the first half of his life story, Chen Pan is guided in his life-choices by his Chinese heritage: "[Chen Pan had] begun insisting on Chinese-only explanations for everything: such as that everyone was born with *yuan*, a destiny inherited from previous lives" (129). Yet he becomes more Cuban in his business and domestic lives. He begins to question "whether he . . . is] genuinely Chinese anymore" (83). He has developed socioeconomic survival skills, transnational values, and humanitarian impulses. He has forgotten most of his Chinese language and culture: "How useless these had been outside of their own geography. Still, it was easier for him to be Cuban than to try to become Chinese again" (245). He cannot go backward in his evolution.

As a Chinese-Cuban, finally, Chen Pan takes pride in his own and his fellow Chinese immigrants' participation in Cuba's war for independence against the Spanish; as soldiers, they become modern Cuban citizens. Fanon's definition of decolonization applies to Chen Pan: "Decolonization . . . infuses a new rhythm, specific to a new generation of men, with a new language and a new humanity. Decolonization is truly the creation of new men" (2). Chen Pan is one of these new men.

As an old man, Chen Pan remains anchored by his love for Lucrecia and firmly rooted in Cuba. On his deathbed, however, he dreams of China, reaffirming his borderland perspective. His boyhood memory of the cranes nesting in his great-aunt's house in China resurfaces; cranes are usually symbolic of wisdom, prosperity, and longevity in Chinese legend, and one legend makes them the vehicles of an immortal soul's transport to heaven ("What Does the Crane Symbolize . . . ?"). Chen Pan's dream suggests that while he has had a full life in Cuba and has gained a cultural-borderland type of wisdom, he feels a "longing . . . for home" (249). Home for Chen Pan may be China, but his soul's home may be his transport to a heavenly place beside Lucrecia. While he carries China within him till death, he dies a better man in Cuba: a New World conclusion to a life of transnational syntheses, sealed by love.

The Lady Matador's Hotel: Lust and Violence Yield to Love and Care

The Lady Matador's Hotel, set in a contemporary, unnamed Central American nation, depicts many cultural and gender border-crossings by its Asian or half-Asian characters. These crossings do not, at first, produce a deeper humanity. As the characters evolve, loving relationships develop. At first, Suki Palacios satisfies her lust in a cold, *macha* way before her bullfights: she uses working-class men for her own pleasure. And at first, Won Kim seems to have taken shameful advantage of his fifteen-year-old mistress, Berta. The Hotel Miraflor itself seems a global microcosm of a loveless, sexualized, and sometimes violent wilderness. The novel's epigraph alludes to these characters' joyless state: "they are a mournful, single-chorded psalm."

Hope, nevertheless, does grow in the initially suicidal Won Kim once Berta becomes pregnant. Love emerges out of lust when the couple's son is born. This emotional transformation recalls the emergence of a butterfly from its cocoon, a metamorphosis of which Won Kim, a passionate butterfly collector, is keenly aware. An ethic of care enters his character. There is also cause for hope when Suki encounters the bull at the end and survives, planning to exchange the *matadora's* dark energy and violence for the resumption of medical school and, with it, the work of healing. García's moments of optimism may conform to Raphael Dalleo and Elena Machado Sáez's description of some post-sixties Latino/a authors: "[T]heir visions of politics are frequently idealistic . . . [and] can move us . . . toward hope for a renewed political Latino/a literature" (11). Conjuring a future beyond *machismo*, the novel creates in Won Kim and Berta the healing practices of transnational love.

Won Kim starts out a reluctant border-crosser; unlike Chen Pan, he is irritated by the Latino/a culture, in which he resides; even the music annoys him: a mariachi band plays "a lively ranchero. . . . Everything in this godforsaken country turns into a fiesta, Won Kim thinks irascibly" (119). His character is preoccupied with death. Peeling wallpaper in his honeymoon suite hotel room "reminds him of a dying moth" (17)—not of the butterflies that he admires. His mother is dying, which contributes to his depression. He imagines escape by electrocuting himself in the bathtub. Other suicide plans are also thwarted. Yet Berta will provide her lover with a "blueprint for his redemption" (19), the mechanism for his evolution into a different kind of man.

His evolution is foreshadowed in a flashback to his one and only night of lovemaking with Berta: "Won Kim remembers every touch and scent and sigh of that night. It was like opening a velvet box from which a butterfly flew out, delicate and iridescent. And he was happy, perhaps for the last time" (20). The reference to the butterfly in this scene (a migrating and evolving species), his butterfly hobby, and his translation of Darwin into Korean all foreshadow his metamorphosis into a more loving, more soulful male than his *macho* father (a serial adulterer). The father criticizes his son's hobby as unmanly (59–60). A gentle humanity comes of Won Kim's migration away from *machismo* and toward love.

Another improving element in Won Kim's character is his gender-bending appreciation of strong women, like his mother and the lady matador. The narrator takes us inside Won Kim's mind: "He does not doubt the lady matador's skills, or any woman's for that matter. Why, he would place odds on his own mother triumphing in the ring" (62). Perhaps he believes in women's evolving skills and strength, much as he believes in Darwin's theory of species' evolution. When Berta—becoming a *macha*—seduces him mid-way through the novel, Won Kim is dazzled (90). During their sex-play, crossing the borders of centuries, she is dressed like an eighteenth-century harlot, and he plays Louis XIV, the Sun King; love enters into their role-playing.

Just after this hopeful scene, news of his mother's death brings him grief. Yet it also frees Won Kim from adhering to the practices of *machismo*; as Basham argues, the macho is born out of a close identification with the mother, in opposition to the authoritarian father, who is often absent, in quest of other women: "It is in the closeness of the mother-son relationship that the crucial role identification problem that results in machismo lies . . . The son . . . is forced into a sharp denial of his natural desire to assume the positive female role . . . He characteristically over-reacts. He is not a female. He is not weak and kind . . . He is el macho" (133). When Won Kim imagines his mother's feminine soul flying off among "clouds of butterflies" (122), her death frees him to evolve from the aggressive masculinity of the *macho* to a softer manliness, one that expresses love of beauty, an affectionate relationship with Berta, and a kindly, engaged fatherhood.

Also redemptive is Berta's act of embroidering a monarch butterfly on his hotel bathrobe (143). Her love for him is conveyed through this act. We gather that he is gladdened by Berta's act of stitchery-witchery. Like a *curandera*, a traditional Native American healer, she cures "the wildness of regret" in Won Kim, banishing his preoccupation with suicide, healing the split between his public reserve and private passions (145–6). When, on her sixteenth birthday, she gives birth to their son, she names him after Won Kim. He expresses his gratitude and affection with a bouquet of flowers to celebrate her birthday and their son's birth. In this moment, which he calls "sublime," the new father feels as if he has come "upon a lost part of himself," a higher self, and he feels whole (188–9). Won Kim experiences cross-cultural love as redemption through this son, harbinger of a new, gentle masculine "species."

Their story's ending affirms life over suicide. It also asserts his integrated identity and agency over his own life: "His life . . . of living outside his skin is over" (204). If Won Kim were a butterfly, he "might be in the last larval stage," with his "pre-wings" getting ready to burst out and fly (205), to "reach the pinnacle of existence" (206). Won Kim envisions a new kind of fatherhood underpinned by his affection for his Korean-Latino son; he imagines introducing his son to his first butterfly (205): a new form of masculinity. He will become as loving a father as *Monkey Hunting's* Chen Pan has been.

Like Won Kim, Suki Palacios takes some time to experience transformation; border-crossings may not immediately create new and better forms of gender performance and love. The narrator notes how bullfighting *aficionados* identify her as a "scandalous woman playing at being a man" (4). She performs *machismo* with swagger, skillfully wielding her phallic sword in the bullring. Like "a disturbingly beautiful man" (6), she publicly crosses gender borders. She behaves sexually, like a selfish *macha*, in private. Her cultural border-crossing is also evident: English, Spanish, and Japanese are her languages and national identities. Before each bullfight she speaks her three-word slogan in Spanish and Japanese: "*arrogance, honor, death*" (5).

At a press conference she admits her feminism, defining it as agency in her life; inside her mind, we hear her *macha* addendum: "'which bulls I kill, and which men I fuck, and how I die'" (40). Her sexual voracity, together with her domination of less virile men who have shapely feet and are hairless (77, 41), is almost a parody of typical *macho* traits. She seduces the waiter who delivers food to her hotel room: "what works best for her: a simple man, not too intelligent, grateful and discreet" (44). This domination is not feminism, but *machismo* in female form. The foods she consumes enhance her masculine qualities, too (71). In the hotel lobby, where a wedding party converges with her group, she is narratively juxtaposed to the traditionally clad and constrained bride, "trussed up in lace" (124). She may not be a traditional feminine bride, but she is, like the bride, trussed up, constrained in the matador suit and in the *machismo* that she feels compelled to perform.

Another way in which the dehumanizing ideology of *machismo* is interrogated in this novel is through a brutal, egotistical character, Colonel Martín Abel, who has sexual fantasies about Suki. García identifies in his fantasies the desire for debasement of women (116). Abel imagines a humble posture for Suki, with himself overpowering her, "stripped naked and begging for her life" (184). His fantasies are tough-man; in Anzaldúa's words, Latino/a "culture makes *macho* caricatures of its men" (43). Actually, this tough man fears Suki's "mocking stance" and is afraid even to ask Suki to dance (95). As Basham notes, "machismo . . . represents a typical male response to fear of dominance by a (perceived) sexually superior and threatening female" (126). Abel's fate is emasculation. His wife divorces him and re-marries in the United States, blocking access to his sons. And Abel is murdered by a female political enemy.

For the *macha* Suki, there is more hope than for Abel. A small detail at the beginning of the novel foreshadows her evolution from *macha* to gentle person. As Suki practices her *matadora's* moves, the narrator tells us that her "reverse slide . . . [flutters] her cape like butterfly wings" (2). The butterfly wings link Suki to Won Kim and promise a metaphorical migration that will improve her prospects for survival and love. Toward the end of the novel, Suki moves beyond an imitation of manliness into a newly gendered space that no longer seems hyperbolic. Recalling the language of evolution, another cross-gendered character, Aura (Abel's murderer), says of Suki: "*La matadora* gives the impression of existing beyond gender—a new, more sublime species" (83). Suki is evolving into a more sublime version of humanity, beyond masculine and feminine.

The setting García creates for Suki encourages this evolutionary interpretation. In an interview with Alissa Nutting about *The Lady*

Matador's Hotel, García notes that the novel's *national* setting is a kind of "Everyplace, Central America. A sort of archetypal place." It is a multicultural place, in which healing from regional or global trauma might begin. Moreover, the *local* hotel setting, transient as most hotel spaces are, becomes a "kind of liminal space," in which the characters are "dealing with issues of identity and belonging" (Nutting), a space in which evolutions of identity may happen.

The bullring may also be a liminal arena in which Suki can recognize her evolving identity, especially as she sees the face of her dead mother each time she meets the bull. These moments of facing her own potential death and also that of her dead mother become the mechanism for birthing a nonviolent, sublime species beyond the strait-jacket of traditional gender roles. In her first confrontation with a bull in the novel, during an exhibition fight, the bull ignores Suki's fluttering cape and seems to mock her arrogance (126). When she is poised to go for the honorable kill, she sees her mother's image in the sky: a sign beckoning her to more nurturing gender performances, a foreshadowing of her future crossing from a world of darkness—the bullring—into a world of light (129). We glimpse a tender side of Suki in her protracted mourning for her mother. Dead ten years, Suki's mother still inhabits her dreams, which fuel her desire to find a cure for the disease that killed her mother (76). Her dreams of gluing her mother back together (149) hint at her resolve to return to medical school. Her goring during this exhibition bullfight seems to warn Suki to renounce the sport, heal herself, and embrace a doctor's life of healing. The narrator, inside Suki's mind during this bullfight, conveys these thoughts: "In giving the bull a chance to fight for its life, everyone is redeemed" (125). Suki seems to become more caring by avowing the bull's right to seek its own kind of redemption. Her brutal coldness is metamorphosing into an ethic of care.

In her second bullfight, the contest of the *matadoras* in the novel's last scene, the other lady matadors do not question the bullring's violence. As she confronts the bull, Suki acknowledges bullfighting's darkness and association with death: "They're well matched, joined inextricably on this November day, in this condemnation of light" (209). Suki questions her participation in "this condemnation of light" when the face on the bull becomes a hallucinatory conjuring of her mother's face. With the face of her mother on the bull itself, Suki cannot ignore the maternal message, calling her toward a nonviolent, life-affirming way of being that contrasts with her *macha* pursuits.

Suki's triumph in the ring during this last bullfight will release her from mourning for her mother, while reinforcing the gentle presence of the mother as role model for her daughter, much as Won Kim's mother's death enables him to become a new breed of male. If she performs successfully "this sacrament of killing," an unholy sport that a *macho* culture worships, she may allow herself to exit from the blood sport. Then she would move beyond her culture's privileging of men and violence and into a newly gendered space of healing after medical school.

Who wins this showdown in the ring is unclear; it seems to be the bull's "terminal" moment. The narrator observes that Suki is talented at killing bulls and implies that she will immortalize this bull by giving him a "death most eloquent" (209). In killing him well, she will participate, for the last time, in a "condemnation of light" (209), a negation of love and care. During her visit to my classroom, García implied that Suki kills the bull and survives because Suki "has the energy and vision to reinvent herself." Like Won Kim, Suki has crossed borders and evolved into a superior "hybridized" species. In this respect, I am reminded of the words of naturalist Dr. Birdseye that Marie Arana offers in her memoir, *American Chica*: "'It's the cross-fertilization that improves things . . . Like you! . . . That's what makes us more advanced'" (155).

In the 1980s, contemplating her own vision of social evolution, Anzaldúa observes, "men, even more than women, are fettered to gender roles . . . I've encountered a few . . . gentle straight men, the beginnings of a new breed, but they are confused, and entangled with sexist behaviors that they have not been able to eradicate. We need a new masculinity" (106), a masculinity "able to show love" (105). Three decades later, García seems to respond novelistically to Anzaldúa's plea for gentle men and women. García releases both

Suki and Won Kim from *machismo*: he to be a loving husband, father, and butterfly-lover and Suki to return to medical school for training in a life of healing.

Both characters are forerunners of a better human species, banishing outworn notions of gender. They join Lucrecia and Chen Pan in this crossover into a new world.

García's novels move us beyond the violence—cultural and historical—of some US Latino/a literary texts. She continues to interrogate *machismo* in her recent portrayal of an elderly Fidel Castro in *The King of Cuba*; Castro is depicted as a narcissistic character longing for the past; reflecting with satisfaction on the violent actions of the revolution; and bemoaning that his youthful, manly exploits are no longer valued. Other Latino/a authors also examine the damage that *machismo* can cause. One thinks, for example, of Dominican American Junot Díaz, whose protagonist Oscar in *The Brief Wondrous Life of Oscar Wao* achieves love while resisting narcissistic, brutal models of masculinity embodied in the narrator Yunior and the Dominican dictator Trujillo. García's vision of a "more sublime species" of human, represented in Suki Palacios, Won Kim, Berta, Chen Pan, and Lucrecia, attests to the power of the artist to advance human evolution beyond violence. Through these characters, García instructs readers in how to raise "humanity . . . to another level" (Fanon 236, 239).

Notes

1. I will switch between the feminine and masculine forms of this Spanish word throughout the essay in order to accommodate Suki's gender identity.

Works Cited

Anzaldúa, Gloria. *Borderlands/La Frontera: The New Mestiza*. 4th ed. San Francisco: Aunt Lute Books, 2012.

Basham, Richard. "Machismo." *Frontiers: A Journal of Women Studies*. 1.2 (Spring, 1976): 126–43. JSTOR. 31 Dec. 2013.

Browne, Janet. *Darwin: The Power of Place*. New York: Random House, 2011.

Caminero-Santangelo, Marta. *On Latinidad: U.S. Latino Literature and the Construction of Ethnicity.* Gainesville, Tallahassee: UP of Florida, 2007.

Dalleo, Raphael & Elena Machado Saez. *The Latino/a Canon and the Emergence of Post-Sixties Literature.* New York: Macmillan, 2007.

"Evolution and Natural Selection, Chapters 15–17." Hoover City Schools, 4 May 2009. Web. 30 May 2012. <http://www2.hoover.k12.al.us/schools/hhsfc/teachers/rhollon/class%20materials/Documents/evolution/evolution%20natural%20selection.pdf>.

Fanon, Frantz. *The Wretched of the Earth.* 1963. Transl. Richard Philcox. New York: Grove Press, 2004.

García, Cristina. *Monkey Hunting.* New York: Alfred A. Knopf, 2003.

──────. *The Lady Matador's Hotel.* New York: Scribner, 2010.

──────. "Buckner Lecture Series: Author Talk." University of North Carolina, Wilmington. Lumina Theater, 7 March 2012.

Gilligan, Carol. *In A Different Voice: Psychological Theory and Women's Development.* Cambridge & London: Harvard UP, 1982.

Moiles, Sean. "Search for Utopia, Desire for the Sublime: Cristina García's *Monkey Hunting*." *MELUS: Multi-Ethnic Literature of the U.S.* 34.4 (2009):167–86. Project MUSE. Web. 30 May 2012.

Morrison, Karen Y. "Creating an Alternative Kinship: Slavery, Freedom, and Nineteenth-Century Afro-Cuban *Hijos Naturales*." *Journal of Social History.* (Fall 2007): 55–80. Web. 14 May 2012.

Nutting, Alissa. "*The Lady Matador's Hotel:* An Interview with Cristina García." *Witness.* 24.2 (2011): n. pag. Web. 30 May 2012.

Rodriguez, Richard. *Brown: The Last Discovery of America.* New York: Viking. 2002.

"What Does the Crane Symbolize in Chinese Culture?" *Wiki Answers.* n.d. Web. 31 May 2012. <http://wiki.answers.com/Q/What_does_the_crane_symbolize_in_Chinese_culture>.

RESOURCES

Additional Works on Gender, Sex, and Sexuality

Drama

Shakespeare, William. *King Lear*. 1606.

Shange, Ntozake. *For Colored Girls Who Have Considered Suicide When the Rainbow is Enuf*. 1975.

Shaw, George Bernard. *Pygmalion*. 1912.

Sophocles. *The Three Theban Plays: Antigone, Oedipus the King, Oedipus at Colonus*. c. 441–406 BCE.

Fiction

Allison, Dorothy. *Bastard Out of Carolina*. 1992.

Adnan, Etel. *Sitt Marie Rose*. 1977.

Allende, Isabel. *The House of the Spirits*. 1982.

Atwood, Margaret. *The Handmaid's Tale*.

Austen, Jane. *Pride and Prejudice*. 1813.

Austen, Jane. *Sense and Sensibility*. 1811.

Brontë, Charlotte. *Jane Eyre*. 1847.

Brontë, Charlotte. *Villette*. 1853.

Brontë, Emily. *Wuthering Heights*. 1847.

Brown, Rita Mae. *Rubyfruit Jungle*. 1973.

Cather, Willa. *My Antonia*. 1918.

Chopin, Kate. *The Awakening*. 1899.

Cliff, Michelle. *No Telephone to Heaven*. 1987.

Cunningham, Michael. *A Home at the End of the World*. 1999.

Cunningham, Michael. *The Hours*. 1998.

Dangarembga, Tsitsi. *Nervous Conditions*. 1988.

Danticat, Edwidge. *Breath, Eyes, Memory*. 1994.

Eliot, George. *Middlemarch*. 1871–72.

Eliot, George. *The Mill on the Floss*. 1860.

Emecheta, Buchi. *The Joys of Motherhood*. 1979.

Erdich, Louise. *Tracks*. 1988.

Eugenides, Jeffrey. *Middlesex*. 2002.

Far, Sui Sin. *Mrs. Spring Fragrance and Other Writings*. 1912.

Flaubert, Gustave. *Madame Bovary*. 1857.

Forster, E. M. *Howards End*. 1910.

García, Cristina. *The Agüero Sisters*. 1997.

Gilman, Charlotte Perkins. *The Yellow Wallpaper*. 1892.

Hardy, Thomas. *Jude the Obscure*. 1895.

Hardy, Thomas. *Tess of the D'Urbervilles*. 1891.

Head, Bessie. *A Question of Power*. 1973.

Hopkins, Pauline. *Hagar's Daughter*. 1901–02.

Joyce, James. *Ulysses*. 1922.

Kafka, Franz. *The Metamorphosis*. 1915.

Kepner, Susan Fulop, ed. *The Lioness in Bloom: Modern Thai Fiction about Women*. 1996.

Kincaid, Jamaica. *Annie John*. 1985.

Lahiri, Jhumpa. *Interpreter of Maladies*. 1999.

Larsen, Nella. *Passing*. 1929.

Le Guin, Ursula K. *The Left Hand of Darkness*. 1969.

Lessing, Doris. *The Golden Notebook*. 1962.

MacDonald, Ann-Marie. *Fall on Your Knees*. 2002.

Mann, Thomas. *The Magic Mountain*. 1924.

Mansfield, Katherine. *The Garden Party and Other Stories*. 1922.

Manzoni, Alessandro. *The Betrothed*. 1827.

Mason, Bobbie Ann. *Shiloh and Other Stories*. 1982.

Morrison, Toni. *Beloved*. 1987.

Morrison, Toni. *Sula*. 1973.

Mukherjee, Bharati. *Desirable Daughters*. 2002.

Munro, Alice. *Hateship, Friendship, Courtship, Loveship, Marriage*. 2001.

Nabokov, Vladimir. *Lolita*. 1955.

Naylor, Gloria. *The Women of Brewster Place*. 1983.

Picoult, Jodi. *My Sister's Keeper*. 2004.

Plath, Sylvia. *The Bell Jar*. 1963.

Pramoj, Kukrit. *Four Reigns*. 1999.

Radcliffe, Ann. *The Mysteries of Udolpho*. 1794.

Richardson, Samuel. *Clarissa, or the History of a Young Lady*. 1747–48.

Sacher-Masoch, Leopold von. *Venus in Furs*. 1870.

Sade, Donatien Alphonse François, Marquis de. *The 120 Days of Sodom*. 1785.

Sade, Donatien Alphonse François, Marquis de. *Juliette*. 1797–1801.

Satrapi, Marjane. *Persepolis: The Story of a Childhood*. 2004.

Silko, Leslie Marmon. *Ceremony*. 1977.

Stevenson, Robert Louis. *The Strange Case of Dr. Jekyll and Mr Hyde*. 1886.

Stoker, Bram. *Dracula*. 1897.

Tan, Amy. *The Joy Luck Club*. 1989.

Tolstoy, Leo. *Anna Karenina*. 1877.

Walker, Alice. *The Color Purple*. 1982.

Weiner, Jennifer. *The Next Best Thing*. 2012.

Wharton, Edith. *The House of Mirth*. 1905.

Winterson, Jeanette. *Oranges are Not the Only Fruit*. 1985.

Winterson, Jeanette. *Sexing the Cherry*. 1989.

Wittig, Monique. *Les Guérillères*. 1969.

Wolf, Christa. *The Quest for Christa T*. 1968.

Woolf, Virginia. *Mrs Dalloway*. 1925.

Zola, Émile. *Nana*. 1880.

Nonfiction

El Sadaawi, Nawal. *Memoirs from the Women's Prison*. 1994.

Kingston, Maxine Hong. *The Woman Warrior: Memoirs of a Girlhood among Ghosts*. 1975.

Korn, Fadumo, with Sabine Eichhorst. *Born in the Big Rains: A Memoir of Somalia and Survival.* 2004.

Lorde, Audre. *The Cancer Journals.* 1980.

Hybrid and Multi-Genre Texts

Anzaldúa, Gloria & Analouise Keating, eds. *This Bridge We Call Home: Radical Visions of Transformation.* 2002.

Lorde, Audre. *Zami: A New Spelling of My Name.* 1982.

Moraga, Cherríe. *Loving in the War Years: Lo que nunca pasó por sus labios.* 1983.

Moraga, Cherríe and Gloria Anzaldúa. *This Bridge Called My Back: Writings by Radical Women of Color.* 1983.

Poetry

Jordan, June. *Directed By Desire: The Collected Poems of June Jordan.* 2007.

Petrarch, Francesco. *Songs and Sonnets.* c. 14th century.

Rich, Adrienne. *The Dream of a Common Language: Poems 1974–1977.* 1978.

Bibliography

Alloula, Malek. *The Colonial Harem*. Minneapolis: U of Minnesota P, 1986.

Anzaldúa, Gloria, and Analouise Keating, eds. *This Bridge We Call Home: Radical Visions of Transformation*. New York: Routledge, 2002.

Armstrong, Nancy. *Desire and Domestic Fiction: A Political History of the Novel*. Oxford: Oxford UP, 1990.

Beauvoir, Simone de. *The Second Sex*. 1949. Trans. Constance Borde and Sheila Malovaney Chevallier. New York: Vintage, 2011.

Bhabha, Homi. "Are You a Man or a Mouse?" *Constructing Masculinity*. Ed. Maurice Berger et al. New York: Routledge, 1995.

Boston Women's Health Book Collective and Judy Norsigian. *Our Bodies, Ourselves*. 1971. New York: Simon & Schuster, 2011.

Browne, Jude, ed. *The Future of Gender*. Cambridge: Cambridge UP, 2007.

Brownmiller, Susan. *Against Our Will: Men, Women, and Rape*. 1975. New York: Ballantine, 1993.

Butler, Judith. *Undoing Gender*. New York: Routledge, 2004.

Carpenter, Edward. *Intermediate Sex*. 1912. LaVergne, TN: Kissinger Legacy Reports, 2011.

Castle, Terry. *The Female Thermometer: Eighteenth-Century Culture and the Invention of the Uncanny*. Oxford: Oxford UP, 1995.

Cixous, Hèléne & Catherine Clément. *The Newly Born Woman*. Trans. Betsy Wing. Minneapolis: U of Minnesota P, 1986.

Collins, Patricia Hill. *Black Feminist Thought: Knowledge, Consciousness, and the Politics of Empowerment*. 1990. New York: Routledge, 2008.

Crimp, Douglas. "Mourning and Militancy." *October* 51 (Winter 1989): 3–18.

Dworkin, Andrea. *Pornography: Men Possessing Women*. New York: Plume, 1991.

Ellis, Havelock. *Studies in the Psychology of Sex*. 1897–1928. 7 Vols. Vols. 1–6. *Project Gutenberg*. Web. 28 Jun. 2014. <http://www.gutenberg.org/ebooks/13610>.

Eng, David L. *Q & A: Queer in Asian America*. Ed. David Eng & Alice Hom. Philadelphia: Temple UP, 1998.

Enloe, Cynthia. *The Curious Feminist: Searching for Women in a New Age of Empire*. Berkeley: U of California P, 2004.

Fanon, Frantz. *Black Skin, White Masks*. New York: Grove Press, 1967.

Fausto-Sterling, Anne. *Sex/Gender: Biology in a Social World*. New York: Routledge, 2012.

_____. *Sexing the Body: Gender Politics and the Construction of Sexuality*. New York: Basic Books, 2000.

Freedman, Estelle. *The Essential Feminist Reader*. New York: Modern Library, 2007.

_____. *No Turning Back: The History of Feminism and the Future of Women*. New York: Ballantine, 2003.

Friedan, Betty. *The Feminine Mystique*. 1963. New York: W. W. Norton & Co., 2001.

Fuss, Diana, ed. *Inside/Out: Lesbian Theories, Gay Theories*. New York: Routledge, 1991.

Gilbert, Sandra & Susan Gubar. *Feminist Literary Theory and Criticism. A Norton Reader*. W. W. Norton & Co., 2007.

Gopinath, Gayatri. *Queer Diasporas and South Asian Public Cultures*. Durham and London: Duke UP, 2005.

Halberstam, Judith. *Female Masculinity*. Durham, NC: Duke UP, 1998.

_____. *The Queer Art of Failure*. Durham, NC: Duke UP, 2011.

Irigaray, Luce. *Speculum of the Other Woman*. Trans. Gillian C. Gill. Ithaca: Cornell UP, 1985.

Jehlen, Myra. "Archimedes and the Paradox of Feminist Criticism." *Signs* 6.4 (Summer 1981): 575–601.

Kipnis, Laura. *Bound and Gagged: Pornography and the Politics of Fantasy in America*. Durham: Duke UP, 1998.

Kollontai, Alexandra. *Selected Writings*. New York: W. W. Norton & Co., 1980.

Krafft-Ebing, Richard von. *Psychopathia Sexualis*. 1886–1903. Trans. Franklin S. Klaf. New York: Arcade, 1998.

Kristeva, Julia. "Women's Time." *The Kristeva Reader*. Ed. Toril Moi. New York: Columbia UP, 1986. 187–213.

Lerner, Gerda. *The Creation of Feminist Consciousness from the Middle Ages to Eighteen-Seventy*. Oxford: Oxford UP, 1994.

Lorde, Audre. *Sister Outsider: Essays and Speeches*. 1984. Berkeley: Crossing Press, 2007.

Masters, William E., Virginia E. Johnson & Robert Kolodny. *Masters and Johnson on Sex and Human Loving*. 1982. New York: Little, Brown, and Co., 1988.

McClintock, Anne. *Imperial Leather: Race, Gender, and Sexuality in the Colonial Contest*. New York: Routledge, 1995.

McKinnon, Catharine A. *Women's Lives, Men's Laws*. Cambridge, MA: Belknap Press, 2007.

McRuer, Robert & Anna Mollow, eds. *Sex and Disability*. Durham: Duke UP, 2012.

Millet, Kate. *Sexual Politics*. 1969. Champaign: U of Illinois P, 2000.

Mohanty, Chandra. *Feminism Without Borders: Decolonizing Theory, Practicing Solidarity*. Durham, NC: Duke UP, 2003.

_____. "Under Western Eyes: Feminist Scholarship and Colonial Discourses." *Feminist Review* 30 (Fall 1988) 65–88.

Moraga, Cherríe. *Loving in the War Years: Lo que nunca pasó por sus labios*. 1983. 2nd expanded ed. Boston: South End P, 2000.

Moraga, Cherríe, & Gloria Anzaldúa. *This Bridge Called My Back: Writings by Radical Women of Color*. New York: Kitchen Table P, 1983.

Oyèrónké Oyĕwùmí, ed. *African Gender Studies: A Reader*. New York: Palgrave, 2005.

Reeser, Todd W. *Masculinities in Theory*. Oxford: Wiley-Blackwell, 2011.

Rich, Adrienne. *Arts of the Possible: Essays and Conversations*. 2001. New York: W. W. Norton & Co., 2013.

_____. *Of Woman Born: Motherhood as Experience and Institution*. 1976. New York: W. W. Norton & Co., 1995.

Rubin, Gayle. "Thinking Sex: Notes for a Radical Theory of the Politics of Sexuality." *Pleasure and Danger: Exploring Female Sexuality*. Ed. Carole Vance. New York: Routledge, 1984.

Sedgwick, Eve Kosofsky. *Epistemology of the Closet*. Berkeley: U of California P, 1990.

Showalter, Elaine. *A Literature of Their Own: British Women Novelists from Brontë to Lessing*. 1977. Princeton: Princeton UP, 2013.

Smith, Barbara, ed. *Home Girls: A Black Feminist Anthology*. 1983. New Brunswick: Rutgers UP, 2000.

Sontag, Susan. "Notes on 'Camp.'" 1964. *Against Interpretation and Other Essays*. By Sontag. New York: Picador. 2001. 275-92.

Spivak, Gayatri. "Can the Subaltern Speak." *Marxism and the Interpretation of Culture*. Ed. Cary Nelson and Lawrence Grossberg. London: Macmillan, 1988.

Steinem, Gloria. *Outrageous Acts and Everyday Rebellions*. New York: Henry Holt, 1995.

Stimpson, Catharine. "Zero Degree Deviancy." *Critical Inquiry* 8.2 (Winter 1981): 363–79.

Vātsyāyana. *The Complete Kama Sutra: The First Unabridged Modern Translation of the Classic Indian Text*. c. 400–200 BCE. Trans. Alain Daniélou. Rochester, VT: Inner Traditions, 1993.

Walker, Rebecca, ed. *To Be Real: Telling the Truth and the Changing Face of Feminism*. New York: Anchor, 1995.

Warner, Michael. *The Trouble with Normal: Sex, Politics and the Ethics of Queer Life*. New York: Free P, 1999.

Wittig, Monique. "The Straight Mind." *The Straight Mind and Other Essays*. By Wittig. Boston: Beacon, 1992. 21–32.

Woolf, Virginia. *Three Guineas*. 1938. Peterborough, Ontario: Broadview Press, 2012.

About the Editor

Margaret Sönser Breen is a professor of English and Women's, Gender, and Sexuality Studies at the University of Connecticut. She specializes in LGBT literature and, more broadly, gender and sexuality studies. Her publications include *Narratives of Queer Desire: Deserts of the Heart* (Palgrave, 2009); *Butler Matters: Judith Butler's Impact on Feminist and Queer Studies*, co-edited with Warren J. Blumenfeld (Ashgate, 2005); and *Genealogies of Identity: Interdisciplinary Readings on Sex and Sexuality*, co-edited with Fiona Peters (Rodopi, 2005). She has also edited or co-edited four collections on evil and wickedness and, most recently, for Salem Press, a volume on good and evil.

Contributors

Michelle Ann Abate is an associate professor of literature for children and young adults at The Ohio State University. She is the author of three books of literary criticism: *Bloody Murder: The Homicide Tradition in Children's Literature* (Johns Hopkins UP, 2013), *Raising Your Kids Right: Children's Literature and American Political Conservatism* (Rutgers UP, 2010), and *Tomboys: A Literary and Cultural History* (Temple UP, 2008).

Lisa Blansett is associate director of freshman English and an assistant professor in residence at the University of Connecticut. Trained as an eighteenth-century scholar specializing in the novel, she has opened her arms to embrace the study of early modern and contemporary rhetoric. Her publications, which focus on the production and representation of gendered space in early modern American and British discourse, include a chapter in Robert Appelbaum and John Wood Sweet's edited volume, *Envisioning an English Empire: Jamestown and the Making of the North Atlantic World* (2005).

Mary M. Burke is an associate professor of English and director of the Irish literature concentration at the University of Connecticut. The author of *"Tinkers": Synge and the Cultural History of the Irish Traveller* (OUP, 2009), she was the 2003–04 NEH Keough-Naughton fellow at the University of Notre Dame and the 2010 Boston College-Ireland visiting research fellow. She has a particular interest in modern Irish drama and has published a number of articles and chapters on Synge's plays, Bram Stoker, and Edna O'Brien, including a piece about two of Synge's plays for *The Cambridge Companion to J. M. Synge* (Cambridge UP, 2009). Her current book project concerns representations of the Scots-Irish (the Ulster Irish in America).

David Gay is a professor of English at the University of Alberta. He is the author of *The Endless Kingdom: Milton's Scriptural Society* (University of Delaware Press, 2002) and co-editor of *Locating the Past / Discovering the Present: Comparative Perspectives on Religion, Culture and Marginality*

(University of Alberta Press, 2010) and *Awakening Words: John Bunyan and the Language of Community* (University of Delaware Press, 2000).

Patrick Colm Hogan is a professor in the Department of English at the University of Connecticut, where he is also on the faculty of the Program in Cognitive Science and the Program in India Studies. He is the author of sixteen books, including *The Mind and Its Stories: Narrative Universals and Human Emotion* (Cambridge University Press, 2003)—hailed by Steven Pinker of Harvard University as "a landmark in modern intellectual life"—*Understanding Indian Movies* (University of Texas Press, 2008), and *What Literature Teaches Us About Emotion* (Cambridge University Press, 2011). His political writing includes *The Culture of Conformism* (Duke University Press, 2001) and *Understanding Nationalism* (Ohio State University Press, 2008). *Conversations on Cognitive Cultural Studies*, a book of dialogues with Frederick Aldama, is forthcoming in 2014 (Ohio State University Press).

Sara R. Johnson is an associate professor of classics and ancient Mediterranean studies at the University of Connecticut. Her primary specialization is in the area of Hellenistic Jewish literature and the uses of historical fiction in Jewish Greek texts. However, through her work on the ancient novel, and as a result of her study of modern and classical Japanese, she has developed a secondary interest in the rise of the novel and the popularity of historical fictions in classical (Heian) Japan. Her first book was *Historical Fiction and Hellenistic Jewish Identity: Third Maccabees in its Cultural Context* (UC Berkeley, 2004). In addition to work on a commentary on Third Maccabees, her current project is a cross-cultural comparison of historical fictions in the ancient Mediterranean and Heian Japan, tentatively titled "In the Shadow of Empire."

Katerina Kitsi-Mitakou is an associate professor in English Literature at Aristotle University of Thessaloniki, Greece. She teaches and publishes on realism, modernism, and the English novel, as well as on feminist and body theory. Her book *Feminist Readings of the Body in Virginia Woolf's Novels* was published in 1997. She has contributed to the "Reception of British and Irish Authors in Europe" series in volumes on Virginia Woolf, Jane Austen, and Charles Dickens. She has also co-edited two special journal issues, "Wrestling Bodies" (*Gramma* 11, 2003) and "Experiments in/of Realism" (*Synthesis* 2, 2011), and three collections of essays, *The Flesh Made Text Made Flesh: Cultural and Theoretical Returns to the Body* (Peter Lang, 2007); *The Future of Flesh: A Cultural Survey of the Body* (Palgrave Macmillan, 2009); and *Bodies, Theories, Cultures in the Post-Millennial Era* (University Studio Press, 2009).

Rachael Sealy Lynch is an associate professor of English at the University of Connecticut. Her research interests are in fiction and women's writing, with a particular focus on contemporary Irish women. She has published many articles and essays on recent and contemporary Irish writers, including Jennifer Johnston, Molly Keane, Edna O'Brien, Mary Lavin, and Liam O'Flaherty, in such journals as *Irish University Review, Twentieth-Century Literature,* and *The Canadian Journal of Irish Studies*. She is currently working on a book about Jennifer Johnston's women, in the hopes that a detailed study of these women will help us to understand the myriad ways in which they are embedded in the larger story of their country's recent history.

Lisa Marcus is an associate professor of English, chair of the Women's and Gender Studies Program, and founding member of the Holocaust and Genocide Studies Program at Pacific Lutheran University. She has published on American writers Willa Cather, Pauline Hopkins, and Anzia Yezierska and has written for the *Women's Review of Books*. A recent essay, "Dolling Up History: Fictions of Jewish American Girlhood," was published in *Girlhood Studies*. Her biographical essay on Yezierska appeared in Salem Press' *Great Lives from History: Jewish Americans*. She is working on a book project, *Finding Zlata Jampolski: Fictions of Jewishness in America*, which links her grandmother's immigration story to the Jewish American texts she studies.

Marlon Rachquel Moore is an assistant professor of English at the University of North Carolina, Wilmington. She teaches courses in African American Literature, LGBT Fiction, and Women's Literary Traditions. Her creative and academic writing has appeared in *African American Review, Gender Forum, Journal of Film and Video, In the Fray Magazine,* and *Black Camera*. She has two forthcoming books: *Geechee to Gumbo:*

Black Southern Womanloving Culture & Politics, co-edited with L.H. Stallings (RedBone Press, 2014) and *In the Life & In the Spirit: Homoerotic Spirituality in African American Literature* (SUNY Press, 2014).

Brenda Murphy is board of trustees distinguished professor of English, emeritus, at the University of Connecticut. Among her nineteen books on American drama and theatre are *The Theatre of Tennessee Williams* (2014); *Tennessee Williams and Elia Kazan: A Collaboration in the Theatre* (1992); *Understanding David Mamet* (2011); *Congressional Theatre: Dramatizing McCarthyism on Stage, Film, and Television* (1999); *The Provincetown Players and the Culture of Modernity* (2005); and as editor, *Critical Insights: Tennessee Williams* (2011) and *Critical Insights: A Streetcar Named Desire* (2010).

Joseph J. Portanova holds a PhD in Byzantine and Hellenistic history from Columbia University. Since 1984, he has taught in New York University's Liberal Studies Program. His articles include "Tokens of Slavery," "Porcelain, the Willow Pattern, and Chinoiserie," "Ann Morgan and the Shirtwaist Strike of 1909–1910," "Darwinism, Nazism, and Same-Sex Desire," and "Rumor and Rule: Shakespeare's Cleopatra, Elizabeth I and Mary Stuart." He is the author of such texts for instructors and students as *Same-Sex Desire in Ancient Greece, An Introduction to Islam and the Caliphate, Athens in the Age of Pericles*, and *Cortes and Moctezuma*. He avidly writes and reads poetry.

Thomas Recchio is a professor of English at the University of Connecticut, where he teaches course on Victorian literature with an emphasis on the novel and Victorian and post-Victorian publishing history. He is the author of *Elizabeth Gaskell's* Cranford: *A Publishing History* (Ashgate, 2009) and the editor of the Norton Critical Edition of Elizabeth Gaskell's *Mary Barton* (2008). His articles have appeared in a wide range of journals, including *Victorian Studies*, *Studies in the Novel*, *Dickens Studies Annual*, *Nineteenth-Century Theatre and Film*, the *Gaskell Journal*, and *College Literature*.

Frederick S. Roden is an associate professor of English at the University of Connecticut. He is author of *Same-Sex Desire in Victorian*

Religious Culture and editor of scholarly volumes on Oscar Wilde, queer Catholic narratives, and Jewish/Christian intersections. He has also written a commentary to the medieval theologian Julian of Norwich. Roden is currently working on a book concerning the borders/limits of modern Jewish identity, as well as an edition/translation of Marc-Andre Raffalovich's 1896 sexological text, *Uranisme et Unisexualite*.

Greg Colón Semenza, associate professor of English at the University of Connecticut, is the author of *Sport, Politics, and Literature in the English Renaissance (U Delaware P, 2004)*; *Graduate Study for the Twenty-First Century: How to Build an Academic Career in the Humanities* (Palgrave Macmillan, 2005; expanded 2nd ed., 2010); the follow-up collection, *How To Build an Academic Life in the Humanities* (2014); *The English Renaissance in Popular Culture* (Palgrave Macmillan, 2010); and with Laura Knoppers, *Milton in Popular Culture* (Palgrave Macmillan, 2006). He has published journal articles on such diverse subjects as Tim Blake Nelson's teen film *O*, the Sex Pistols, the globalism of silent Shakespeare films, *Shakespeare: The Animated Tales*, and wrestling in *The Canterbury Tales*; he also edited the 2010 forum "Shakespeare After Film" for *Shakespeare Studies*. His current project, co-authored by Robert Hasenfratz, is *The History of British Literature on Film: 1895–2010* (Bloomsbury, 2014). It will be the only comprehensive narration of cinema's one-hundred-year-old love affair with British literature.

Roger Travis is an associate professor in the Department of Literatures, Cultures and Languages of the University of Connecticut. He received his bachelor's degree in classics from Harvard College, and his PhD in comparative literature from the University of California, Berkeley. He is a founder of and contributor to the collaborative blog Play the Past, where he writes about the fundamental connection between ancient epic and digital games. He also works on developing and studying a form of game-based learning, practomimetic learning, in which learners play the curriculum as an RPG (role-playing game) wrapped in an ARG (alternate reality game).

Barbara Frey Waxman is a professor of English at University of North Carolina, Wilmington, where she teaches courses in US ethnic literature, multicultural US memoirs, food memoirs, women in literature, US Latino literature, Victorian literature, and literature about later life. She has written two books on aging in literature and edited a collection of essays using the critical lenses of poststructuralism and feminism. Many of her essays, on works by authors such as May Sarton, Toni Morrison, Eva Hoffman, Alice Walker, Richard Rodriguez, and Marie Arana, appear in scholarly journals and essay collections.

Index

Abbey Theatre 195, 198, 202
Abel, Martín 255
Abrams, M. H. 35
Adelman, Janet 133, 136
Adelman Komy, Hannah 179
African American Literature 68
Āgamaḍambara xii, 106, 110, 111
Agrippina II 4
Aguilar, Grace 17
ahiṃsā 117
AIDS xviii, xxv, xxvi, xxvii,
    xxviii, xxx, xxxi, xxxii, 218
Alcibiades 84, 85
Alexander the Great 188
Allen, Norm 68
Alvarez, Julia 244
Alys of Bath 9
American Dream 168, 174
Americanness 169
ancestral genealogy 51
Anderson, David A. 226, 242
Anderson, Robert xii, 181, 183,
    193
Andreolle, Donna Spalding 68
Andrews, Edward 193
Andrews, William L. 68
Anselm, Saint 11
Anzaldúa, Gloria 244, 258
Aphrodite 4, 24
Apollo 39
Arana, Marie 257
Aristophanes ix, x, xi, 20, 73, 75,
    76, 77, 78, 79, 80, 81, 85, 86
Artemis 4
Āryas 117
Aspasia 75
Asp, Carolyn 129, 137
Athenian women xi, 76, 79, 81

Athens 20, 73, 74, 77, 79, 80, 81,
    82, 83, 84, 86
Atwater, Richard 19
Audley, Alicia 160
Audley, Robert 156, 159, 160
Audley, Sir Michael 160
Augusta 4
Augustine 12
Augustus 4
aura viii, xxix
Aurora Leigh 15, 19
Auschwitz and After xv, xviii, xix,
    xxii, xxv, xxx, xxxi, xxxii
Austen, Jane 14
Aydede, Murat 120, 122

Bagemill, Bruce 68
Bailey, Edward 213
Baldwin, James 55
Barchester Towers 156, 166
Barrett Browning, Elizabeth 15,
    19
Barsalou, Lawrence 120
Basham, Richard 258
Beauty Queen of Leenane, The
    196, 197, 205, 209
Beckford, William 49
Beowulf 6
Bible, The 8, 12, 14, 54, 58, 61,
    67, 138, 139, 141, 150, 170,
    175
Big Daddy 189, 191, 192, 193
Big Mama 190, 191, 192, 193
Bigote, El 248
Bildungsroman 169, 170, 174, 179
binary, binarized 3, 24, 48, 124,
    130, 220, 230
Bishop, Jane 19

279

Black Blankets 115
Black, Joseph 19
Blackwater Lightship, The 217, 225
Bleeding Nun, The 42, 51
Blessing, Carole 151
Blythe, Ernest 200
Boleyn, Anne viii
Booth, William 209
borderland consciousness 247
Borderlands/La Frontera: The New Mestiza 258
Bowen, Elizabeth 212
Bowlby, Rachel 35
Braddon, Mary Elizabeth 156
Bradley, Katharine 16
Bread Givers v, xii, 167, 168, 169, 171, 174, 175, 179, 180
Brigit, Saint 6
Bristow, Joseph 33
Brodum, William, MD 52
Brontë, Charlotte 29
Brooke, Rupert 27
Broom Tree, The 96
Browne, Janet 247
Bryer, Jackson 193
Burgis, Nina 34
Burke, Mary 209
Burke, Mary M. vi, xiii, 195
Butler, Judith xv, xxxi, 18, 30, 40, 48, 52, 106, 120, 227, 234, 242
Butler, Octavia xi, 55, 61, 68

Callirhoe 104
Caminero-Santangelo, Marta 259
Carney, Frank xiii, 198, 199
Carpenter, Edward 24, 27
Carraway, Nick 167

Caruth, Cathy xxi, xxxi
categorial identity 106
Catherine, Saint 11, 13
Cathleen ni Houlihan 195, 196, 197, 199, 205, 207, 208
Cat on a Hot Tin Roof xii, 181, 187, 193
Celtic Tiger 196, 219
Chariton 104
Chatton, Barbara 230, 242
Chaucer, Geoffrey 8
Chow, Whym 16
Christianity 5, 6, 10, 16, 54, 57, 63, 125, 141
Christine de Pizan 9
Christoval, Don 40
Church of Hagia Sophia 5
Chuujou, Tou no 94
Cisneros, Sandra 244
Civil Rights Movement 54
Cixous, Hélène 32
class viii, xviii, 7, 9, 10, 14, 15, 22, 23, 24, 30, 45, 55, 57, 61, 88, 153, 154, 164, 165, 168, 171, 179, 199, 201, 202, 203, 213, 231, 251, 259
classical (Greek) 14, 30, 86, 87, 91, 100, 101, 102, 138, 149
classical (Japanese) 87
Clerk's Tale 9
Coats, Karen 234
Cockburn, Alexander 108
Cohn-Haft, Louis 86
Coleman, James 68
Collins, Eoin 224
comedy xi, 20, 23, 37, 73, 74, 75, 76, 77, 78, 79, 80, 81, 83, 85, 86, 205
Common Era 4

companionate 44
Connery, Sean 205
Cooper, Edith 16
Copperfield, David 22, 34
Cox, Don Richard 166
Cravath, Lynne Woodcock xiii, 226, 243
Crosby, Fanny 14
Cross, Ezra 56
Cross, Horace 56
Cuddy, Amy 121
cultural border-crossing 247, 254
Curtis, Edward E. 68

Dalleo, Raphael 252
Daly, Mary 18
Daniélou, Alain 270
Dark Rosaleen 195
Darwin, Charles 245, 246, 247, 252, 253, 258
Davis, Colin xxii, xxxi
Days and Memory xix, xxiii, xxxi
Delbo, Charlotte xv, xviii, xix, xxiv, xxx, xxxi, xxxii
de Valera, Éamon 199
Devlin, Albert J. 194
Devoted Ladies 212
Dezső, Csaba 121
Dhairyarāśiḥ 113, 118
Díaz-Diocaretz, Myriam xxxii
Díaz, Junot 244, 258
Dickens, Charles 22, 153
disgust 36, 47, 48, 107, 109, 110, 113, 116, 117, 118, 119, 212
Divine Love 11, 16
Donoghue, Emma xiii, 211, 216, 219, 225
Dorcey, Mary xiii, 213, 220

Doty, Mark xv, xviii, xxiv, xxv, xxx
Douglas, Alfred 24, 26
Druid Theatre 208
Drummle, Bentley 154
DuBois, Blanche 185
Duckitt, John H. 120
Dudach, Georges xix
Duran, Angelica 152

Edelman, Lee xvii, xx, 50
Eliot, George 14
Emperor Claudius 4
Emperor Ichijou 89
Emperor Justinian 5
Empress Shoushi 89
epic xii, 6, 32, 102, 138, 147
equality 7, 125, 142, 149, 151, 224
Erickson, Leif 193
ethic of care 245, 247, 248, 249, 252, 256
Ethnicity 259
Evans, Mary Ann 14
expression vii, viii, 26, 29, 49, 55, 62, 64, 65, 66, 134, 153, 155, 156, 157, 158, 161, 166, 183, 201, 212, 216, 220, 222
Eyre, Richard 209
Fanon, Frantz 259
Feher, Michel 34
Fell, Margaret 141, 150, 152
Female Sexuality 32, 34
Femininity 32, 34, 126
Ferguson, Margaret W. 152
Field, Michael 16
fin de siècle 16, 27, 33
Fiske, Susan 121, 122
Fitzgerald, Alexis 209

Fitzgerald, F. Scott 180
Flannagan, Roy 139
Foster, E. M. 27
Foucault, Michel 34, 53
Frederico, Annette R. 152
Freud, Sigmund 26
Fujiwara 89, 93, 95, 98, 99
Fuss, Diana xxxi, 120

García, Cristina vi, ix, xiii, xiv, 244, 259
Garden of Eden 143
Gaskell, Elizabeth 155, 156
Gates, Jr., Henry Louis 68
Gatsby, Jay 168
Gatz, James 168
Gay vi, xii, xiii, xxxi, 33, 120, 138, 180, 211, 217, 219, 224, 242, 243
Gay, David v, xii, 138
Geddes, Jennifer L. xxxi
Gee, Susan 226, 242
Gender Identity Disorder vi, xiii, 226, 228, 236, 237, 238, 239, 240, 242
gender passing 62
gender performativity 30
Genesis 58, 138, 139, 140, 141, 142, 145, 146, 148, 150, 152
Genji ix, xi, 87, 88, 89, 90, 91, 92, 93, 94, 95, 96, 97, 98, 99, 100, 101, 102, 103, 104, 105
Gilbert, Sandra and Susan Gubar 28, 29, 34, 140, 141, 151, 152
Gilman, Sander 110
Gilovich, Thomas 122

Girlhood vi, xiii, 226, 227, 229, 231, 233, 235, 237, 239, 241, 243
Gitomer, David 121
Goldberg, Jonathan 137
Goldstein, Max 173, 175
Gooden, Angela M. 226
Gooden, Mark A. 226, 242
gothic x
Gothic Tales 166
Graham, Lucy 159, 160
Gray, Allen 185
Great Expectations 153, 155, 166
Great Gatsby, The 167, 180
Greece, Ancient xi, 4
Greek (sentimental) novel 88, 104
Greenberg, Judith xx
Grey Woman, The 156, 158, 163, 166
Griffin, Dale 121, 122
Grimes, John 121

Haggerty, George 47, 49
Halberstam, Judith xxxi, 242
Hall, Radclyffe 16
Hamel, Debra 86
Hamilton, Mykol 226, 242
Hankin, James 121
Hare, David 203
Harris, Alice Kessler 169
Harris, Lasana 121
Harris, Trudier 57
Haunting xvii, xix, xxiv, xxx, 29, 43
Heaven's Coast x, xv, xviii, xix, xxv, xxvi, xxx, xxxi
Heian era (794–1185) xi, 87, 88, 89, 91, 92, 93, 95, 96, 97, 99, 101, 103, 104, 105

Heian/Kyoto xi, 87, 88, 89, 91, 92, 93, 95, 96, 97, 99, 101, 103, 104, 105
herms 84
heterofemininity 241
heterogender 241
heteromasculinity 230, 241
heteronormative xiii, 39, 47, 169, 182, 183, 234, 241
heteronormativity 46, 47, 49, 50, 51, 212
hierarchy 8, 139, 140, 141, 142, 146, 148, 149, 150, 151
Hijuelos, Oscar 244
Hikaru, Genji 94
Hilda of Whitby 6
Hildegard of Bingen 6, 19
Hildegard, Saint 6, 11
Hirsch, Marianne xxxi
Hogan, Patrick Colm v, xii, 106
Holocaust xvii, xix, xxii, xxvii, xxx
homoeroticism 7, 62
homophobia 184, 219
homosexual, homosexuality xiii, xxvi, 49, 59, 182, 183, 184, 185, 187, 212, 213, 239
homosexuality xiii, xxvi, 49, 59, 182, 183, 184, 185, 187, 212, 213, 239
homosocial 155, 156, 159, 160, 162, 163, 166
Horney, Karen 32
Hotel Miraflor, The 251
Houghton, Walter 153
Houston, Natalie M. 166
Hurly, Robert 34

immigrant xii, xiii, 167, 169, 170, 177, 200, 204, 206
Importance of Being Earnest, The 23, 24, 26, 35
Indigo Blankets 115, 117
Inés de la Cruz, Sor Juana 12
Infantile Sexuality 34
Ingraham, Chrys 241
In Search of Our Mothers' Gardens 180
Irigaray, Luce 32

Jackson, Agnes Moreland 68
Jackson, Sue 226
Jayánta, Bhaṭṭa xii, 106
Jenkins, Christine 242
Jewishness xii, 167, 176, 177
Johnston, Jennifer 211, 212
Jonas, Regina 17
Jones, Ernest 32
Jones, Wendy 43, 45
Jouvet, Louis xix
Joyce, James 197
Juana Inés de la Cruz 12, 19
Judith xv, xx, xxiv, xxxi, 6, 18, 19, 28, 30, 33, 40, 48, 52, 106, 120, 173, 227, 228, 234, 237, 242
Julian of Norwich 10, 11

Kacandes, Irene xxxi
Kahneman, Daniel 121, 122
Kashmir xi, xii, 106, 120, 121
Kazan, Elia 182, 192, 276
Keats, John viii
Keith, Arthur B. 121
Kelly, William 49
Kempe, Margery 9, 11
Kenan, Randall xi, 55, 61

Kertbeny, Karl-Maria 27
Kessler Harris, Alice 169
Kim, Won 244, 245, 246, 247, 251, 252, 253, 254, 255, 257, 258
King David 151
King Duncan 125
King Lear 176
Kirkpatrick, Kathryn 225
Kitsi-Mitakou, Katerina x, 20
Kolin, Philip C. 193
Konstan, David 104
Konzett, Delia Caparoso 180
Krafft-Ebing, Richard von 27
Kristeva, Julia 32
Kullman, Colby H. 193
Lady Audley's Secret 156, 158, 163, 166
Lady Matador's Hotel, The vi, x, xiii, 244, 247, 251, 255, 259
Landing 185
Langer, Lawrence L. xix
Lanyer, Aemilia 141
Laqueur, Thomas 30, 34, 130, 137
Larsen, Nella 68
Latino/a literature 244, 252
Laugh of the Medusa, The 32, 34
l'ecriture feminine 33
Lee, Joseph 209
Lee, Tom 181
Lehr, Susan S. 242
Leonard, John 152
lesbian, lesbianism ix, xiii, xv, 16, 18, 48, 136, 188, 189, 193, 211, 212, 213, 214, 215, 216, 217, 219, 220, 221, 223, 224, 235, 238, 239, 244
Levy, Amy 17
Lewis, C. S. 152

Lewis, Matthew x, 36, 37, 39, 41, 43, 45, 47, 49, 51, 53
Literary Imagination xxxi, 28, 34, 152
Livia 4
Lonergan, Patrick 209
Loraux, Nicole 86
Luxon, Thomas 149
Lydon, John 209
Lydon, John Joseph 203
Lynch, Rachael Sealy vi, xiii, 211
Lysistrata ix, xi, 73, 74, 75, 76, 77, 78, 79, 80, 81, 82, 83, 84, 85, 86

Macbeth ix, xii, 123, 125, 126, 127, 128, 129, 130, 131, 133, 134, 135, 136, 137
MacGregor, Donald 122
Machismo 245, 246, 252, 253, 254, 255, 258
Madame Neroni 156, 157, 158
Madigan, Shawn 19
Madwoman in the Attic 28, 34, 151, 152
Magdalene, Mary 5
Malden, Helen 158
Man of Law's Tale 9
Marie de France 8
Marks, Elaine 34
Martin, Catherine Gimelli 141
Martin, Ellie 181, 186, 187
masculinity 29, 55, 56, 58, 59, 61, 64, 65, 66, 79, 85, 125, 126, 127, 128, 131, 133, 135, 150, 227, 229, 230, 233, 234, 235, 240, 241, 245, 253, 254, 257, 258
masochism 154

Mason, Bertha 29
Maynard, John 155
McBrien, William xxxii
McColley, Diane Kelsey 146
McConache, Bruce 193
McDonagh, Martin 209
McKay, Nellie 68
memoir x, xv, xvii, xviii, xix, xxi,
    xxii, xxiv, xxv, xxvi, xxx,
    xxxi, 17, 257
Merck, Many 243
Meredith, George viii
Milton, John 152
Minnelli, Vincente 193
Minter, Shannon 238
Moiles, Sean 248
Monette, Paul xxvi
Monier-Williams, Monier 121
Monkey Hunting vi, ix, xiii, 244,
    245, 247, 248, 254, 259
Monk, The x, 36, 37, 39, 41, 42,
    43, 44, 45, 47, 49, 50, 51, 53
Monroe, Kristen Renwick 121
Montagu, Lily 17
Moore, Marlon Rachquel xi, 54
Mouzell for Melastomus, A 152
Munstdorp, Janneken 12
Murasaki ix, xi, 88, 89, 90, 94, 96,
    97, 98, 99, 100, 101, 103,
    104, 105
Murphy, Tom xiii, 198, 200, 202
Murrary, Tony 209

Nicholson, John Gambril 25
Nightingale, Florence 14
Noise from the Woodshed, A 213,
    217, 224
normative, non-normative xii,
    xxvi, 21, 26, 32, 36, 38, 39,
    40, 41, 42, 43, 45, 46, 51,
    61, 106, 110, 116, 118, 119,
    234
Nussbaum, Martha 121
Nutting, Alissa 255
Nye, Robert A. 34
Nyquist, Mary 142, 152

O'Brien, Kate 212
O'Carroll, Ide 224
Ochello, Peter 189
Octavius, Caius 4
O'Hagan, Sean 195
Olamina, Lauren 62
one-sex model 130, 136
Orlando 21, 22, 29, 30, 31, 32, 34,
    35, 180, 224
O'Shaughnessey, Síle Sunita
    Siobhán 219
O'Toole, Fintan 196

Palacios, Suki 244, 251, 254, 258
Pan, Chen 244, 245, 246, 247,
    248, 249, 250, 251, 252,
    254, 258
Pandit, B. N. 121
Parable of the Sower xi, 54, 55,
    61, 68
Parable of the Talents xi, 61, 68
Paradise Lost xii, 138, 139, 140,
    142, 143, 149, 151, 152
Parker, Michael 225
Patrick, Saint 6
Peck, Louis F. 49
Peden, Margaret Sayers 19
Pelagia, Saint 6
Peloponnesian War xi, 74, 76
performative, performativity 30
perpetua 5, 6, 19
Perpetua, Saint 5
Peters, Ellen 122

Phallus xi, 73, 75, 77, 79, 81, 83, 85
phantasmagorical 50
Phrases and Philosophies for the Use of the Young 24, 35
Pillay, Sunita 219
Pinn, Anthony 68
Pogues, The 204
Polanski, Roman 134
Pollitt, Brick 182, 188
Polydorou, Desma 141
Portanova, Joseph J. x, 3
postpartum psychoses 9
Post-War Irish Emigration to Britain 197
practical identity 106, 107, 108, 118
prehomosexual 239
Prentice, Deborah 121, 122
Prince Edward 24
Procopius 5, 19
Pronin, Emily 122
Puccio, Carolyn 122
Puette, William J. 105

Queen Elizabeth II 196, 204, 205
queer x, xi, xv, xxiv, xxv, xxx, 18, 33, 37, 49, 50, 52, 58, 61, 183, 184, 185, 187, 189, 192, 221, 222, 228, 234, 241
Queer Gothic 47, 53
queer subjectivity 61
Queer Time x, xxiv, xxxi, 36, 37, 39, 41, 43, 45, 47, 49, 51, 53
Quinn, Antoinette 225

Reardon, Bryan P. 105
Recchio, Thomas xii, 153
Reform Act of 1867 24

Reid-Walsh, Jacqueline 227, 243
Religion xi, 3, 54, 68, 111, 121
Renold, Emma 227, 230, 238
repression 43, 55, 143
Reynolds, Laura 181
Rich, Adrienne viii, xv, xxxii
Richardson, Samuel 37, 53
Robbins, Philip 120
Robinson, Mary 219
Roden, Frederick S. x, 3
Rodriguez, Richard 248
Rokujou Haven 93, 98
romance plot 179
Room of One's Own, A ix, 28, 35, 171, 174, 180
Rosenberg, Edgar 166
Rossetti, Christina 15, 19
Rotten, Johnny 195, 203, 209
Rottnek, Matthew 239, 242, 243
Roughgarden, Jane 69
Roulston, Chris 53
Rubin, Jay 105
Ruether, Rosemary 18
Rusten, Jeffrey 86

Sackville-West, Vita 16
Sáez, Elena Machado 252
Said, Edward 110
Same-sex desire 124
Sanskrit Drama xii, 106, 120, 121
Santería 54
Sappho x, 4, 16
Sedgwick, Eve Kosofsky 228, 237
Segal, Naomi 243
Seidensticker, Edward 90
sensation fiction 155
Sex Pistols 203, 204
sexual fluidity 65, 66

sexuality ix, x, xii, xiv, xv, xvii, xix, xxi, xxiii, xxv, xxvii, xxix, xxxi, 26, 32, 33, 34, 53, 69, 106, 138, 147, 153, 155, 157, 159, 161, 163, 165, 166, 243
Shakespeare, Judith 28, 173
Shakespeare, William 137, 263
Shikibu, Murasaki ix, xi, 88, 89, 96, 103, 104, 105
Shirane, Haruo 105
Showalter, Elaine 35
Slope, Obadiah 156
social evolution 257
Some Physical Consequences of the Anatomical Distinction between the Sexes 34
Sommer, Doris 248
Sonnet 20 123, 125, 126, 130
Sontag, Susan xxvi
Sparta 74, 84, 85
Speght, Rachel 141, 142, 152
Spurlin, William 228, 237, 238
Strachey, James 34
Strachey, Lytton 27
Straw, Jack 189
Superman 237
Swain, Simon 104
Swetnam, Joseph 142
Symonds, John Addington 27
Synge, J. M. 202

Tacitus 4, 5
Talboys, Clara 162
Talboys, George 159, 160, 161, 163
Talboys, Helen 159
Tale of Genji ix, xi, 87, 88, 89, 90, 92, 94, 100, 105

Talboys, George 156
Tarantino, Quentin 202
Tea and Sympathy v, xii, 181, 182, 183, 190, 192, 193
Teresa of Ávila 11, 16
Teresa, Saint 11
Ternan, Ellen 23
Theatre of Dionysus 73, 74, 85
Theodora 5
third sex 20, 21, 24, 27
This Sex Which Is Not One 33, 34
Thucydides 84, 85
Tischler, Nancy M. 194
Todorov, Alexander 122
Tóibín, Colm xiii, 4, 211, 216, 217
Tomboy vi, xiii, xiv, 226, 227, 228, 229, 234, 235, 236, 238, 240, 241, 242, 243
Tomboy Trouble vi, xiii, xiv, 226, 227, 228, 229, 234, 235, 236, 238, 240, 241, 243
transgender xiv, 227, 228, 241
Transgender xxiv
Traub, Valerie 137
trauma x, xv, xvii, xviii, xix, xxi, xxii, xxiv, xxx, 125, 256
Travis, Roger xi, 73
Trollope, Anthony 155, 156
two-body system 39, 51
two-sex model 20, 21, 130
Tyler, Royall 90, 105

Uji sisters 96
Ulrichs, Karl Heinrich 24
Uranian love 24, 27
Utsusemi 96

Valera, Éamonn de 212
Van Steen, Gonda 86

Varley, H. Paul 86, 105
Vechten, Renée van 121
Virgil 101, 138
Virgin Mary 4, 199
Visitation of Spirits, A xi, 54, 55, 56, 61, 67, 68
Voodoo 54

Waley, Arthur 90, 105
Walker, Alice 174
Wallace, Alfred Russel 247
Waller, Margaret 34
Walpole, Horace 49
Wasserman, Suzanne 168, 180
Waxman, Barbara Frey vi, xiii, 244
Weekes, Ann Owens 211
Weird Sisters 125, 129, 134
Wheatley, Phyllis 174
Whistle in the Dark, A 200, 201
Whitmarsh, Tim 105
Wife of Bath 8, 10
Wilde, Oscar x, 21, 22, 23, 27, 35

Wild West, The 195, 209
Wilentz, Gay 180
Williams, Tennessee 193
Williams, William Carlos ix
Wittreich, Joseph 152
Wollstonecraft, Mary 15
Wolpert, Stanley 122
Women, Jewish 17, 18
Woods, Susanne 152
Woolf, Virginia ix, x, 21, 22, 27, 34, 171
Wright, Elizabeth 243
Wright, Richard 69
Wyeth, Sharon Dennis vi, xiii, 226, 241

Yeats, W. B. 195
Yezierska, Anzia xii, 167, 171, 174, 179, 180
Young, Bertha 26

Zavala, Iris xxxii
Zeitlin, Froma 86